D0677257

**AN
EYE
FOR
AN
EYE**

New York   Chicago   San Francisco

AN EYE FOR AN EYE

H. Jack Griswold   Mike Misenheimer
Art Powers   Ed Tromanhauser

Holt, Rinehart and Winston

Copyright © 1970 by H. Jack Griswold,
Mike Misenheimer, Art Powers, Ed
Tromanhauser

All rights reserved, including the right
to reproduce this book or portions
thereof in any form.

Published simultaneously in Canada by
Holt, Rinehart and Winston of
Canada, Limited.

Library of Congress Catalog Card
Number: 72–108668

First Edition

SBN:03–084519-X

Printed in the United States of America

365.9772
E y 3 l g

2 5 7 l d a

To James L. Hyatt,
Fay C. Smith,
Father Joseph Sedlak,
and all the women who wait

FUNDERBURG LIBRARY

c. 1

MANCHESTER COLLEGE

CONTENTS

Preface

> We have been judging and punishing ever since Jesus told us not to; and I defy anyone to make out a convincing case for believing that the world has been any better than it would have been if there had never been a judge, a prison, or a gallows in all that time.
>
> —GEORGE BERNARD SHAW

There have been enough books written about *crime* and *punishment* to fill a prison cell. Unfortunately, most of them were written by men who have either never given in to their felonious proclivities or were never caught or served as much as a day in prison. One might therefore wonder—as I have—where and how these men gained their expertise in such matters.

To learn about crime and the criminal, a criminologist must rely on the one-sided information supplied by the police or some federal agency. In the same way, a penologist must rely almost entirely on surface information. It's a little like the newsman who visits Russia and, after being taken on a guided tour and allowed to read selected booklets and circulars, comes away an expert on the Soviet Union.

It's true, of course, that an occasional social scientist will become well enough acquainted with a few inmates of a prison to get below the surface; but even then, he usually hears only what the "convict" wants to tell him, which I know from personal experience is something less than the truth.

By the same token, an occasional criminology major from one of the universities will frequent the so-called criminal hangouts—sleazy nightclubs, all-night restaurants, and third-rate hotels—and get to know a few hoodlums on a first-name basis. But here again, the information he gathers is rarely worth his efforts.

Realizing that their information is less than complete, these crime and penal "experts" will use data and statistics resulting from a myriad of surveys and polls in much the same way that secretaries shower the heroes in a ticker-tape parade. The result is usually a book so jammed with esoteric theorems and anachronistic misinformation that even a social science professor would hardly think it worth his time. Little wonder then that such books rarely reach the general public.

In the spring of 1969, I and the three other staff members of the *Lake Shore Outlook* (the inmate-written and -edited newspaper of the Indiana State Prison) decided to pool our knowledge and writing talents—such as they are—to correct this situation. As a result of that decision and subsequent efforts, this book has become a reality.

While all of us have taken college courses in sociology and criminology, it is doubtful that any of us would have elected to write on these topics had it not been for our own criminal histories and penal backgrounds. Here then are our credentials for writing this book: Taken together, we have served more than fifty years in a dozen different prisons on charges ranging from burglary to forgery, from armed robbery to kidnaping.

It all began when the four of us sat discussing the *pros*

and *cons*—no pun intended—of our writing such a book. At first, a couple of us were reluctant to undertake such a formidable task; but, the more we kicked it around, the more interested we all became. Following this bull session, our discussions about *crime* and *punishment* became somewhat more formalized, and in a matter of a few days we had actually begun to write.

This was really only the beginning, however, for it then fell to me to contact Miss Ellen Levine of Paul Reynolds, Inc.—a New York literary agent with whom I had previously corresponded—to determine the best approach to such a book. Miss Levine was most helpful in this regard. As I look back, it is doubtful that we would have succeeded with this project without her help and encouragement.

As editor of a prison newspaper, I had long felt that it was the inmate's—especially the inmate journalist's—responsibility to verbally kick the affluent cushions from beneath the sleeping public, tell them what's really going on in this nation's prisons, and inform them that they're victims of a gigantic fraud with regard to the so-called "rehabilitation" programs in vogue today. And because I hadn't been very successful in doing this with the *Outlook,* this book seemed the ideal way to reach the general public—the tax-paying public, who have every right to know what *is* happening behind prison walls.

The present state of affairs in corrections in this country is appalling, and nothing *can* or *will* be done until you demand something more workable and humane. The four of us hope, therefore, that after having read this book, most of you will agree that the huge, outdated institutions in this nation that we call prisons and reformatories are in reality catacombs of misery and perversion, caldrons of bitterness and hatred that must be torn down and replaced with scientifically oriented centers of social readjustment.

This book is a series of essays, profiles, and sketches

written by men who, though presently serving time in prison, have lived both in society generally and on the outskirts of so-called decency. And while you may be anxious to get on to the chapters dealing in sex, violence, and the utter despair of prison living, I hope you will read the first section of the book, as it will serve to remind you that although man is and has been, in many ways, a bastard since the beginning of recorded history, there is still some hope for him—for *us*.

As might be expected from four people from varying backgrounds, our writing styles vary considerably. I think, however, that this fact adds to rather than detracts from what is sandwiched between the covers of this book. I would hope, therefore, that the reader would judge each selection on its individual merits and then consider the whole a smorgasbord upon which he is invited to feed to his mind's content.

—H.J.G.

**AN
EYE
FOR
AN
EYE**

1

Man's Greatest Folly

The problems of crime bring us together. Even as we join in common action, we know there can be no instant victory. Ancient evils do not yield to easy conquest. We cannot limit our efforts to enemies we can see. We must, with equal resolve, seek out new knowledge, new technique, and new understanding.

—MESSAGE FROM PRESIDENT JOHNSON
TO CONGRESS MARCH 9, 1966

A crime is simply an act or omission forbidden by law and punishable upon conviction. Yet the reasons for the social phenomenon referred to as "the rising tide of crime" are vastly more difficult to understand. But, understand it we must if we are to avoid total chaos in the United States. For a social problem, like a cancerous sore, has a tendency to spread, and—if not treated in time—to destroy.

That crime and violence have been an integral part of man's social order is borne out by his many wars of acquisition. Hardly a decade has elapsed in the whole of man's history when he hasn't, in the name of nationalism, encroached on his neighbor. And just as the major proportion of all individual criminal acts are crimes against property, these criminal aggressions perpetrated by one nation against another have almost always centered around territorial disputes and/or the almighty dollar.

Crimes of violence garbed in the full battle-dress of war or the shabby cloak of isolated incidence have been so prevalent down through history that man has socialized warfare and enshrined the heroes of such dubious activities —both factual and fictional.

Such heroes have been many in name, yet only a few of the more illustrious and infamous should suffice to make the point. Who that is familiar with Homer's epic poetry doesn't quickly recall the deeds and misdeeds of Hector and Achilles? Likewise, who isn't at least vaguely familiar with the antics of Beowulf or the conquests of Genghis Khan? And finally, what man-child hasn't played Robin Hood or Jesse James?

In the distant past, a young tribesman was first a hunter, then a warrior, and finally, if he possessed rare talents for rape, pillage, and slaughter, a great war-lord to be praised for his ruthless feats of conquest. And this was the case up to and including World War II. However, with the advent of nuclear bombs, which have rendered full-scale, declared wars obsolete, how is a young man to satisfy his primeval urge to join the pack and act out his feelings of aggression?

Certainly, the police actions (?) in Korea, Viet Nam, and other trouble spots afford a handful of young men the opportunity of wearing a uniform and venting their hostilities against an alleged enemy. But what about the hundreds of thousands—yes, even millions—of young men who are for one reason or other denied the aforementioned avenues of release from their socially imposed inhibitions? What will they do? Or, more to the point, what are they doing? The answer is obvious: they're stealing, burning, cutting, shooting, raping, fighting, and just generally raising hell. In short, they have turned to isolated incidents of crime and occasional mob actions as a means of demonstrating their masculinity, their gut reaction to the oppression and brutality of modern life. In this instance, however, they aren't decorated for killing and maiming their enemy, as they would be if they were members of the armed forces; rather, now that they are killing and molesting members of their own communities, they are branded as criminals.

In my opinion, we must look at and treat the whole patient and not merely what appears on the surface to be the affected member. For crime, whether we like it or not, is very much a part of the individual and national character of the United States. It is, in fact, deeply rooted in the very foundations of our so-called free enterprise and democratic system of business and government.

Even now I can hear the pious pleas of innocence to such a blatant charge. ". . . and made by a common criminal! A no-good thief!" Yet the fact remains that property crime, which makes up the bulk of our annual statistics in this country, is an outgrowth of the profit motive deeply embedded in the very texture of our culture. In short, it has a tendency to bring out the worst in all but the most saintly people, and they are so rare as to be practically nonexistent.

The best illustration of this is the increasing number of crimes reported in our daily newspapers—crimes that involve people from all walks of life. They range in seriousness from price fixing by corporation heads to small-time payola; from bank embezzling to check forgery; from armed robbery to charity fund pilfering; from political graft to income-tax cheating; from burglary to shoplifting— which incidentally, accounts for a greater loss in dollar volume than all the aforementioned combined.

Yet according to the report made by President Johnson's Commission on Law Enforcement and Administration of Justice, "Many Americans take comfort in the view that crime is the vice of a handful of people. This view is inaccurate. In the United States today, one boy in six is referred to the juvenile court . . . about 40 per cent of all male children now living in the United States will be arrested for a nontraffic offense during their lives."

The report went on to say: "An independent survey of 1,700 persons found that 91 per cent of the sample admitted they had committed acts for which they might have received jail or prison sentences."

Crime then, it would seem, is a common occurrence in this country and touches the lives of all of us in one way or another. Therefore, it would behoove us to quit paying lip service to such myths as "One Nation Under God" as if the Omnipotent Master had for some strange reason granted us a corner on goodness or absolved us of all guilt for our wrongdoings. Let's try to see ourselves—individually and collectively—as we really are.

It does no good whatever to ignore our faults while looking down our noses at the neighbor across the street. Nor does it solve anything to curse a headlined member of the Cosa Nostra while filching a can of anchovies from the local supermarket. Honesty, like charity, must begin at home. Only the sinless may condemn.

If indeed our history has been a "bath of blood" and, as John Steinbeck said, we are now a "sad and sick and destructive society," then how, you might ask, can we change appreciably? Or better yet, if we are by nature violent and self-seeking, how can we ever hope to control our ruthless and selfish natures?

The answer is, of course, that we are not all base or negative; on the contrary, we also have a positive side to our natures and therefore desire—alas! even yearn for—the approval of our society and will, as a result, go to very great lengths in our quest for the acceptance of our social groups. Even to the extent of obeying the law.

To warrant this desire to conform on the part of its individual members, however, a society must itself conform to certain ideals inherent in the positive side of man's nature. It must be a society wherein every citizen is made to feel that he belongs—a society wherein every baby born receives as his birthright the "golden ring" of full opportunity.

It is all too obvious that our social institutions—the home, the school, the church, and the government—have not met their respective responsibilities insofar as properly socializing the new members (children) of our society—especially those from the minority segments of our population. As a result, many teen-agers are refusing to try the status quo and are behaving in anti-establishment, anti-social, revolutionary ways.

This rebellion has taken many forms. Yet the most apparent is so-called juvenile crime, which—according to FBI Director J. Edgar Hoover—accounted for 49 per cent of the over-all crime picture of 1967. And this picture didn't improve during 1968 and '69. The fact is, as the months and years go by, those under twenty-five years of age seem less and less inclined to identify with our social institutions, which they consider anachronistic. And to expect other than that tens of thousands of these youngsters will of necessity crowd our already overcrowded prisons during the seventies and eighties is naive in the extreme.

To cope with the growing problem, we can continue to jeopardize our remaining personal freedoms in our country by enacting more and more state and federal laws (criminal codes) and exact ever-increasingly severe punishment for the violation of same. This, of course, will necessitate continued and ever-accelerated construction of vast new systems of penal and correctional (*sic*) institutions. Or, on the other hand, we can merely ignore the "skyrocketing" crime rate and give free rein to our criminal inclinations.

Quite obviously, neither of these proposals is realistic, the first being a questionable palliative only, and the second, of course, an absurdity.

A few of the "die-hards" who still subscribe to the nineteenth-century "punitive punishment" school of thought obviously feel that the criminal is possessed of evil spirits and must, therefore, be put to death or imprisoned for life. One such is J. Edgar Hoover, who is reported to have said that modern penologists are "coddling criminals."

On the other hand, men like James Vorenberg, the executive director of President Johnson's crime commission, feel that our present penal systems are totally outdated and fail, as a result, to rehabilitate the offender. Said the commission: "Experts are increasingly coming to feel that the conditions under which many offenders are handled, particularly in institutions, are often a positive detriment to rehabilitation."

My own feeling is that most of our present penal institutions (and I've served time in four of them) are nothing more than seed beds of hatred. They are, in reality, institutions of higher learning in crime and violence. The fact is, if I were a member of a "Communist conspiracy" who sought to undermine the government of this country I would forthwith lend my voice to the cries for "an eye for an eye and tooth for a tooth" and shout, "Let the offender be damned!" But because I love my country, I would prefer to see a more rational approach to our problem.

Just such an approach might be to liken crime in this country to malaria in the vicinity of a stagnated pond. If we were trying to eliminate malaria in such an area, we would have to inspect the pond and devise a way to drain it of material defilement. So it is with crime: we must sanction selective birth control, eliminate poverty, do away with slum and ghetto areas, close the cultural lag—that area where social institutions such as the church, the school, and the government lag so far behind technological and scientific advancement—do away with the outmoded means of handling those who are caught violating the law, abolish for all time the grisly, inhuman practice of capital punishment, which begets an atmosphere of violence that can only regenerate the taking of human life . . . and, last but by no means least, come to realize that the man who falls by the wayside is indeed our brother, who, if not helped, will become a burden many times over.

Only when all the aforementioned have been accomplished will we be able to say with any degree of certainty that we have done what the forward thrust of humanity demands of us. Only then can we afford the smugness of the self-righteous—if even then.

I would be the first to agree that such giant steps forward in the area of human equality and social justice will take time; yet we must begin now while there *is* still time.

If ever in history man has been faced with a supreme challenge, now is that time. We are engulfed in a series of social revolutions of which crime is only a symptom—albeit, an extremely important one. How we face up to this challenge will in large measure decide man's future course here on earth.

—H.J.G.

2

First Day

I know not whether Laws be right
Or whether Laws be wrong;
All that we know who be in gaol
Is that the wall is strong
And that each day is like a year,
A year whose days are long.
—OSCAR WILDE

It was a day just like any other when I took the Blue Goose down to Joliet. It was autumn. The leaves were turning gold and orange and brown. They floated lazily down from the trees, covered the grass, and blew about the streets.

The Blue Goose turned off the main highway just east of the business district of Joliet and aimed its blunt nose toward the outskirts of town. The scenery was just as depressing as the general mood within the beat-up old schoolbus. Street after street of weatherbeaten frame houses, auto junk yards, vacant lots, and small marginal commercial concerns.

But none of the men in the bus minded the drabness

of the scenery. This was the last free-world scenery they would see for a long, long time. After rotting for several months in the county jail awaiting trial, just about any sight other than steel and concrete looked pretty good to them.

You could not see much anyway because the windows of the bus were covered by a thick black screening and the glass had not been washed for months.

I was one of forty-odd men chained and handcuffed together on the bus. Why they called it the Blue Goose I never did find out, though I do recall someone saying that it had been the proud possessor of a coat of bright blue paint at one time in its life.

Some of the men were laughing and joking, others were conversing in low tones. But most were just sitting hunched up in the small seats gazing out of the windows or staring into space. That bus was carrying over a thousand years up to the state penitentiary.

Everyone stopped talking as we neared the prison. There was an air of nervous tension in the bus which had been mounting steadily since we had left the county jail. Up ahead next to the driver, on the other side of a heavy screen door, sat our shotgun guard, cradling a Remington pump in his skinny arms. In back of us a black county sheriff's car nosed the rear bumper of the bus. You could look down and see the stubby, notched noses of the Thompson submachine guns sticking a few inches above the window level of the car.

Then someone said, "There it is." All heads swiveled in unison, and some bent low craning their necks to see. Yes, there it was, a sort of midwest Gothic monstrosity of rust-colored limestone outlined against the slate sky. It reminded me of something right out of an old Frankenstein movie, just about the most depressing sight I had ever seen.

The bus was quiet now. The only sounds were the rattle of chains and handcuffs, and the shuffling of feet on the pimpled steel floor of the bus. We slowed and swung into a short concrete drive which led to a barred truck entrance in the high stone wall. The bus lurched to a stop. The shotgun guard stood up and growled something about our new home as he unlocked our cage and backed carefully down the three steps to the ground, the shotgun at port arms.

Slowly, awkwardly, stiffly, we got up, one row at a time, our exit governed by our place on the long chain, and worked our way down the aisle to the door. You had to go down the steps sideways because you were handcuffed to another man and tied by a four-foot length of chain to a pair of men in front and behind you.

We lined up outside the bus in a long double row and waited. Behind us were two deputies with pumpguns. To our left two county detectives with the choppers. We were not going anywhere.

Two men in brown uniforms came out of a door in the truck gate and stood talking with the deputy in charge of the transportation detail. We watched them laughing and joking. It was just another day for them. Then they turned to us, and one of them waved his hand and pointed to the gate. "OK, through the gate there. No talkin' and no smokin'."

We stumbled wearily through the gate into a kind of sally port, through another gate, and emerged in a large concrete courtyard. The walls, about forty feet high, were on three sides. Directly in front of us was a dirty limestone three-story building with bars on all the windows. A sign over the building entrance said: ILLINOIS STATE PENITENTIARY—JOLIET BRANCH, and just below this: DIAGNOSTIC DEPOT.

A couple of the guys started whispering, and one of the men in brown yelled out, "Knock off that talking!" Now the courtyard was still. They clanged the gates shut

behind us and walked down the rows, unlocking our handcuffs, letting them fall with a clank on the concrete at our
feet. As soon as our hands were free they motioned us toward the entrance to the limestone building.

I looked up at the wall as I walked toward the building and saw a guard in the gun tower over my head. He
had a carbine pointed at me. I looked down quickly and
stepped through the doors into a wide light-green corridor
with benches along the walls. None of the men ahead of me
sat down so I didn't either.

Two more men in brown uniforms stepped out of a
door about midway down the corridor and stood staring at
us, shoulders together. One was tall, about fifty, with a set
of silver bars on his shoulders. The other was short, fat,
and was wearing sergeant's stripes on the sleeve of his badly
rumpled shirt. When the last of the busload straggled in the
door, the sergeant tugged on his pants and stepped forward.
"Empty yer pockets an' put all yer belongins in these here
envelopes," he yelled as he waved a batch of brown manila
envelopes.

We lined up and got our envelopes. I put my watch,
comb, wallet, belt, and handkerchief in the envelope. As
each of us turned in his personal property, the sergeant
handed us a pencil stub and told us to write our name on
the front of the envelope.

An old convict in faded blue denims, his number stenciled in black ink on the front and back of his shirt and
pants, shuffled down the corridor toward us, dragging two
heavy gray canvas bags. These were for our shoes and
clothes.

"Everybody strip bare-ass!" yelled the sergeant. We all
stripped standing up and stuffed our belongings in the bags,
which the old convict dragged off down the corridor.

The fat sergeant bellowed again and jabbed his thumb
in the direction of a gate halfway down the corridor. We

lined up along the wall by the gate. As we stepped one at a time through the gate, the one with the silver bars greeted us with a flashlight. He looked in our hands, under our arms, at the soles of our feet, and then in our mouths and anuses for "contraband." When he had finished this routine he sent us down the hall to stand in front of a door marked: SHOWER ROOM.

After we had been standing bare-assed on the concrete for about half an hour the sergeant strutted down the corridor and unlocked the door. It was a large square-shaped room with shower heads jutting out from the walls at four-foot intervals. The floor sloped toward a large drain in the center, and a small concrete rim ran around the room three feet from the wall.

"In and out," the fat sergeant shouted. "Two minutes."

There were about twenty shower heads. A man got under each one, and the rest stood milling about in the center of the room.

"*Everyone* in," the sergeant screamed. "Two men to a shower . . . three men to a shower. *Everyone* in."

The rest of the men jammed into the space under the shower heads until we all stood elbow to ass waiting for the water to come on.

A Negro con in a blue denim jacket passed down the line giving out one-inch cubes of yellow soap to every other man. When he reached the end of the row he reached above his head and turned a wheel.

Ice cold water spat from the shower heads and struck us about the shoulders. I jumped forward out of reach of the jet of water and stood shivering by the drain. Now the old Negro was turning another wheel and hot water began to mix with the cold.

I stepped over the trough and waited for the man with the cube of soap to finish lathering. He stepped aside and handed me the soap. I stepped under the water just as the sergeant shouted, "Rinse off and get out!"

I looked up in disbelief. The man next to me said, "Hurry up," so I stepped aside to let him under the water.

"Water off!" announced the sergeant, and the convict whipped the wheels, shutting down the shower. A few men stood under the heads with soap covering their bodies.

"Out of the showers," said the sergeant. We moved like a herd of cattle into the middle of the room, dripping soap and water.

The convict picked up a Campbell's Soup carton and ambled into the group. The box contained small hand towels, about the size and texture of dish rags. We dried ourselves, if you can call it that, and stood in a shivering mass of nakedness watching the fat sergeant, who was obviously enjoying his work.

He herded us out into the hall and lined us up before a door marked CLOTHING ROOM. We stood in front of this door for another half-hour before a con came down the hall and entered the door. He gave us all brownish gray overalls and gray canvas slippers. My coveralls were too small and I asked for a larger size. The con laughed and said, "Tough shit man."

I started to argue with him when one of the guys behind me tugged on my arm and pulled me away from the door.

"You crazy?" he asked. "Argue with that rat and you'll wind up in the hole." He grinned. "Nobody gets the right size anything in this joint."

I nodded and leaned against the wall, back hunched because I couldn't straighten up in the small coveralls. The sergeant and the one with the silver bars, who I later learned was a captain, walked down the hall toward us. As they came abreast of me I said, "Excuse me, but I'd like to get another pair of coveralls. These are too small."

The fat sergeant stared at me for a moment, slowly shifting the snuff in his mouth with his tongue. Then he grinned and walked on. The captain said, "Where do you think you are, the Ritz?"

I flushed. "No, but I . . ."

"Awright, you'll get another pair of coveralls on laundry day." He walked off down the hall.

"See," said the guy who had pulled me away from the clothing room door.

I jammed my hands in the pockets of the coveralls.

"Better get your hands out of them pockets."

"I can't put my hands in my pockets?"

"Nope," he replied. "From now on you can't do *nothing* without permission. They tell you when to eat, drink, piss, wash, go to bed, get up, pray, and breathe."

"You been here before?"

"Yah." He bobbed his head up and down. "Three times."

I shook my head.

"You'll get used to it," he said. "Just keep your mouth shut and your eyes open. Learn the ropes."

"Hey you!" someone shouted in my ear. I turned and looked into the face of the fat sergeant, which was growing uglier with each passing moment. "I done tol' you about talkin'. Catch you again and you git the hole, unnerstan'?"

I nodded.

"What?" he shouted again, his face beet red. "What?"

"Yes," I said. "I understand."

"Yes what!" he screamed. "Yes what?"

The guy behind me poked me in the back. "Yes *sir*," I said.

"That's better," he said, and turned away with a grin on his face. I watched him strut off down the hall and stop in front of another man to begin the same routine all over again.

I turned to the little guy behind me.

"They're gonna rehab-ill-tate your ass." He grinned. "It's all part of the *treatment* program."

I stared glumly at the floor.

"Aw, don't worry about it," he said. "He just seen you was a cherry. He knows you ain't been in no joint before." He leaned closer and spoke almost without moving his lips. "I know how to handle these dumb rednecks. You got to go into a little act is all. You say 'yes *sir,* cap'n,' and 'right away, cap'n,' and he'll leave you alone. All screws are 'cap'n sir,' and you hate their guts *inside.*"

"Pair it up and knock it off," yelled the sergeant from down the hall. We assembled in a double row. "Eyes front and git them hands out of yer pockets!"

They marched us down the hall to a flight of stairs behind a set of steel bars. We passed two officers where cons in blue denim were sitting at desks typing and shuffling papers. The sergeant unlocked the gate, and we climbed the stairs to another gate at the top, then into a cellhouse, where we assembled in the middle of the floor in two long rows.

"Hands at yer sides and knock it off," bellowed the sergeant, who stood with arms folded across his chest and legs spread apart. His fat gut hung down over his belt like a basketball, and a small stream of snuff dribbled down his chin.

The floor was concrete. So was the ceiling, some thirty feet above our heads. Two tiers of cells ran along the walls with solid steel doors painted battleship gray. In the middle of each door was a small barred window with a slot at the bottom to shove in food tins. I could see faces looking out at us from many of the windows.

"Aw right," shouted the sergeant. "Line up down there." He pointed to the end of the cellhouse where a sign hung on the wall proclaiming the area as the BARBERSHOP.

We stood behind a red line painted on the concrete and stepped two at a time into the jerry-built barber chairs. They used the clippers to shave all the hair off our heads down to the gleaming white skin. It took about two minutes per man. The con barbers went about their work in silence; the fat sergeant leaned against the wall watching the operation.

When we were sheared we were passed on to another con, who told us to drop our overalls around our ankles. He sprayed our armpits and genital areas with a powdered pesticide and told us to button up and go back to the center of the cellhouse floor. There we waited for the barbers and the "sanitation" worker to complete their job on the whole crew. We stood with hands at our sides in silence, thinking about that wonderful beautiful free world we had just left behind us. Boy, did we feel sorry for ourselves.

Now the sergeant and the captain paced back and forth in front of us, looking us over. "Aw right," snarled the sergeant, "pay attention now. Cap'n's gonna talk to yo'll."

The captain cleared his throat. "You're now *inmates* of the Illinois State Penitentiary. We didn't send for you. We didn't bring you here. You brought yourselves. But we're gonna see that you stay here until your sentence is complete or you are paroled."

He scratched his buttock and continued. "We don't stand for any crap from no *inmate* here, so get that through your heads right now. Step out of line and we'll come down on you hard. My advice to you is to do your own time, mind your own business, and obey all the rules. That'll make your time easier and our job easier."

He spoke in a dull, flat monotone, with a slow, southern Illinois accent. He had obviously given this little speech a thousand times before and knew every word by rote.

"You'll find some *inmates* who'll try to lead you

astray. Don't listen to 'em. You'll find some *inmates* who'll tell you how to beat the system and get around the rules. Don't listen to 'em. You'll find some *inmates* who'll try to escape. They won't make it. We ain't had no escapes in twenty years. Remember what I said. Do your own time. Obey all the rules. You'll find a rule book in your cells. Study it. Memorize them rules. You got no excuses if you break one. We got a place for rulebreakers and troublemakers in here, and it ain't pleasant."

He coughed and shifted his weight. "OK, Sarge," he said, and walked away.

"Aw right," said the sergeant. "Stand here till yer name is called by the clerk. He'll give you a doorcard and assign ya to a cell." He started to walk away, then paused and yelled over his shoulder, "An keep yer mouths shut!"

The cellhouse clerk was a balding lifer. A tall gangling stringbean with a built-in stoop who walked so far bent forward you thought he was going to fall over any second. He handed me a strip of white cardboard with my name and number stenciled on it and pointed down the row of cells.

"At the end," he said. "Cell twenty-nine." I shuffled down the concrete in my canvas slippers and stood in front of cell number twenty-nine. A face looked out at me from the barred hole in the door.

"You comin' in here?" it said.

"Yes," I said.

The face continued to stare at me. Down the concrete the sergeant locked a man in a cell. He slammed the door and jammed the key in the lock. Then he started walking toward me.

"You go here?" he asked when he reached me.

"Yes *sir*," I replied.

He scowled and jammed the huge brass key in the

lock, gave it a savage twist, and jerked the door open. "Inside," he said.

I entered the cell and the door slammed, the key grating in the lock. I heard him trudge away.

The cell was about nine feet long and seven feet wide. Directly opposite the door was a heavily barred window which overlooked a yard. A toilet was mounted on the wall near the door, and just above it was a wash basin and single faucet. Two metal slabs jutted out from the wall, each fitted with what could pass for a mattress. A thin gray blanket and a sheet were folded at the foot of the top bunk. On the bottom one lay a boy of about twenty with blue eyes and a slight build. He had a blond stubble on his chin, and of course he had been shaved bald.

"Where you from," he said.

"Chicago," I said.

"Rockford," he said.

"Been here long?"

" 'Bout three weeks."

I walked over to the window and sat down on the floor with relief.

"Chow in a few minutes," he said.

"I'm starved," I said.

"Yah," he said. "You guys missed lunch. Beans."

I groaned. "I'm sick of beans. That's all they seemed to give us in the county jail."

He laughed.

"What's funny?" I asked.

"You are. Sick of beans. That's a laugh. You gonna be a lot sicker of 'em before you leave this hellhole. They bean you to death around here."

I didn't say anything.

"Yah," he continued, "beans and macaroni, beans and greens, beans and spaghetti, beans and rice, beans and noodles, and beans and beans."

I smiled. "I guess all jails are alike."

"Yah, in this state," he nodded. "Want a cigarette?"

"Sure."

He tossed me a bag. I looked at it. "What's this?"

"Egyptian," he said. "State tobacco. They get scrap stuff, mix a little molasses and iodine with it, and grind it up for us."

I opened the bag and looked inside. It smelled faintly of tobacco but looked like wheat chaff. He tossed me some cigarette papers. "If that don't give you lung cancer nothing will."

I tried to roll one. After the third try I was still making no progress and had a pile of tobacco in front of me on the floor.

"Here, let me roll it," he said. "It takes practice." He took the tobacco and papers from me. "My name's Bill," he said.

"Mine's Ed."

"OK, Ed, just watch me." He spilled a little, but not nearly as much as I had. He handed it to me. "Next time you roll, put a paper under you," he said. "They only give you one bag a week. Besides, they inspect the cell every day. There better not be any tobacco on the floor, or your ass has had it and mine too."

I nodded. He tossed me a book of matches and I lit the thing. It tasted like I don't know what. I guess it tasted like I imagined dried manure tasted. I coughed and gagged and shook my head.

"I'll finish it," Bill said. "You'll get used to it."

I shook my head again. "Oh no I won't."

He smiled and took a drag. A bell rang in the cellhouse. "Chow," he said. "They hand it through the window." He got up and walked to the door.

I looked out the barred window at the yard below. It was just after Halloween, but a light snow was coming down, partially obscuring the distant wall and gun towers.

Sounds at the door made me turn my head. I got up to receive a bowl of whatever was thrust through the opening. I looked at it. I smelled it. The bottom of the metal bowl was filled with watery navy beans on the surface of which floated a solitary piece of fat with hairs sticking out of it like the chuck of a hairbrush. Two pieces of bread were jammed down the side of the bowl halfway into the watery beans. I took the bowl over to the window and placed it on the sill.

Bill walked back to his bunk and sat down. He began to eat.

"What's that stuff in the beans?" I asked. "That stuff with the hairs sticking out of it?"

"Fatback," Bill said. "Fatmeat is for protein, man. They got to give you some protein. Whatsamatter, don't you like hogfat?"

I shook my head.

"Well, I'll eat it," he announced.

I handed him the bowl. "Eat it all. I'm not hungry."

"I had a hard time gettin' used to it at first," he said.

"How often do you get that stuff?"

"Oh, you get fatback in all your beans and all your greens and in most all vegetables. They cook about everything in hog fat. Boil it, fry it, you know."

I was silent.

"Couple times a week they give you a meatball. Sometimes they call it hamburger, sometimes sails-bary steak. 'Bout the size of a silver dollar and mixed with filler like bread or crackers. Tough as golf balls."

The steel door of the cell reverberated as someone banged it. Bill jumped up. "Coffee time," he said. "Coffee comin' up." He rinsed his bowl in the sink and walked to the door, where he held the bowl out the hole. Someone poured coffee in it, and Bill drew it back.

"Hey," he said. "Here, take this coffee since I'm eatin' your dinner." He handed me the bowl.

"Thanks," I said glumly.

He smiled. "You'll get used to it. Me, I adapt easy. It ain't much worse than the boys' school."

"Oh."

"Yah, before this rap for stealing a car I done time in the boys' school for runaway and truancy. Three times."

"Oh."

"Yah, give me twenty years for taking a car."

"Twenty years!" I exclaimed.

"Well, that's the max. But I see the board in three-nine."

He ate my beans. "Whatcha in for?" he asked.

"Robbery," I said.

"How much you bring down with you?"

"Five to fifteen years."

"See, I get twenty for a car and you get fifteen for robbery. If I'd a been in Chicago I'd a got maybe five years."

"It doesn't seem fair, does it?" I said.

"Fair," he said. "Fair? What's fair? Nothing's fair in this world. They give you the shaft whenever they can, that's all. Makes 'em feel good and holy."

"Looks that way," I said.

"Sure they do," he nodded and finished my bowl of beans. "Gimme the bowl and I'll wash it. They'll be coming by for 'em in a minute."

I nodded.

"Try out the Beautyrest." He gestured toward the top bunk.

I climbed into the bunk, kicking off the canvas slippers. The mattress cover was stuffed with straw. It was old straw, lumpy and hard in places, loose as sawdust in others. I beat the lumps, trying to smooth out the mattress, but quickly gave up the idea when a huge cloud of dust, dirt, and lint swirled around my face. I folded the blanket and using it as a pillow, stretched out on the hills and valleys beneath me. The steel plate behind my head chattered and hummed as someone flushed a toilet, and the clanking of keys and buckets and steel doors resounded through the cellhouse.

There was no reading material, not even the ubiquitous Bible. I gazed at the ceiling and began counting the cracks and lines in the plaster. Well, I thought, just about got my first day in. Only fifteen-hundred to go.

—E.T.

3

Rehabilitation

It is a problem that allows people to go through all sorts of folderal to avoid thinking about it. It is a repression of reality—when you begin talking about rehabilitation when you don't know how to rehabilitate, you can defend anything you want to do.

—Francis Allen
Dean of the School of Law
University of Michigan

Measured by any standard the American penal system is a scandalous flop. Two thirds of the population of our nation's "correctional" institutions are not "corrected." They are repeaters, that is, inmates who have previously received the prescribed "treatment" but are not corrected, reformed, resocialized, or rehabilitated.

In spite of all the obvious evidence that it does not work, the American people continue to operate a system of prisons that have never done even a halfway decent job, and never will until some drastic changes are made. All of this has been pointed out time and time again, yet the public continues to fly in the face of tons of statistics, mass documentation of gross economic, social, and human waste, logical arguments, reason, and reality. It seems rather pathological on the surface, but when we begin to analyze this strange and contradictory set of attitudes and behavior, we begin to understand that things are as they are because the public wants them that way.

Orwell's *1984* and Huxley's *Brave New World* are not just around the corner in some parts of our society. They have been here for a long time in the field of corrections. For example, think-speak, the double talk of those predicted new eras, is already hoary with age in our present approach to crime and criminality. An outstanding example of the new eras' fraudulent double talk is found in the field of penology, where terms like "reform," "resocialization," and "rehabilitation" have been bandied about for decades.

The most popular word of the trilogy today is "rehabilitation." The criminologist and the penologist talk about it, the prison warden and his staff talk about it, the judges and the courts talk about it, and even the community mentions it once in a while.

Of course, none of them has the faintest conception of what he is talking about. The whole concept as it is used in the field of corrections is a huge sham and a great fraud. It is a big "put-on" because while all the talk about rehabilitation goes on and on and on, the whole system keeps right on doing what it has been doing for a century—demeaning, degrading, dehumanizing, and punishing.

With the absolute certainty of offending many people, I have to say that the American people want, desire, lust for, and need crime and criminality. They need, albeit on a subconscious level, an easily identifiable group whom they can look down upon, feel superior to, castigate, segregate, and inflict emotional, psychological, and physical punishment upon. The public needs its criminally deviant individuals so that through an act of catharsis they can expunge their own guilt feelings, and every once in a while call up from the darker side of their souls all the repressed hate and savage fury that dwell within.

We have, all of us, socially deviant and criminalistic thoughts and urges. It is normal to the human condition. But, writes Sidney Harris, "We are then forced to punish ourselves for these illicit and untamed feelings—and so we impose harsh penalties upon the perpetrators of such crimes. All realistic evidence shows that harsh penalties do not act as a deterrent, but we pretend they do, in order to justify our actions and to mitigate our hidden sense of guilt."

The criminal functions as a sort of "built-in" outgroup and contributes to the solidarity of the social group as a target for its aggressions in the same way as do witches, devils, or hostile foreign powers. It was the anthropologist George Herbert Mead who pointed out fifty years ago that ". . . the attitude of hostility toward the lawbreaker has the unique advantage of uniting all members of the community in the emotional solidarity of aggression."

This, the most criminogenic society of modernity, has quite literally clapped millions of persons into its prisons in the last few decades under an archaic system of vengeful law and alleged corrections. And the reason for the stagnation and perpetuation of this madness is that the people need it. The community knows full well that prisons do not "reform" or "resocialize" or "rehabilitate." They know that prisons poison and destroy a man's spirit, degrade him, and turn him into a worse human being than he was before he entered the tool steel gates.

"It is unbelievable," writes Karl Menninger, "that anyone familiar with our prisons, let alone with the history of punishment, supposes that confinement in prison reforms or rehabilitates. The truth is, at the end of their terms, many prisoners are likely to be more dangerous than they ever were before. . . . Almost every warden says so, and all but the most somnolent and hypocritical judges knows and regrets it." Unfortunately, Karl Menninger reflects the viewpoint of only a small percentage of the general public. The vast majority are quite happy with things as they are.

The American correctional system is a felicitous product of all the inequities, all the injustice, all the glib and trite hypocrisy, all the double and triple standards to which the society is heir. And while I speak of the collective responsibility when I use the words "society" or "public," it all really boils down to individual responsibility in the final analysis. Nothing so aptly illustrates the darker side of man's nature as the facility with which individuals consent to the most wicked acts. Everyone hides behind the anonymity of the group. Nobody is held personally responsible for the evil that is done. While abhorring crime and violence and vengeance, and adoring justice and humanity and compassion, the individual too often encourages acts of crime, injustice, and vengeance.

By lecturing and cajoling—but certainly not by setting any kind of example—the society seeks to provide a pitifully small adjunct to its system of retribution, punishment, and dehumanization. This adjunct is the admonition to "straighten up" or "go straight," by seeking socially approved goals and ways of behaving.

But here we have another of those paradoxes that keep cropping up in any discussion of crime and criminality. Society admonishes us to seek socially approved goals! But society does not provide socially approved access to the goals or the means to achieve these goals in the prisons. They teach the prisoner to hate and ask him to love. They strip the prisoner of all responsibility and ask him to be responsible. They degrade the prisoner and ask him to have some self-respect. They teach a man how to make license plates or wield a broom, then say they've given him a trade, toss him out the front gate with twenty dollars in his pocket, and say—survive!

And once he is released the society continues to discriminate against and stigmatize him. With the cachet "once a thief, always a thief," they perpetuate all the abuses heaped upon him since the first day he became a socially "acceptable" target. Two sociologists, Richard Schwarz and Jerome Skolnick, conducted a study of hiring practices and found that only four per cent, or one out of twenty-five employers, would hire a man who had been convicted of assault. Make a man covet something and then bar him from access to legitimate means of obtaining it. Good show! Smart thinking! And then try to convince the average prisoner that the whole system is not "rigged." They know exactly what the society thinks of ex-cons, and that the society will continue to treat him as a pariah for the rest of his life. Thirty or forty years after release he will still be defined as a "risk," won't be bonded, won't be given any job involving trust, won't be knowingly hired by ninety per cent of the business and industrial community.

As a consequence of community attitudes, rehabilitation is virtually nonexistent in our prisons. And as a further consequence, "treatment" is largely a vague, undefinable process in which "someone does something for, or to, someone else." Thus our prisons operate with revolving doors, the same people continually going in and out. Once you pass through these doors, the "treatment" program virtually insures that you will be back. Thus our systems of correction are bastions of injustice, monuments of economic and human waste, and fortresses of indifference and hypocrisy.

To this environment, writes Martin Mayer, ". . . without thinking much about it, we banish about 100,000 people each year—20,000 of them for sentences of five years or longer, unless a parole board intervenes. What society wants is an institution that will be primarily punitive to the convict while he is there, yet will prepare him for release to sin no more. It can't be done—but nobody cares much, because the society is prepared in these matters to accept defeat."

Thus the most modern, most "enlightened" country in the world, operates a system of jails and prisons which are wretched pestholes, indecent crime-breeding swamps of iniquity into which are jammed the poor, the socially outcast, the ignorant, the emotionally disturbed and the mentally ill. There, confused, self-contradictory, antisocial beings are turned into the truly alienated sector of our populace.

Many prisoners, possibly the majority, are accidental or circumstantial criminals. They do not, consequently, enter prison, hardened, embittered, hate-filled, or completely alienated men. Generally holding the conventional values of their society, they feel great shame in what they have done and identify closely with the aims and mores of the general society and the prison administration. They are actually an integral part of this society.

But how many times have I seen these same men slowly change as they are subjected to the degradation of the prison system day after day, only to leave the institution a changed man. Rehabilitated, you say? Oh, yes, he has been "rehabilitated" all right. Within the course of his incarceration he has been taught that he is some humanoid thing that doesn't belong in the same company as "honest" people. He has been taught to hate, to sneer at the hypocrisy of the "system" and the society, to identify with the "have-nots" and the "I'm gonna get me somes." He will never again accept his society, and he knows that his society will never accept him. He has become a cynic and a rebel.

I do not mean to leave the impression that the inmate bears no responsibility for getting himself into the cesspool that is the American correctional system in the first place.

He does. But I happen to believe that what the society does to a man after it gets him in a prison is much the greater wrong. It is so much the greater wrong that it seriously ameliorates and offsets what the individual has done to get there in the first place. And biases aside, all but the most dense, ostrich-like, head-in-the-sand individual in the society knows that what is done to this individual *after* he arrives at the prison, and before he *leaves* it, is the absolute responsibility of the society.

There are many prisoners—I would estimate some ten per cent—who *are* completely impervious to just about anything that the society or its correctional system might do for them. They are emotionally stunted individuals who will be in and out of pens all of their lives. But that's ten per cent. What about the other ninety per cent? Those who can be reached, and helped, who can learn to lead normal, productive, and rewarding lives? For the general society and for the prison administrations there is no real difference between the ten per cent and the ninety per cent. So they are all lumped together and all treated the same. Even the ten per cent should not be punished, since punishment just makes them worse. But in fact the whole one hundred per cent are punished, degraded and dehumanized. And then the society is shocked when the great majority of them react to "treatment" upon return to the community by rejecting its values, striking out in the fury of blind rage, and returning to prison. The prisons have done such a good job of "rehabilitation" that they have insured that the majority of these people will plague the society for the rest of their lives.

The indifferent and hypocritical society pays handsomely for all of this in the long run. Incarceration provides a very short-term protection for the community. Eventually it compounds the danger from which the society seeks some relief. In the revolving doors passes a young car thief, and out that same door passes a well-indoctrinated, well-trained burglar, safe-cracker, or armed robber. If the society is lucky. He could be an aggressive sexual psychopath or a future killer by now if the society is not so lucky.

It has taken one hundred years for the American correctional system to move, however slightly and cautiously, beyond the rat-infested dungeons and the ingenious forms of corporeal punishment which have been the tradition. Yet public acceptance and approval of implementation of a scientific and humanistic program of rehabilitation is still light-years away. Who dares speak of "modern" correctional practices or "treatment" programs when the minimum recommendations of the Declaration of Principles of the American Prison Association Convention of 1870—a century ago—have yet to be put into practice!

Spend just one twenty-four-hour period in the typical jail or prison in this country, then listen to the talk about "rehabilitation" and you will understand the key to the problem—hypocrisy. The poor know about the spirit-crushing miasma of hypocrisy which permeates so much of our society. The black man knows it full well, so does the Indian, and so does the convict—with or without the "ex" as a prefix. These people know with a keenness and an awareness made raw by experience that the society wants it that way. They need it that way.

The "need to punish" lies at the heart of our correctional policies. There seems to be, deep within all of us, a caldron of aggressions which we are able to repress most of the time, and which we can work off in various socially permissible ways. All of us have at some time or other desired to deviate from the legal norms of our society. But this rouses strong guilt feelings and brings into consciousness the impulses that have been so rigorously repressed.

The stage is set for reaction-formation; we turn on the so-called criminal deviant with fury and insist that he be harshly punished. By so doing we demonstrate our own goodness and affirm that we are truly the enemies of evil. We deny our own repressed impulses. At the same time we obtain expression of our evil impulses, our own antisocial feelings, and our own aggression. This aggression, these antisocial feelings, we displace onto the criminal in the ill-disguised form of justice.

Prisoners are seen as simple, relatively unchangeable creatures of a more or less humanoid character (reminiscent of the old attitudes toward our slave population, isn't it?), and they are herded like cattle or zoo creatures—except that zoo animals are much better cared for, much better fed and housed. Oh, yes, they now provide three high-caloric, if relatively unpalatable, meals and even clean sheets once a week. They've done away with the shaven heads, the silent system, and the lock step. And probably a majority of the prisons in this country now have a counselor or sociologist lurking somewhere, about the halls of the administration building to be seen by visitors. It's too bad they don't pass through the gates to see the men very often and are kept busy writing reports all day long which won't be read.

Unfortunately there is no substantive relationship between a reduced number of cockroaches and recidivism, between clean sheets and reform, or between a lonely window-dressing counselor or sociologist and rehabilitation. Not while the majority of prisons supply "treatment" as an adjunct to punishment and degradation, however subtly applied, and not while some prisons in this country supply "treatment" with the blackjack and the sawed-off baseball bat, with the goon squads and the hole.

Prisons cannot, in fact, be anything but a negative, immoral, unreforming influence so long as they are assigned the principal task of punishment. Prisons cannot rehabilitate as long as the majority of prison administrators, reflecting the attitudes of the society in general, sincerely believe that inmates are sent to prison *for* punishment and not *as* punishment.

Prisons will never be able to resolve, all by themselves, all the difficult problems which they face. The solutions must come, in the final analysis, from the community. Prisons merely reflect the community, its standards, its norms, its goals and priorities, its interests and understanding. No prison administration, tied up in politics, working with low-grade personnel, lacking funds, lacking public support and cooperation, can make a dent in the crime rate in this country.

The general public must be made to understand that effective rehabilitation cannot take place in the American correctional system as it exists today, as long as all other goals—the deterrence of crime, the effective and long-term protection of the society, and the resocialization of the offender—are subordinated to the single goal of punishment. The consequences of criminal behavior cause the public to focus on revenge rather than prevention.

That punishment is capable of deterring some individuals is entirely possible, although this has never been subjected to any form of scientific investigation. Obviously, punishment does not succeed in deterring very many or crime would have long ago ceased to be a major problem. A cursory inspection of our crime statistics and our prison population should convince even the most skeptical that those whom punishment is intended to deter are not being deterred. Any psychologist will tell you that it has long been known that the emotionally maladjusted, the frustrated, and the mentally impaired are notoriously incapable of an appreciation of deterrence.

The American correctional system—heir of a corrupt history that blends savage revenge, gross hypocrisy, neanderthalic philosophy, and worn-out ideology, a system in which the intelligence of man has stooped to becoming the servant of vengeance, hatred, and oppression—that system, starting from nothing but its own negation, has no place to go and nothing to offer.

The stagnation within the correctional milieu can no longer be tolerated by a society that is landing rockets on the moon and attempting to create the "Great Society." The decision to reshape the philosophy and the practices of corrections must be forced by the realization that the human and economic waste that inevitably follows in the wake of a punitive approach completely disregards all our accumulated knowledge concerning human behavior and human potential and is inconsistent with real rehabilitation and human needs.

—E.T.

4

Administration

We called him "Bull." He stood six foot and weighed 240. He could fight, drink and chew tobacco with the best of us. He was mean. His favorite stunt was to argue a man down and then tell him: "Git out my face, you sorry ole *thing!*" When the humiliated victim would turn to leave, Bull would kick him hard, not in the soft part of the buttocks, but higher, on the end of the spine. I never did see a man turn around and argue with Bull after he had kicked him. But it did finally cost him his job.

Bull was the superintendent of a North Carolina road gang for youthful offenders. When I "fell" there in 1956, I was sent to Newton, which was Bull's camp. I was nineteen, and there were many there who were younger than I, even though it was felony camp. Three years later, a small item in the newspaper told of Bull being fired for mistreatment of prisoners. He had kicked a "Yankee Boy" who had told his parents. They had enough influence to cause an investigation and get Bull dismissed.

As road gang superintendents go, Bull wasn't bad. He was certainly well qualified for the job. Had you called him a progressive penologist, he would have probably growled at you, but Bull did things on instinct and common sense that northern prisons try to do with classification committees and treatment programs . . . and botch.

Bull would look a man in the eye to determine whether or not to place him on trusty status. My "rap partner" and I had been there for three days when Bull spotted us boxing in the "yard" on the weekend. He called us aside and, after asking a few abrupt questions about boxing, appointed us as trainers to form a boxing team that could beat cons on the other road gangs. He wanted some trophies to put in his office. We were excused from all road work to accomplish this. Every day, after the other men had gone on the road to work, the camp gate would swing open for the boxing team, and we would go outside the compound to train for the rest of the morning. In the afternoon we rested. This freedom was granted after we had been there only three days.

Eventually we traveled to other road camps all over the state, taking on all comers. Bull was proud of his fighters. At every eating stop along the way he let it be known that he had the toughest cons in the state. At fight time he would be looking over the judges' shoulders as they scored every match. Out of seven fighters we won him five state championship trophies.

Bull's "Store Boy" was doing a life sentence. (In North Carolina every camp has a canteen that is managed by one inmate who assumes responsibility for the inventory. In Indiana they pay three civilians almost twenty thousand dollars annually to do the same thing. The service was better in Carolina.) One afternoon the Store Boy learned that he had been turned down by the parole board for the third time. As Bull sat in a rocking chair on his office porch, the Store Boy stormed into his office, stayed for only a couple of minutes, and stormed back out, slamming the door both ways. Bull never left his rocker.

We watched from the cellblock windows as the Store Boy paced angrily back and forth in front of the office, obviously waiting on something. After a quarter of an hour had passed, a taxi pulled up in front of the camp and we heard the horn sound once. The Store Boy stalked toward the cab but stopped when Bull called his name.

"You aimin' to come back?" Bull asked.

"Yeah," said the Store Boy. Then he got into the taxi and rode off.

Bull was still in the rocker when the same taxi brought the Store Boy back forty-five minutes later. He walked into the compound carrying what was obviously a fifth of whiskey in a brown paper bag. He walked past Bull without saying a word and went into his one-room "store." We didn't see him again until morning.

Bull could judge a convict. That Yankee Boy that told on him was probably the only one he ever misjudged.

Later I served under "Blackjack" Griffin at Gatesville. I won't elaborate on his nickname other than to say he earned it. This was the hardest working camp in the state. (I've talked to some cons who argued for "Red Eye" Meadows at Ivy Bluff, but I'll stand by Gatesville.) Under Blackjack, I dug ditches in one-hundred-plus-degree heat until I passed out. (For some reason, you don't have to work when it drops below twenty degrees, which it seldom does; but no matter how hot it gets, you work.) We shoveled dump truck after dump truck full of sand, a ten-man squad averaging two and a half minutes per truck. On our thirty-minute lunch break, we ate beans that had been spoiled by the heat and later threw them up as the foreman growled at us to "quit wastin' time."

Escapes were a common thing in North Carolina, but so were captures. One guard, armed with a .38-caliber pistol and his choice of a shotgun or a 30-30 rifle, provided security for an eight-to-fifteen-man squad. A foreman also accompanied the squad, but his job was basically to supervise the work. When a squad of men had to be stretched out too far when cutting a right of way around a curve in the road, the guard would give one of the weapons to the foreman and send him to the head of the line.

Beating the gun was not hard. It was simply a matter of picking the right spot along the road where cover was nearby, and running like hell. Many times other cons who knew of the attempt would station themselves between the guard and the path of the escapee. When the break was made, the obstructing cons would appear to be slow in comprehending what was taking place, hoping desperately that the guard wouldn't fire his weapon anyway.

Once you had beat the gun though, your troubles were just beginning. Then you had to beat the dogs and the farmers who lived nearby.

I remember watching two men throw down their bush axes and run down a side road. The guard snapped off two quick shots with his 20-gauge shotgun, hitting one about forty yards away. The "rabbit" only yelled and picked up speed. The dogs were brought from camp and put on the trail. The men were captured about 2 A.M. the following morning when a farmer spotted them running across one of his fields and called the law. That same morning, as we prepared to go to work, the guards brought the two escapees to the cellblock and I helped gouge buckshot out of one man's back. They both went back on the road with us that morning with Blackjack's challenge to "try it again" ringing in their ear. Neither of them accepted.

During the mid-1950s, the North Carolina road gang offered nothing that even vaguely resembled the northern states' so-called rehabilitation programs, but the recidivism rate was no higher. Now there are educational and vocational courses available at most of the camps. In Newton, Bull's old stomping ground, there is a brick masonry class and school classes through the twelfth grade. All over the state, trades are being taught in conjunction with local technical schools in the community. Eventually North Carolina will be able to boast of a lower rate of recidivism than most of the northern states because of the size of the prison unit (less than one hundred men in each camp), allowing some degree of individual treatment.

Even Georgia has started a training program for state prisoners with a $624,336 federal grant. The word "rehabilitation" has become fairly popular in Georgia since a young con, who was serving as a duck retriever for a road-gang guard, drowned in cold water one December when he failed to reach the shore while carrying a duck in his mouth.

When I came to the Indiana State Prison, with a life sentence in 1959, Alfred Dowd was the warden. Shortly after I arrived I was called to his office for a "talk." The conversation turned quickly to football, and Warden Dowd explained that he had arranged to borrow some used equipment from Notre Dame and the prison would field a team for the first time in many years. He was quite proud of his accomplishment and emphasized his love for sports. I left the "talk" very unsure of why I had been called out in the first place. It was the only time I had occasion to speak to the warden. He was replaced two years later after a new political administration took office.

In the meantime I received the full benefit of the prison's treatment personnel. I was given a battery of tests which occupied a week of my time. Then I lay in a cell in the Admission & Orientation section for three months waiting for the results of the tests to be determined so the classification committee could assign me to a job.

The only break in that confinement came the day my counselor interviewed me. After referring to my past record and present charge, he told me I probably needed psychiatric help; but he added that it was doubtful that I would receive any such help unless I got into some kind of trouble. I must admit that he summed the situation up very accurately. And so far, since I have managed to avoid any serious trouble, I have also avoided the psychiatric help I allegedly need. I keep promising myself though that someday I will try to get into enough trouble to deserve help.

When the big day finally came and I was called before the Classification Committee, they told me I was going to be assigned to the Education Department. Since I had a high school diploma and the eighth grade was the highest level offered at that time, I asked them what I would be doing there. The Classification Director seemed to take affront at my question, grumpily pointed at Mr. Buck, the school principal, who was also on the committee, and told me to report to him when I was assigned.

A week later, when I was released from A&O, I did as I had been told. Mr. Buck seemed uncertain as to what my duties were to be, and he finally referred me to his assistant, Mr. Winn, who openly admitted that he didn't know where to place me. He asked if I wanted to be a teacher. I certainly didn't feel qualified to teach. I couldn't type, so that eliminated being a clerk. Finally, Mr. Winn told me to look around for a few days and find something I wanted to do. After three days of "looking" I selected the drafting class because there was a window fan in the classroom. I spent a lot of time in that room wondering just what it was that indicated to the Classification Committee that the Education Department was where I belonged.

After serving ten years here, I still can't explain how they determine what a man's job assignment should be. There is one factor in their behavior though that has remained fairly constant. Every time I have requested a job change I have been met with resistance or a flat denial. At one point I had been assigned to the shoe shop after being returned from escape. The foreman and I didn't get along. We rubbed each other wrong from the first day I entered the shop. I controlled my feelings for several months, but I eventually found myself thinking more and more of smacking him right in the mouth. This is an unhealthy attitude, in any prison.

I sent the Classification Committee an interview slip requesting a transfer, and I had the supervisor of the medical lab write a request asking for me to be assigned there. The Classification Director, Mr. Dave Sweet, told me I was needed in the shoe shop. (I worked fifteen minutes daily there.) I explained that I wanted a transfer to avoid trouble, but I didn't tell them with whom. Mr. Sweet told me to try harder to get along and sent me back to the shoe shop. I went instead to my cell, packed my toothbrush, and went to a cell on the Idle Gang. A week later I appeared before the Classification Committee from the Idle Gang. This time I asked to be assigned anywhere in the prison except the shoe shop. Mr. Sweet reminded me that I was in prison and I had to work where I was told to work. (Hell, Bull could have told me that!) He again assigned me to the shoe shop. When I refused this time, it constituted a violation of the rules, and my next appearance was before the institutional court. They found me guilty of refusing to work and gave me ten days in lockup, but they also transferred me to the tag shop, where I got along fine. It might have been simpler to have smacked the foreman.

Within six months the shoe shop foreman had been fired because he had trouble with so many men, and Mr. Sweet was reassigned when it was discovered that he had only three hours of college credits instead of the degree in sociology he had claimed when applying for his job. I can't take any credit for those dismissals, but I shed not a tear.

Once, while still assigned to the drafting class, I heard my name called over the recreation loudspeaker with instructions to report to the cannery right away. I walked over there, wondering who could possibly want me at the cannery. The foreman met me at the gate and told me I was now assigned to the cannery. I protested that I hadn't requested a job change and certainly hadn't appeared before the Classification Committee.

"You been to Classification," he said. "You just didn't know it."

I helped can tomatoes until eleven o'clock that night. The next day I went back to school to find out why I had been transferred. The Director of Education, Paul Payne (Buck had been transferred to another institution), angrily told me of the many warnings he had given me about my failure to turn in assignments. I sat there amazed as he told of promising me that the next lesson I missed, I was to be transferred. The thing was, I had yet to even be late with an assignment and had never even talked to Mr. Payne about lessons.

After checking the grade book with my instructor and examining my lessons, Mr. Payne finally admitted that he had made a mistake; he concluded that he had gotten me mixed up with another student. There were six of us in the class.

Mr. Payne isn't with us any longer either. He resigned suddenly last year. As a matter of fact, Anthony Kuharich, then Corrections Commissioner, entered Mr. Payne's office at noon one day and, after only a brief conversation, escorted him to the front gate.

Even while I was enjoying the window fan in the drafting class, I was trying to find something in this prison that would interest me. I eventually decided on the hospital medical lab, where an inmate can become a certified technician. After talking to the lab personnel and getting their OK to work there, I sent my request to the Classification Committee. They denied my request but would give no reason. During the course of my ten years here, I have attempted to transfer to the medical lab three times, with the results always the same.

A short time ago a friend of mine, who is a clerk, showed me an information card that contains the results of the battery of tests I took when I arrived. On the front of the card was listed my name, number, charge, IQ, grade level, etc. Typed on the back was this recommendation: "This man has a high average in intelligence and operates on an 11th grade scholastic level. It may be to the best interest of this man to place in hospital technician training thus providing a vocation."

Though some inmates have surely had better luck with the Classification Committee, I have found it to be a useless stumbling block. Even its intended function is a farce under existing prison conditions. There is simply no place within the confines of these walls where the rehabilitation potential is great enough to warrant having a five- or seven-man committee spend two mornings a week doling out the "good" jobs to those men who have not displeased the committee. To be sure, there are "good" and "bad" jobs behind the walls of the prison, but neither category has anything to do with rehabilitation. The collective wisdom of this committee can only serve to keep a certain number of men assigned to a certain number of industry shops (which are the financial backbone of the prison system) and occasionally move a man to another shop or shelter for his own protection. Old Bull would be amazed at the aggregate salary paid these men for this function.

There was, at least, one other avenue open for a man who wanted a "good" job when I came here. The deputy under Warden Dowd was Robert Hock. He was a bigger man than Bull in more ways than one. Hock weighed more and knew more about hustling a con out of a dollar than

Bull's limited imagination would ever let him learn. Hock sold jobs, cells, punks, and freedom to any con who had the cash to lay down.

Hock's favorite target was the inmate bookies. When one of his "rats" tipped him off about a bookie that was making good money, Hock would send a couple of his select officers to shake the man down. Because an inmate is only allowed to have so many packs of cigarettes in his possession, the officers would confiscate the bookies' excess cigarettes. Most bookies also dealt with actual cash, and this is what the officers really searched for. When they found it, the officer who discovered it would quickly pocket it and tell the inmate that he was going to give him a break and not write him up. Of course the bookie couldn't argue. The officers split the money with Hock, and the rat got the cigarettes. The bookie had to start from scratch, but he realized that under an honest administration he would have been locked up.

Hock was known to sell a "good" job for ten or twenty dollars. He was also known to have one of his officers "bust" the man off the job soon afterwards so Hock could sell it to him again. If you were caught violating a rule and locked up, you simply sent word to one of your friends to "see Hock for me." If they could come up with five or ten dollars, you would do very little time in lockup.

Hock once called a lecherous old friend of mine to the deputy's office and told him that five fine young "kids" had just been transferred up from Pendleton and were locked up upstairs in Seclusion. For fifty dollars my friend could go up and take his choice, and the kid would be moved into his cell immediately. They argued about price for a while, with my friend pleading that he didn't have but twenty dollars. Hock finally settled for twenty-five and let my friend go upstairs and take his pick. The two of them celled together for several months before my friend lost the kid in a crap game, betting him against a ten-dollar bill. I was in the game but not the pot.

It was about this time (1961) that Ward Lane was appointed by the new governor to replace Alfred Dowd as Warden of ISP. We called Lane "Cool Tom." He was also called "Old Stone Face" and "Big Tom," depending on the situation. Before another governor was to replace him in 1969, he was to be cursed, praised, feared, respected, smacked, and worshiped by the cons he controlled. I think it's a safe bet to say that he was respected more than anything else.

Word of Lane's appointment preceded his arrival here by several days. He had a reputation that caused unrest among the cons. Cons that had served time under him at Pendleton claimed he was a tough, gun-toting, club-swinging, up-from-the-ranks warden that would take no shit from any man. The word was that he had killed a man at Pendleton. His one virtue, they said, was that he wouldn't lie to you. If he told you "yes," that was it. If he told you a mouse could pull a house, just harness that little critter up.

Their assessment of the man was probably as accurate as it could be considering that it was based strictly on his past actions. What it failed to consider was that some men mature as they grow older. (The parole board makes most of its judgments on past record also.)

Cool Tom strolled the yard for three weeks. He did it without the usual entourage of officers that had accompanied Dowd everywhere he went. And Lane forbade anyone to call ahead and announce him. (When Dowd was coming inside the walls he would call for an escort. They would call various departments and let them know the warden was coming. The department officers would tell the cons the warden was coming. He never saw anything he wasn't supposed to see.) Lane listened to hundreds of cons voice their complaints. He said very little. Old Stone Face.

One of the first results of his "listening" was the dismissal of Deputy Hock. The very rats that had set up the bookies for Hock were instrumental in getting him fired. But six of them were suspended along with him.

Another of Big Tom's early moves was to put the prison tough guys right in the palm of his hand. He called each of them out as he became aware of them and gave them The Speech: *I'm not afraid of you. Act like a man, get treated like a man. If not, I've got a place for you.*

They came away from The Speech impressed. They accepted it as a statement of fact rather than a threat. They told their friends about it. Their friends believed too. It was true.

Cons that had only stared when Dowd and his entourage had passed began to say, "Good morning, Warden." They tested him by approaching him on the street with a minor request. He told them "Yes," "No," or, "I'll look into it." Whatever the answer, it could be depended on.

Under Lane, a full-time band director was hired. Palmer Myran, a clown-faced shrimp of a man, was given an abandoned laundry as a concert hall. He was given the malcontents and troublemakers as musicians. The troublemakers rebuilt the laundry. They cleaned old brick from a nearby prison wall that had been torn down. They knocked out old walls and built new ones, making about twenty individual practice booths, a half-dozen combo rooms, an office, and a large concert-size practice room. They painted the building inside and out.

The troublemakers blew scales and beat rudiments for the funny-looking little man. They played Puccini and lost. There was talk of a concert for the free people and even rumors of outside trips. So the troublemakers stayed out of trouble; many of them began to build "clear time" for the first time.

It paid off. Within a year there were regularly scheduled outside trips to two state hospitals. There was a concert for the free people. Eventually the band traveled all over the state. It played in the Indianapolis-500 parade; it backed Miss Indiana at a Strawberry Festival; it played AA dances; it played the Summer Festival in Michigan City and parades all over the state. I eventually traveled with them, playing drums in the dance band and the concert band.

In the beginning, every time the band went out the other cons made bets as to how many would come back. There were men doing life that traveled. "Big Steve" was traveling. He was doing life for murder and was one of the "tough guys" that Lane had talked to. Big Steve had whipped officers. He had been chained to a concrete slab and beaten senseless by prison guards and then sent to a mental institution. But there he was, blowing second clarinet in the band, playing "Él Capitan" on the main street of Fort Wayne for that funny-looking little man. And he came back to the prison with the band. Every time.

A lot of Lane's underlings didn't like to see the band travel. The deputies didn't like the high escape potential. Some of the officers who accompanied the men on trips seethed with resentment when the band members mingled politely with free people without incident. It made their job as keeper of the dangerous, wild animals a little less glamorous.

The band gave men hope. It helped us to believe we weren't animals. It helped us to hope that someday someone else would believe it too.

Last week, under our new warden, I watched them tear the band room down.

Last November a Republican governor, Edgar Whit-

comb, was elected in Indiana largely on a campaign promise not to raise taxes. In order to keep his promise, he ordered a ten per cent cut in state employees and ordered that
budgets be trimmed wherever possible. The band director
was informed that he would have to take a cut in salary. He
resigned. Soon afterwards, Warden Lane was replaced by the
governor.

Under Lane, the prison had been run on an open-door
policy. The public came in and viewed concerts, attended
club functions, and watched sporting events. The inmates
went out and played baseball, softball, music, and chess;
they boxed, wrestled, and lifted weights. Over the years of
travel with Lane, hundreds of inmates participated regardless of their charge or how much time they were doing or
even how many previous escapes they had. A man was allowed to travel because Cool Tom had faith in him. No
other reason. Lane accepted full responsibility.

Cool Tom was as good or better than old Bull in his
judgment of men. His prison gates were open for five good
years. During these years, there were five escapes made
from trips. (I accounted for one of those; see Chapter Nineteen.) In the past two years, since traveling has been
stopped, eight men have escaped from *inside* the walls. The
hope is gone.

As warden, Lane was forced to officiate at the last execution held in Indiana, which was in 1961. Afterwards
Lane vowed he would resign rather than witness another
one. He was almost put to the test.

The court-appointed attorney for Jay Dull, who had
been convicted in the murder of a Muncie, Indiana, taxi
driver, made a statement to the press that he had exhausted
all available legal remedies in behalf of his client. This was
forty-eight hours before the scheduled execution of Dull.
The prison custodial staff began moving men out of the Seclusion Unit, where the execution was to take place.

After the law school graduate had given his client up for delivery to the gods, a jailhouse lawyer named Johnny Bennett took the case. Inmate Bennett began preparing not one but two writs. He researched the opinions to be cited and assigned different sections of the brief to three other inmates who worked nights at various locations throughout the prison and had access to typewriters. Bennett received permission from Warden Lane to stay at his desk throughout the night in order to complete the writs. Shortly after daylight on the morning of the scheduled burning, Parnell finished his task and Lane expedited the "filing" of the writs. About two in the afternoon, the federal court granted Dull a stay, and the state court did the same an hour later, both on the strength of the writs that Bennett had written.

That was five years ago, under Warden Lane.

Today, two custodial officers went to death row and demanded that Dull give up a bird that he had raised from a baby and trained.

When Lane arrived at ISP, he inherited a typical northern prison's version of solitary confinement. After an inmate had been found guilty in the institution court, which was comprised of three or four officials serving as the prosecution, but no lawyer for the defense, he was stripped, given a pair of coveralls, and placed in a bare cell for three to seven days. In the cell, the surface of four stone walls was broken only by a small, barred window, too high off the floor to reach, and a narrow doorway at the front of the cell. The doorway was covered with a barred steel door and a solid wooden one. The surface of the floor was broken only by a round hole, six or eight inches in diameter, that served as toilet facilities. It was covered with a piece of cardboard that did little to prevent the odors of human waste from permeating your abode. The only other items in the cell were a handful of loose toilet tissue and a small paper cup.

Your breakfast consisted of two pieces of toast and that cup full of milk. If you saved one of those pieces of toast, you could also have lunch, or even dinner if your will power was that great.

There was nothing in the cell to bother you. It was boring, and yet if you could live with yourself for seven days, you could make it. You got hungry but you didn't starve. What you did mostly was pace the floor and wonder just what the hell this week of isolation was supposed to prove. You eventually decided that they were trying to break you, but you also decided that you could take it. You left the hole determined to show them that they hadn't proved a goddamn thing to you: fuck 'em!

While working at the Parole Office, I went through the court records to check the effectiveness of solitary confinement as a deterrent to the violation of institutional rules. The recidivism rate for the hole was greater than that of the prison. Like prison, the hole was only effective as long as you were in it. You came out of it bitter and angry.

The real abomination of ISP's prison discipline was the "dungeon." Transgressors were stripped and chained to a concrete slab in the basement of the Seclusion Unit. That's where Big Steve was beaten senseless. (Tonight, as I went to the evening meal, the "Hack" that broke his nose with a club was directing traffic in front of the mess hall.) That's where many cons were beaten and left chained down to suffer in their own urine and excrement. Seven days wasn't the maximum sentence in the dungeon. There was no maximum.

When word occasionally leaked to a member of the press about this method of punishment, and when a reporter bothered to inquire, Dowd and his regime denied the very existence of such a place. No journalist ever pushed the inquiry far enough to be able to walk down the Seclusion stairs and see for himself.

When Warden Lane took over, he curtailed the use of the dungeon greatly but, for some reason, couldn't bring himself to eliminate it completely. He did eliminate the beatings, but kept the slabs.

Once, when the prison newspaper editor came to the parole office and asked me to give him an article on something, I proposed writing about the Seclusion Unit, including the dungeon. The editor gave the go-ahead but expressed doubt that Warden Lane would allow it to be printed. It was while writing that article that I did the research on the recidivism rate of solitary confinement. I wrote the article, stressing the obvious futility of trying to change a man's behavior pattern by taking away his food, clothes, toilet, and dignity for seven days. I cited the large number of repeat offenders who went back to the hole time after time for petty offenses, indicating that solitary confinement, like prison, had no deterrent value.

After going that far, I had no qualms about condemning the dungeon, even though its existence had never been acknowledged to the public. I fully expected, though, to be called on the carpet by Lane, told to stay in my place, and watch him tear the article up. What did happen was that Lane returned the article to the editor with an OK to run it only *if* I changed one word in it. I had written about a man being chained to a *cement* slab. Cool Tom struck out the word "cement" and wrote the word "concrete" in its place. Of course I made the change.

Eventually, Lane abolished not only the dungeon but also solitary confinement. He maintained discipline by revoking a man's recreation privileges. Some offenders were allowed to go to work but were made to return to their cell in the evening and on weekends while other men were playing ball or watching a movie. A more serious offense might result in ten days in your own cell without being allowed to leave except for meals. The flagrant violators were placed in a Seclusion Unit cell but were fed three meals a day and had a bed, toilet, and sink.

Many of Lane's staff resented these changes. They were afraid it would cause an atmosphere of permissiveness —hence, disruption. Some of the staff reacted by ignoring an inmate who was seen violating a rule, thus perpetuating the very thing they feared.

Lane forbade brutality. He authorized violence only in self-defense. This does not mean that there were no beatings, but they did become a rarity. Once, a drunk and angry inmate smacked the Warden in the face. When the man was locked up, Cool Tom came to the Seclusion Unit to make sure the man was not harmed. Today that inmate expresses respect for the former warden.

Lane knew the evil and uselessness of America's prison system. He stated this many times in many ways. While speaking before an Achievement Forum group in South Bend, Indiana, he said: "Half of the inmates at the Indiana State Prison are drunks or vagrants. Except for the AA program, we have nothing to help them." Lane estimated that no more than twenty per cent of the prison's population should be behind walls. He also knocked the patronage system whereby a warden is appointed by the governor. Lane said, "I would resign tomorrow if I could be assured that all prison jobs would be filled by means of the Civil Service examinations."

Lane begged the legislature for funds and facilities but was ignored. He asked the public for support and was met with indifference. He was quoted in the South Bend *Tribune* as saying, "With the right personnel and the right programs we can do much to reduce the prison population in the coming years. And to get the personnel and programs we're going to ask the people of the state to give us their

FUNDERBURG LIBRARY

c. 1

MANCHESTER COLLEGE

backing. A prison is an expensive facility, but greater expenditures now will mean much greater savings for the Indiana taxpayer of the future."

The guards' meager wages were raised only after so many of them had quit that Lane had to draft the band director and the Director of Education as guard towers rifles. All treatment programs had to be temporarily closed because of the shortage of guards.

Even though it has been several months since Governor Whitcomb replaced him with another warden, Lane is still in Indiana. The man with thirty years of experience in the correctional field is working in a local steel mill, a victim of the same political patronage system that was responsible for his appointment as warden eight years prior to his replacement.

The new warden's name is George Phend. We call him "The Fiend."

He was sent here by former Corrections Commissioner Anthony Kuharich, almost a year before Lane was replaced, and although his title was Assistant Warden, Phend ran the prison from the day he came. He effectively isolated Lane from the pulse of the prison by screening all written communications directed to Lane by the cons. Men who sent Lane interview slips expecting the usual prompt action received no reply at all. When they would see him on one of his increasingly infrequent trips inside the walls and ask him about the matter, Lane would admit that he had received no request slip.

During this period of the Lame Duck Warden, I was, after several denials, transferred to the prison newspaper by the Classification Committee. The afternoon of my first day on the job, the Director of Education came to the office and told me to pack my things. Since I hadn't yet written that first subversive word, I pressed him as to why I was being transferred. He told me that Warden Lane had ordered it and they were making out my transfer in the office of the Deputy. Lane's action did not greatly surprise me. I had recently written several critical articles attacking Indiana laws and the prison system. Lane had not agreed with the articles.

Accompanied by the editor, I went to the D.O. to try to influence where I was to be transferred. There, Assistant Warden Phend called Lane on the phone and suggested that I remain assigned to the newspaper. Lane angrily said no. (Both the editor and I could hear his response over the phone.) Phend politely insisted. Lane slammed down the receiver, and I kept my job. The incident left little doubt in my mind as to who was running the prison.

Phend's first hundred days as warden were very impressive (to the conservative, budget-conscious Republican governor, Edgar Whitcomb).

His first act that affected cons came three days after his appointment. He reopened solitary confinement under the name of "Strip Cells." The wording on the Court Sheet was terse: "Strip Cell 30 days. No Shave or Shower. No Lights. No mail. No visit. Meals and medication only."

Phend's next move was food rationing. The prison butchers and cooks were told to allot eight ounces of meat per day per man. (If that much meat ever reached the serving line, it would be a rare treat!) There were no seconds to be given out on any item, whereas in the past a man could receive all the potatoes, gravy, beans, or cabbage he wanted.

At this point, the February parole board met and released the lowest percentage of eligible men it ever had, whereas at their two previous monthly meetings the percentage was over 60. The cons regarded the parole board's action as an obvious effort to please the "law and order" governor. The hard-rock cons began planning a riot.

It was called off that same week when Phend called

out a group of inmate club officers, cooks, clerks, etc., and explained that food was being rationed on a temporary basis because of a budget deficit that he had inherited. He went on to tell of his plans for inmate committees to better conditions in the prison. This was interpreted by most of us as some form of inmate council, the members of which would be elected by the cons. What it turned out to be in reality was a hand-picked group of boot-licking yes-men who were told to make up a set of rules to govern the inmates. Intoxicated with this unaccustomed responsibility and power, they gave birth to many modern breakthroughs in progressive penology such as: Do not engage in any form of sexual perversion; Do not steal; Do not engage in horseplay; and Do not lie to any institutional personnel.

There were other changes during The Fiend's first hundred days. The inmates' meager monthly wage was cut, items of comfort such as soft chairs were confiscated and destroyed, television sets were taken out of the hospital wards, etc. etc.

Warden Phend believes in the "chain of command." He has stated that he considers himself an administrator and not a father confessor. He wants an inmate to take his problem or request to a counselor, or the department head concerned, and let the request reach Phend only as a last resort.

But just as you can't judge this nation's President on the basis of one hundred days in office, you can't accurately predict the future of the prison under Phend's administration. It's obvious that he intends to remain in full control of his wards. But it is not obvious how long he will last with his methods. Guards who resent his demands, and who can sense an eventual inmate rebellion, are quitting their jobs. Many of them have joined Lane in the steel mill. The AA coordinator has resigned. Sadistic guards use Phend's policy of tight discipline as an excuse to gas, mace, and beat prisoners, while other guards, who have qualms about mistreating other human beings, denounce any brutality and express their own concern about a riot.

To the delight of some inmates, and the sadness of others, there are fewer "troublemakers" walking the prison streets under Phend. They are locked up in D.O. Seclusion or sentenced to the I-Cellhouse Detention Unit for as long as a year. In IDU they remain in their cells twenty-four hours a day, seven days a week, with the only exceptions being a weekly shower (if the guard has time) and a monthly haircut.

Twenty-four hours in a cell with nothing to do is a long time. Multiply twenty-four by seven days a week, and the product of that by four weeks in a month, and the product of that by twelve months in a year and you have . . . what?

You have a bitter goddamn monster whom you had better not release from this prison!

But you have to release him. When his time is up, you can't hold him no matter how bitter he is. You eventually release 98 per cent of us. And over half of us go out and rob you, rape you, or murder you and then come back here for more *rehabilitation.*

All of these minor, petty things that I have written of —the different methods and ideas of Bull, Blackjack, Dowd, Hock, Cool Tom and The Fiend—these petty things are important to me in the sense that they have been my life for a decade. The whims of these people have determined the extent of my comfort or discomfort, my immediate happiness or unhappiness.

But in the final analysis, all of it is meaningless. Both to me and to you. Whether I work in the tag shop or the medical lab; whether I dig ditches down South or repair shoes up North; whether I spend seven days in the hole or twenty-five days in a strip cell; whether I play drums in a parade in Fort Wayne or watch the band room being torn down; none of these things matters to me in the final analysis. And you out there don't have to be concerned with them either.

But there is one thing, one tiny little omission that might concern you.

I have spent over twelve years in three state prisons under numerous administrations. During all that time not *one* prison official has ever bothered to ask me to live decently when I'm released. Not one has bothered to tell me *why* I shouldn't rebel from an unjust, hypocritical society that takes advantage of one man's ignorance and poverty while rewarding another man for his parentage and political connections. No one has told me *anything*.

You out there had better damned well hope that someone talks to me before I walk out of the front gate of this prison.

—M.M.

5

Are We Communicating?

Blessed be letters—they are the monitors, they are also the comforters, and they are the only true heart-talkers.
—DONALD GRANT MITCHELL
Second Reverie

Indianapolis, Ind.
January 1, 1960

Dear Son:

Your mother and I are simply heartbroken, son, over your being sentenced to prison. We are optimistic that your sentence can still be probated. We have been talking to the lawyer and he thinks perhaps he can get you out of there on a hardship plea.

Mother and I went over to visit Gloria and the children shortly after your trial. She is heartbroken. They are getting along as best as can be expected under the circumstances. Mother and I are going to see that all their needs are cared for, at least until Gloria composes herself.

The two boys miss you very much. David asks for you frequently. Gloria told the three of them that "daddy has gone North to work for a while." I agree with her that there is no sense in trying to explain your circumstances to them. Ten and eight is too young to attempt to explain something so sticky. And, of course, the little one can't possibly understand.

Didn't you tell me before your trial that you had an understanding with your lawyer about the fee? Two weeks after you left mother and I received a bill from him for "final services." Rather than raise any argument about the matter, we paid him. He mentioned briefly that the bill was for personal pleas he made with the sentencing judge in chambers.

He told us to keep in touch for possible consultation on your pre-parole hearings. I assume he wants to continue representing you. What is your view on this? Remember, son, that year to the parole board hearing will pass before you know where it went. Keeping the lawyer on retainer, then, might be something for you to think about in the meantime.

Son, your mother and I want to remind you to apply yourself constructively and keep out of trouble while you're in that place. We haven't lost faith in you. Everything is going to work out for the best. We're planning on a trip up as soon as we can get away. Gloria has told mother and me that she wants to visit you.

If we have any important news, we will write immediately, son. You take care of yourself, now, and write us.

Mother and Dad

Indiana State Prison
January 30, 1960

Dear Mother and Dad:

Sorry I haven't written to you before this, but I have been very busy since I got here. My time is entirely taken up with interviews, physical and mental examinations, aptitude tests and a dozen other things. I don't mind admitting, this prison scared the daylights out of me when I got my first look at it: the walls are 50-feet high with gun towers interspersed along the top, and the custodial officers are so grim looking. All the convicts look so vacant-eyed and bewildered. I simply can't understand why. The atmosphere is absolutely unbelievable. I have talked with many of the convicts who have been here for a long time, and without exception every single one of them is full of hatred and bitterness. I feel sorry for them: they have no family ties, no outside help—nothing. One fellow in my unit only last week received notification of his wife's divorce proceedings. It hit him very hard, too.

The warden gave us an indoctrination talk here in New Admissions last week. He certainly is an impressive man. I'll admit I was feeling very depressed, hearing all those dreary prison stories, but the warden reassured us by the nature of his talk. He assured us that so long as a man "kept his nose clean" and served his sentence—"don't nose into the other man's business!"—he wouldn't have a single thing to worry about. The warden said that a good institution record goes a long way toward parole consideration. He said that when we go to the Classification Committee from this unit, we would be assigned jobs in the prison in accordance with our outside employment classification.

I am glad to know that I'll be working as an auto mechanic. The warden also told us that quite often the Classification Committee will assign first term prisoners directly to outside the walls trusty assignments. Maybe I will be one of the lucky ones.

I've been attending church services every Sunday. It's a real comfort. I do miss taking Gloria and the children as I used to. I do have confidence that everything will be alright. In the meantime, you both pray for me. I'll be back with you shortly, for you're right: this year will pass so quickly none of us will know it slipped by.

Your son

Indianapolis, Indiana
July 4, 1960

Dear Son:

Your mother and I are busy packing for our annual vacation. We expect to be gone for a month. California this time. You know how mother always wanted to visit out there. We thought to invite Gloria and the children along—you know, maybe the trip would take her mind off your being there—but she said no. The children were certainly in favor of the trip. Gloria says they've been running like wild horses during school vacation. Too bad she wouldn't make the trip.

Gloria is acting rather strangely toward your mother and I, son. We have been out to the house several times since we brought her up to see you, but we don't seem able to catch her in very often. Several times we've found the children with baby sitters. David told us once that "mother has gone bowling with Tom Duggan." Remember Tom, son? I recall the first time you and Gloria brought him by the house. You were trying so hard to cheer him up about his impending divorce. It is nice, though, that Gloria has somebody to pick up her spirits occasionally, but I hope she doesn't neglect the little ones. Gloria is a good mother, so I don't think you have any worries on that score. The children seem to like Tom. David calls him Uncle Tom.

No sense rambling on about Gloria. I know she has told you about Tom. I do wish she would return mother's phone calls. (You know how mother worries, son!)

I thought I detected a change in your attitude when we were up to see you. Don't let your spirits sink. Keep on with your church attendance. Remember, prayer helps. What was that you told us about some of your convict buddies ridiculing your praying at the dinner table? Terrible, just terrible! Don't pay any attention to that sort of thing, son.

You must have been disappointed about not being assigned outside the walls, and even more so by being assigned to the kitchen scullery. You must remember, son, that the prison officials know what's best. No doubt they had reasons we know nothing of for putting you there.

The lawyer contacted us and reminded us that your parole hearing would be scheduled shortly. Soon as we come back from vacation we are meeting with him to see what can be worked out. His fee for representing you at the hearing is $250, reasonable if he can get you paroled. He advised against filing a hardship release plea with the judge.

We'll drop you a card from California, son. In the meantime, keep smiling. The lawyer told us that your charge, receiving stolen property, is considered a "lesser" felony, and that you should, with your four dependents and excellent employment background, be a very good parole risk your first time to the board. Write soon and let us know how you are getting along. Enclosed is our California box number.

Mother and Dad

Indiana State Prison
August 3, 1960

Dear Mother and Dad:

Sorry I haven't written sooner. The situation with Gloria worsened for a time. She is very discouraged. Having trouble making ends meet, she said. Evidently the children are too much for her. David, she says, is getting impossible to handle. He is doing well in school; that's a relief. The little one was hospitalized for three or four weeks; I suppose she told you that. Ran from between parked cars into the street—broken left arm, contusions, and severe bruises. Tom Duggan helped Gloria with the hospital arrangements and took care of the more bothersome details of getting the little guy checked in and out. That must have been a blessing, having Tom around to lean on in time of emergency.

Gloria wrote that she had to sell the car to pay the hospital bills. (Had to let the Blue Cross lapse.) She told me she and the children may move to a smaller place: rent's too high where they are. She also wrote that she may have to go back to work. The bank account is depleted. Do you think you and mother could help her out with a small loan?

Still attending church. It helps. I haven't given up hope of being out with all of you by this time next year. I asked the chaplain if he would speak a word on my behalf to the Classification Committee so I might be transferred to the auto-mechanic shop. He refused. Said those matters were best left to the committee members to decide, and that he didn't want to influence them in any way.

Yes, if you and mother can afford the lawyer's fee, it would help to have him present at my parole board hearing. I wasn't aware parole applicants could be represented by counsel at their hearing, but if he says yes, then it must be so. I don't think it's absolutely necessary, for everyone has told me I'll be granted parole. Still, it won't hurt to have added assurance.

Did I mention this before? Occasionally I hear some of the more disreputable convicts claiming that some parole board members take bribes from the convicts. Did you ever hear anything so ridiculous? No wonder these guys are in prison. I certainly don't intend to let this place affect my reasoning to that degree.

You might remind Gloria to write more often. Her letters don't come as frequently as they once did. She must have her hands full out there. Someday I'll make all this up to her and the children. Enjoy yourself in California. Next year Gloria and the children and I can have our vacation together. Write soon now.

Your son

Indianapolis, Indiana
December 25, 1960

Dear Son:

We miss not having you with us for Christmas. It just isn't the same. This is the first Christmas in your life that you haven't been with mother and I. We invited Gloria and the children over, but she told us that she had already accepted an invitation from Tom's sister. They have a tree and all the decorations there, too.

Now for the good news! Mother and I made an appointment with Mr. Rudikell, the parole board chairman. Believe me, son, he is a fine Christian man. He told us that your chances for parole are excellent. He said that you would be home within the next 30 days. How about that! Our prayers have been answered.

Too bad your parole couldn't have been arranged two months earlier. Mother and I didn't want to worry you unduly what with the problems you've been having with Gloria—all that foolish talk about filing for divorce. Whatever is wrong with her, son? Your preoccupation with Gloria and the children is one reason mother and I never mentioned in our letters about the finance company foreclosure on your shop. Several companies sued for judgment, and the court awarded 95 per cent of the claims. Amounts to about $8,000.

All of your tools were sold at auction. Perhaps you'll have to go into some other business when you're out. Anyway, son, you're all squared with your creditors. You don't owe a cent. As Mr. Rudikell told mother and I, your only debt now is to the state—and that's about paid, too.

We are getting all your personal belongings out of

mothballs. Gloria sent us most of your clothing months ago. It's all ready for you. Perhaps when you get out, Gloria will get some sense into her head and you and her can make a family again. Write soon.

Mother and Dad

Indiana State Prison
February 1, 1961

Dear Mother and Dad:

I'm dumbfounded. Simply dumbfounded. I can't believe that my parole was denied for another year. Everybody here told me I was going to be paroled. I was stunned when Mr. Rudikell denied me. He was furious with me for not having gone to school and for not having learned a trade. I told him that I had a high school education, had my own auto mechanic shop outside (or did have once) and had worked as a master mechanic for 10 years. He said working as a mechanic was how I met bad companions and got in trouble. He said that due to the foreclosure proceedings against me, I would no longer be permitted to work as an auto mechanic. What will I do?

Mr. Rudikell said it was obvious that I was financially irresponsible. He had a transcript of the foreclosure and wouldn't hear my explanation that the foreclosure squared all my creditor accounts. He was quite disturbed, he said, that I was misleading you and mother. (What did he mean by that?) He also said I was being denied parole because of the nature of my crime. Said I should join some hobby clubs in here. Another board member recommended that I join Alcoholics Anonymous and attend meetings regularly, and when I reminded him that I didn't have a drinking problem, he said it was obvious that I wasn't interested in solving my character problems.

Two of the other members seemed very interested in

my marital history. One asked me if my wife was "still with me" and I told him that, yes, she was, for the time being, but that my being away had unsettled her very much and that she had in the past few months been threatening divorce. I told him that if I were paroled now I could possibly bring my family back together before it became too late.

Mr. Rudikell informed me that I didn't qualify for a hardship parole. Evidently somebody had contacted Gloria, and she wrote Rudikell a letter saying she was working part time and receiving state aid for the children. Mr. Rudikell seemed to think that was sufficient for the time being.

My heart simply isn't in writing. I'll close for now.

Your son

Indianapolis, Indiana
March 15, 1961

Dear Son:

Your mother and I feel bad too, son. We have tried several times in the past week to contact Mr. Rudikell but his secretary says he is out of town. Perhaps he could tell us something further on his decision to deny your parole. We certainly shall inform you of any developments along this line. In the meantime, son, keep your chin up.

Mother and I went by your old place, son, and Gloria and the children have moved—bag and baggage. We don't know where. The caretaker said she left no forwarding address. What do you suppose she has on her mind? Well, you probably know her circumstances better than mother and I.

We had a letter from the lawyer last week. Actually it was more a bill for "services" than it was a letter. Mr. Hughes said he was sorry that he could not persuade Mr. Rudikell that you were deserving of a parole. We weren't aware he had talked to Rudikell. Mr. Rudikell's secretary told us sometime back that parole applicants weren't allowed to be represented by counsel at the parole hearings. So we thought it strange that he should send us a bill, since he obviously didn't accomplish anything. We did pay him the $250, though, and informed him that his services would no longer be needed.

Don't despair, son. Keep praying; keep attending church. In the meantime, you join those hobby clubs and AA like the board advised. And since you won't be able to work as a mechanic when you are finally paroled, get in school there and take up another vocation. Write soon.

Mother and Dad

Indiana State Prison
May 1, 1961

Dear Mother and Dad:

I'm sorry that I don't have any good news for you. Let me give you the worst of the bad, then. You recall our discussing Gloria's not writing and her moving away without leaving a forwarding address? Last week Chaplain Flaubert called me to his office and read a citation for divorce proceedings. Seems Gloria has a lawyer and is filing immediately. She wrote the chaplain a letter concerning her reasons, but Flaubert wouldn't let me read it. He seemed to think it would only further unsettle me. Gloria has a court restraining order against me, also judgment of $45 weekly support payments for the children, effective 30 days after my release.

The chaplain was nice about his unpleasant task. He advised me to keep faith and said that "things would turn out OK." Gee, I'm so confused. The chaplain took me to task for not attending church regularly. Justifiably, I'll admit, for my faith has been flagging lately.

Now for the other news. I took a battery of aptitude

tests for vocational training and the instructor says I passed with flying colors. He placed my name on the barber school waiting list. That is what the tests indicated I was best suited for. I had hoped for trusty assignment outside the walls, but my counselor advised against that. Said learning a trade, joining hobby groups and regular church attendance was especially important in parole consideration. In the meantime, the scullery work is going along about as well as can be expected. It is a job—something to pass the time. There are about 100 men assigned to the dining room and messhall, mostly disciplinary cases and incorrigibles working here as punishment. The mental attitudes are something else! There are 10 men for every job opening, so most of us sit around all day, loafing or playing dominoes.

Don't worry about me. Write when you can.

Your son

Indianapolis, Indiana,
July 4, 1961

Dear Son:

Not much of an Independence Day for you, is it? Your mother and I are spending a quiet vacation at home this year. Not much doing around town right now. The city is changing so fast. Lots of construction projects going on downtown. You won't know the city when you get back. It's impossible to drive downtown now without being detoured through miles of alleyways.

Your mother and I have been quite worried about you, son. We had a short note from Chaplain Flaubert. He says your church attendance has stopped. What's the problem, son? You can tell your mother and me. We know you must have a lot on your mind with the divorce becoming final next month, but don't let that make you bitter, son. You still have your health, and the end of your sentence is in sight. Only six more months for parole consideration again. All of your old friends have been asking about you. (Why, just last week Tom Duggan called us to ask if we knew when you would be out.) Also on the plus side, son, you will have a new occupation, and you know you will always have a home here with your mother and I.

Get that head up in the air; get back in church. Hear me? I don't mind telling you, son, that your mother and I are very worried about your health, and about your mental attitude. Mother especially is quite shocked at your language. And now that I'm reminded of it, you looked to be 15 or 20 pounds underweight. What's the matter? Loss of appetite from working in the scullery? Write soon, now.

Mother and Dad

Indiana State Prison
December 25, 1961

Dear Mother and Dad:

I hope that you and mother weren't overly worried when you came up and were unable to get in to see me. I was, as the warden informed you, in solitary confinement. I had a disciplinary report for eating a sandwich in my cell. The night captain wrote me up for having contraband food (a baloney sandwich) in my cell.

Yes, Chaplain Flaubert is correct. I haven't been to church lately. It is difficult to explain, dad, but the fellows ridicule and razz and continually haze anyone who shows any inclination to attend. Makes it difficult at times. These are the guys I live with every day. The chaplain only works here. His sermons, too, are lukewarm, insipid monologues on the evils of man, not exactly the kind of "meat and potatoes" sermon convicts want to hear. I suspect Flaubert has his orders from the warden on what to preach and on what not to preach. At least all the convicts accuse our chaplain of being a status quo man, a conservative bedrock fundamentalist—not much on the hell's fire and brimstone type of church conversation. Strictly establishment. Know what I mean?

Well, now for the good news! If everything develops as expected, I will be home this time next month. Think of that! Two years in here has taught me plenty. These Hoosiers don't need trouble themselves about my returning to prison like 85 per cent of all parolees do in this state. First thing I plan to do is enroll in barber school and get my license. That should take no longer than a couple months at the most. Then, I want to persuade Gloria to remarry me and make a home for the children.

My counselor talked with me recently. He said everything is favorable for parole. He called me in to inquire if I wanted to be considered for an outside the walls trusty assignment. When I told him I was eligible for parole in another few weeks and that, anyway, I was frozen in vocational barber school, he realized that he was looking at another man's case history packet. The counseling staff is in the middle of a hectic reorganizing of their administrative procedures. (My counselor said he had a caseload of 250 men.) I knew he was busy, for I have sent him about 10 interview requests and he never acknowledged any of them. This is the third time I've seen him in two years.

Christmas doesn't have much meaning in prison. Other than looking forward to a once a year turkey dinner, the day is like a hundred others. Volunteer convict workers strung colored streamers overhead in the messhall and decorated the tree, but it was a futile gesture. It didn't soften the atmosphere a bit. I heard some convicts remarking that the state would have done well by investing the money it spent on the decorations for food. I will admit the food here is very coarse. Anyone in this prison who doesn't like beans and baloney is in trouble! We have that combination here at least three times a week. And greens and asparagus. Lord, you never saw the likes. The warden and his staff were in the messhall today, passing out to each man a cigar and a bag of Salvation Army candy (along with frozen-faced smiles and Merry Christmas, men).

I will write more later. Right now I am at loose ends with this parole hearing coming up in less than two weeks. Have a nice Christmas and a good New Year. I'll be out there to share this one with you and mother.

Your son

Indianapolis, Indiana
March 1, 1962

Dear Son:

Your mother and I are just sick. How could the parole board deny your parole for the second year in a row? It doesn't make sense. Are you absolutely certain the board gave you their real reasons? Don't hold back anything from us, son. It doesn't figure that you should be continued another year because you were disciplined for eating a contraband baloney sandwich. And for Mr. Rudikell to tell you that it would be better for you to remain in prison until you finish your barber training—well, that is ridiculous. (Is a man ever better off by staying one extra day in prison?) Didn't you inform him that your mother and I were going to finance the balance of your training outside while you lived with us? And whatever in the world did he mean by saying that you were "con wise?" What does that mean, son?

When Gloria married Tom Duggan, your mother and I thought that was the worst thing that could happen to you, but obviously we were wrong. (Did you read about their wedding in the newspapers?) Well, son, your mother and I don't approve of the way she has done you since you've been in prison, but give Tom his just dues. He is a hardworking fellow, and he'll be a good father to your children. Not that you weren't before your trouble.

Your mother and I are trying to arrange an appointment with Mr. Kuhetric, the corrections commissioner. Only recently we read in the paper where he said in a speech before the local Rotarians that Hoosier corrections were making "great strides" in prisoner rehabilitation. Kuhetric stressed prisoner rehabilitation and told the Rotarians that his personal philosophy was that prisoners shouldn't be denied parole because of their past criminal history. Any first term prisoner, Mr. Kuhetric said, would, if he showed an inclination to "better himself and develop a healthy attitude toward correcting his faults," be released in the minimum time. I should think, son, that you qualify on all these accounts. Your mother and I intend to have a talk with him about this. Perhaps Mr. Kuhetric will intervene in your case. It is worth a try.

Son, we hope to have good news the next time we write. Lord knows your being in prison hasn't been easy for your mother and I. We would like to continue giving the officials up there the benefit of the doubt about knowing what is best for you—but, frankly, son, sometimes that is very difficult. We will write again soon. You do the same.

Mother and Dad

Indiana State Prison
July 1, 1962

Dear Mother and Dad:

I haven't been writing lately because my visiting and corresponding privileges have been suspended since you were last up to visit me. Too, I'm working in the auto tag shop now—10 to 15 hours a day during the rush season for licenses. A convict friend paid me a package of cigarettes for a haircut and the instructor wrote me up—for being an institution "hustler." The captain locked me up and recommended that I be transferred to the auto tag shop. Same captain who disciplined me for eating that contraband sandwich.

My counselor sent for me again. It seems Gloria wants Tom to legally adopt the children. He is willing, but according to the counselor, they will need my signature. I refused to sign at first. Then the counselor warned me that the parole board has a rule against granting parole to an applicant who has pending court litigation. Their policy is to wait until court hearings are over. Counselor said these adoption proceedings usually drag out a year or so until they become final. Rather than take a chance on being denied parole again, I signed the waiver.

Mr. Rudikell also called me out for an interview shortly after you and mother had your interview with Mr. Kuhetric. He was very angry. Accused me of inveigling you and mother to intercede. What's his objections to that? Mr. Rudikell said he was putting my case before the parole board next month for rehearing instead of making me wait my full year's continuance until January. I had to sign a waiver stipulating that I was voluntarily appearing for rehearing and that should I be denied, the denial would date from August instead of January. Rudikell was very noncommittal about what action he would take at the rehearing.

All the convicts say Mr. Rudikell is a man of his word. He's personally acquainted with most men here. Despite his complete lack of professional qualifications and his limited education, he has succeeded in achieving a capable position, chairman of the parole board. A lot of convicts accuse him of being more "convict" than the most hardened con here. Some say he was a brutal, sadistic guard when he began his career in corrections 30 years ago. I don't know about that. He seems to me to be a very simple man. How did he impress you? He and the warden are very good friends. Both started in corrections as custodial officers and worked their way up. Lots of convicts say the Warden was a brutal man, too, in the early days of his career. Like Rudikell, he has a very limited education. He's a schoolhood chum of Governor Melsh, I understand. Melsh appointed him under the odd Hoosier spoils system of politics. (All patronage employees of the state pay a 2 per cent "tax" into the political coffer. Sort of a "thank you" offering for their jobs, I guess.) The warden is a wary man; that's for sure.

Enough of prison gossip. Write when you can.

Your son

Indianapolis, Indiana
August 30, 1962

Dear Son:

What in heaven's name is going on up there? Denied parole for the third time! And after your mother and I had talked with Commissioner Kuhetric. He promised us that you would be paroled this time. We are simply at wit's end. (Why would the commissioner lie to us? He seemed like such a sincere, conscientious man.) Two days after your hearing we managed to get Mr. Rudikell on the phone. He was a different person from the last time we spoke with him. Very discourteous. Told us that paternal interest was one thing, meddling another. Whatever did he mean? We only asked him on what basis you had been denied parole and reminded him of what Kuhetric had said about first termers being released from there in their minimum time. He said rather abruptly that he wasn't, as chairman of the parole board, required to justify his decisions. I wasn't asking for justification, only a simple explanation. Besides, I told him that mother and I were paying his salary, that he is a public servant and that he *does,* indeed, owe us if not an explanation, then the courtesy of treating me as a gentleman.

No wonder you talked so strangely when mother and I

were up last. Son, you have a side to your disposition now that you never had before. When we stopped off to talk with your counselor (he led us to believe he knew you well, that's why your disclosure that you had talked to him only three times came as a surprise) and he said you couldn't make the proper adjustment to prison. Whatever that means. Do they expect you to adopt those surroundings as a normal part of your future life? From all we've seen of that place, we wouldn't want you bringing home any applications to living you had picked up there.

Your mother and I tried to arrange an appointment with Governor Melsh to talk over your case, but we couldn't get through to him. His appointments secretary said that as a matter of policy, the governor doesn't discuss those matters. He refers them to his corrections commissioner. There's little use to speak to Mr. Kuhetric. We know what he will say: "I leave those matters to Mr. Rudikell, my parole board chairman." It's a vicious, albeit short, cycle.

Son, we simply don't know what to tell you. Do the best you can. I am tempted to tell you to pray, but you might logically counter with "to whom?" Keep your spirits up the best you can, son. If there is anything mother and I can do, let us know.

Mother and Dad

Indiana State Prison
January 30, 1963

Dear Mother and Dad:

Well, after three years it happened. *Parole!* As unexpectedly as a heart attack. I wasn't scheduled to appear before the board until August, 1963. You may recall I told you I signed a waiver on my regular January appearance. Some convict filed court action against the parole board, declaring that procedure was coercion and illegal, and that it deprived him of his rights as stated in Burns Indiana Statutes. The court ruled in his favor; that automatically rescinded all the waivers ever signed by convicts.

They didn't do me a favor, though. Three years on a sentence for which 95 per cent of the offenders are sentenced under a misdemeanor law. I shouldn't have been sent here to begin with. What a lousy system. Less than $100 involved in my crime and the state takes three years of my life, not to mention my wife and children, my business, my community standing and my dignity. I consider my "debt" to the state paid in full.

My counselor called me for an interview yesterday. (Why does he call me only when he has bad news?) Seems Gloria and Tom have a peace bond against me. That means not going around to see the children. The counselor informed me that one stipulation of my parole was that I wasn't to annoy Tom and Gloria. The parole officer has found me a job in Hancock County. The counselor says that later, after I've adjusted, I can leave Hancock County to visit you and mother. So, temporarily, I will be living at the Salvation Army Home and working for Goodwill Industries. I won't be able to change jobs, until after a six month job stabilizing period.

I will be free within a week or two. That is the important thing. These Hoosiers will never get me back in this prison. That is the truth. I will write again as soon as I get settled over in Hancock County. Looking forward to seeing you real soon.

Your son

Indianapolis, Indiana
February 10, 1963

Dear Son:

Your mother and I are happy for you. We know how glad you must be, getting out of there after three years. We are disappointed that you couldn't come home to live with us. Not being able to visit your children must have been a bitter pill to swallow. After all, son, they legally belong to Tom now; they have his name. He supports them.

Remember, there are worse jobs than working for the Goodwill people. Besides, it is temporary. You will get something better as soon as your six months probationary period is over.

Mother and I still want to put you through barber school if it is permissible with the department of corrections. You will be able to move from Hancock County here with us. You will see.

We have all your clothes out of storage. You looked so skinny and underweight when we last saw you that you may just have to buy all new clothes or have your old ones altered. They may be out of style right now, but at least they are functional. Don't be angry with yourself, son, or hold a grudge against anyone for your being in prison. It's all over now.

It is nice out here, and as soon as you see the outside again, you'll forget all about prison. Write from Hancock County.

Mother and Dad

Hancock County, Indiana
April 1, 1963

Dear Mother and Dad:

It was wonderful seeing you again. You both looked great. You were right about one thing: the outside is just fine. Fine. I've missed it too—more than I thought I had.

Got off on the wrong foot with my parole officer. He caught me drinking a beer in the town's only tavern; now he's mad as hell. Said if he caught me drinking again I would be violated. How about that?

I asked him for permission to come to Indianapolis on the weekends to visit you and mother. No soap. Later on, maybe. And absolutely no visiting the children, ever. The parole officer has a letter from Tom and Gloria saying they are afraid I'll cause trouble. How about that?

The job at Goodwill isn't going so hot, either. A dollar an hour isn't much wages these days. And sitting through those damned sermons over at the Sally doesn't sit well with me. A house rule—everyone living at the Sally is required to get one sermon a week under his belt.

I'll write more later. Take care.

Your son

Indianapolis, Indiana
July 4, 1969

Dear Son:

Your mother has been in the hospital seriously ill for the past three weeks. I've kept it from her that you are back in prison. She couldn't take that kind of news right now. Frankly it hit me pretty hard when the parole officer came to the house looking for you. And when he told me you were wanted in Hancock County for parole violation, I could hardly believe my ears.

What happened, son? Did you really do all the things they said you did? Will withhold further comment until I hear from you.

Dad

—A.P.

6

Disparate Time

Let's make believe.

Let's assume that you, John Q. Citizen, are forced to commit a crime with the foreknowledge that you will be caught and sentenced to prison. The only detail left to your choosing is which state you will commit the crime in—Indiana or North Carolina.

Being enlightened and aware, you will naturally choose the northern state. Everyone knows of the brutality and deplorable prison conditions that exist in the South. Everyone knows that the northern penal systems offer educational benefits, vocational training, modern counseling, Dale Carnegie classes, alcoholic programs, and a highly paid, full-time parole board.

If you choose Indiana, John Q., you're a sucker! Any con in the know would go South and sweat and toil on the road gang. Because he knows if he keeps his nose clean, he will get out in about a third of the time that it would take him up North. He knows that there is no good time given on an indeterminate sentence in Indiana, whereas North Carolina gives good time on all sentences *if you earn it*.

A man's past record would have little bearing on the

sentencing in Indiana. If convicted of robbery, the sentence is ten to twenty-five years. You, John Q., receive the same sentence as my buddy, Big Sam, who is a five-time loser! Indiana law prescribes a set law for each crime, regardless of the circumstances surrounding the crime or even the past record of the criminal. The only deviation from this is in the case of a man being placed on probation.

In North Carolina the law is more flexible. The judge can let you off with ten months or slap twenty-five years on you, depending on your past record and the nature of your offense.

The con in the know also understands that if he is caught pulling an *unarmed* robbery in Indiana he will be given a ten- to twenty-five-year sentence. But if he's smart enough to take a pistol along he can get off with ten years flat, which means that he will be discharged in six years and eight months. His poor muscle-headed cell partner who didn't use a weapon will just be appearing before the parole board when he leaves.

Let's look at the "good time" in the two states. You'll be on your best behavior, won't you John Q.? Certainly. Therefore, you deserve to get out a little sooner than Big Sam, who fights, takes pills, has a "punk," and tries to escape. Surely Indiana will give you a fairer shake on this issue than North Carolina. Right?

Forget it!

On any indeterminate sentence in Indiana your time runs out when the maximum number of years runs out, no matter how good, or bad, your conduct within the institution is.

Take a good, hard-working burglar. The second-degree burglary rap in Indiana is two to five years. Reasonable enough, right? In North Carolina he might even get the same sentence.

The Hoosier in Indiana will go to the parole board in

twenty-one months. The Tar Heel in North Carolina will go in six months. If the Tar Heel doesn't make parole but keeps his nose clean anyway, he will be *discharged* in seventeen months and seven days. Discharged four months before the Hoosier even gets an audience with the Wise Men. In penal terms, the word "discharged" means that the inmate has no further responsibility to the prison system. He is free to go or do anything that any other citizen can do. A man on parole (as the Hoosier would be if the parole board decided he was a good risk) must report to his parole officer regularly; secure permission to buy a car, change jobs, marry, or move; stay out of taverns; and arrive home by a certain hour each evening. Go South, John Q., go South!

Thieves in Indiana have been known to bargain with the prosecutor to obtain a ten-year flat sentence rather than a one to ten because they would rather have the certainty of going home in six years and eight months than take a chance on the parole board's releasing them sooner than that. A quick check at the records department would show you that it's a good gamble. Many men have done every day of that one to ten in spite of a spotless prison record. Indiana judges have often expressed their amazement upon learning that men whom they have sent here with a one- or two-year minimum have served five or more years without being offered a parole.

North Carolina has many paradoxes within its own prison system. It is a forerunner in the progressive work release program in which the participants have lowered the recidivism rate to a remarkable nine per cent. And yet it still has sixty-three road camps within the system that are nothing more than chain gangs with the chains removed. The work and conditions are much the same.

A North Carolina road camp contains about ninety men who are leased to the Department of Public Roads for five dollars a day. The money goes to the prison system rather than the inmate. He is paid nothing for his labor. The prisoner's job is to maintain all of the roads in the particular county he is confined in. That means cut right of way, dig or clean drainage ditches, repair roadbeds, lay culvert, etc.

The inmate receives one clean change of clothing per week. (OK John Q., so digging ditches in the same pants and shirt all week is a bit unpleasant. So is sitting in your cell with clean clothes on year after year after year after. . . .) The noon meal is eaten on the road out of a "bean can," and the typical meal would consist of navy beans, fatback, biscuits, and collard greens.

If an inmate is placed in solitary confinement, it is usually for a period of thirty days. He subsists there on a hashlike item that the prison officials call Monotonous Diet. The cons call it dog food, and one whiff would convince you of the accuracy of the latter term.

Educational and vocational facilities are nonexistent at the road camps.

A northern prison will allow a man to join AA, DC, fish clubs, record clubs, and teach him shoe repair, but it will confine him endlessly while doing this. A southern prison will work an inmate harder than he's ever worked in his life but will release him in a much shorter period of time.

If the miracle of rehabilitation takes place in either state, it is by accident. Shoe repair or a high school diploma does no more than digging ditches to change a criminal's thought patterns, his improper channeling of bitterness and hate. In neither state does the prisoner come into contact with people he can respect, who can teach him to handle his emotions and problems.

The kind of man that the inmate can respect does not

last long in any prison system. The occasional priest or psychologist or doctor who wins the admiration of the con will soon find that he has become an outcast from the remainder of the staff. When he attempts to right the many wrongs to be found in any prison, he will come to work one morning and find that his door has been locked; he has been locked *out* of prison to preserve the status quo *inside* the walls.

The evil of disparity of sentencing is not confined to any geographical area. It prevails in different areas of any given state—from county to county and from judge to judge.

In Oklahoma a man was sentenced to forty-five years for stealing one cow. In the same state, a banker drew three years for stealing $750,000. In Wyoming a thief in the northern part of the state was given a ten-to-twelve for a $7.50 armed robbery. In the southern part of the state, an armed robbery netted another rascal $124. He was given a two-to-three-year sentence.

The Chicago *Tribune* recently editorialized about such a lack of uniformity in sentencing. One judge sentenced a man to five to fifteen years for the strong-arm robbery of a bus driver which netted $13. In the same city misappropriation of $2,000,000 resulted in three men being fined heavily and given suspended sentences.

The great majority of state penal systems throughout this country are in need of some form of modernization and revision. They don't all have the same faults, but they all have some. The only practical means of obtaining some form of unification is by calling on that old standby, *Big Brother*.

The federal government would do society a tremendous service by stepping in and setting up a set of standards that would end the inequality of sentencing, time served, and prison conditions in general.

In the meantime, John Q. Citizen, my advice stands. To you and all of my thieving friends I say, go South, where the livin' ain't easy but they cut you loose a hell of a lot faster!

—M.M.

7
Education

Only the educated are free.
—EPICTETUS
Discourses

Joe Bell Williams is a twenty-eight-year-old black man from Andalusia County, Alabama, who is serving a term for grand larcency. It is his fourth felony conviction and probably will not be his last. I spent six months teaching Joe how to write his name, learn the alphabet, and read a first-grade primer. You see, Joe is a functional illiterate. He is one of an estimated eighty thousand functional illiterates warehoused in the U.S. correctional system every year.

One of the first requirements of being an "average" convict is to have little or no education. Fifty per cent have never completed grade school, more than 90 per cent have never completed high school, and less than 1 per cent have ever attended college. According to a recent study of 56,-200 inmates done by Dr. B. S. Brown of the National Institute of Mental Health, 96 per cent of the group were school dropouts, and 20 to 25 per cent were functional illiterates. Moreover, the Brown study found the median IQ for the group was 95, a full 5 points below the national average, and 40 per cent of the group had IQs below 85, as compared to 16 per cent of the national population.

Thus, those unfortunate enough to be incarcerated in the prisons of this country are in dire need of basic education. For their own well-being and self-respect, and so that the men, upon release, can compete with even the most niggardly chance of success in the job world today, they need education.

Unfortunately, prison education is poor, low-grade stuff on the whole, and made worse because it traditionally has been chained securely to the "rehabilitation" image that prison administrators like to foster on the naïve public— the false image of a successful rehabilitation program, backed up by largely artificial statistics.

Since the prisons of this country have failed miserably in what they consider as their dual job of protecting the public and rehabilitating the offenders in their charge, many prison administrators turn with a sort of frenzy upon whatever program of education is to be found within their institutions. They demand that it produce results that the administrators can take down to the legislature or use in a speech at the local Lion's Club luncheon—the "we have graduated one hundred men from elementary school and sixty from high school" type of statistics. Never mind that half of the grade school "graduates" still can't read a comic book, or that half the high school "graduates" could not pass a ninth-grade equivalency test in the schools of the free community. It's a nice round number, 160. And next year give us 200 graduates. Throw in the cooks and bakers and the barbers too. Have the print shop run off a bunch of diplomas. Damn it, man, we need statistics.

Some prison administrators are so hung up on statistics that just about anything you do in the prison is considered a part of the rehabilitation program. So we find such ridiculous things as giving a man who swings a mop across a concrete floor a "diploma" in "janitorial engineering," and calling every inmate clerk up to the auditorium rostrum to receive a certificate in "office management." We should not forget the tailors, barbers, cooks, and bakers. They all get rehabilitated just by being on an assignment.

There is also the fallacy that passing a course in arithmetic or social studies will make a bad citizen into a good citizen. Unfortunately, what they wind up with, all too often, is an unrehabilitated burglar or robber who knows a little more about arithmetic or social studies. Prison education is not attacking the central problem of changing attitudes and value systems. And until these are modified or altered, all the academic education in the world is not going to do very much good when it comes to keeping the men out of prison.

The prison administrator's obsession with favorable statistics and with "front" or facade is just one of the many problems pressing on the well-intentioned correctional educator. He must work within a sick bureaucracy which subverts its stated missions and goals and has a pathological resistance to the smallest accommodation to changing demands or changing realities. Within this protectionist feudal barony, inbred upon itself for so long that a form of "penological idiocy" has become its main characteristic, the correctional educator must battle against stalling and delay, negative attitudes and poor relations with the custodial staff, lack of funds, lack of space, lack of staff, and lack of understanding. Under this heavy burden, the prison teacher staggers about his task like Sisyphus, performing a seemingly senseless task, against seemingly hopeless odds, unto eternity.

Why does he do it? Possibly because it is always possible to see a little light far down the long dark corridor. Some men benefit greatly from prison education programs.

I know many who have left prison never to return because of the new worlds opened up by a prison education. There has been a plethora of studies done which offers evidence of the value of education in prison, evidence that men who have taken advantage of the opportunities offered by a prison school have greater parole success rates and greater chances of staying out of prison permanently. So, I think it is the fact that education *does* make a difference with some of the men that keeps the conscientious correctional educator battling against such heavy odds every working day of his life.

The average public school teacher has no conception of the problems of the prison school teacher, who must work within an abnormal community of involuntary inhabitants in a rigidly ordered and controlled environment. He must attempt with one hand to reach out to the inmates, while with the other fend off the restricting controls of the prison administration. To implant a degree of learning, self-confidence, and hope in men with "born to lose" tattooed on their arms is, in this atmosphere, less a pedagogical feat than it is a working of miracles.

And yet it is done. That the prison educator is mildly successful in spite of all the obstacles in his path, is to his credit. The average prison teacher is head and shoulders above the rest of the prison staff. He is more intelligent, better educated, sensitive, aware, humanitarian, and more optimistic than the wardens, supervisory staff, and guards. He is also, in many cases, the most misunderstood and maligned member of the prison staff. He is resented by other prison employees as being too liberal, a mere "college boy" (even if grayheaded), and an "egghead." He is often held in contempt by the old-line custodial people who think that teaching an inmate to read and write or how to lay bricks is somehow "mollycoddling" him and turning the prison into a "country club."

It is surprising to realize that with few exceptions, the

role of education as a rehabilitative tool has been accepted by the majority of correctional institutions in this country only within the last few decades. Not that there haven't been places labeled "school" in many prisons for a long long time, but no real, no serious attention has been given to the value of convict education until recently.

This is even more surprising when it is realized that education, whether academic or vocational, is the *only* form of rehabilitation going on in any U.S. prison. Not one correctional institution in this country has a rehabilitation program capable of reaching 10 per cent of its prisoners. There are no total therapy programs, almost no psychologists or psychiatrists, counselors or guidance experts, no individual or group therapy, no prerelease programs, and no employment programs. The only thing remotely resembling a rehabilitation program which is capable of reaching the majority of the inmates in our prisons is education. And there are still prisons in this country, especially in the South, where there are no schools, where education is felt by officials to be a "waste of time and money."

There was a time when they set aside a corner of some old cellhouse, shop, or warehouse in a prison, threw in some rickety donated furniture, and nailed up a sign: EDUCATION DEPARTMENT. Then they hired an old retired schoolmaster to come in and direct the school. They used inmate teachers exclusively and wrote begging letters to school districts in the state asking for old textbooks. Then they went out and grabbed all the inmates who were not working but lying around in their cells and labeled them "students."

Well, things haven't changed much. Prison schools still do not have decent physical plants. They still use inmate teachers almost exclusively, and they still write begging letters. But attitudes have changed somewhat, and a little more is being done.

Prison schools were not a part of the funding or design of prisons when they were built. Consequently they've had to move into quarters designed for something else—the old smokehouse, tobacco warehouse, or soap shop. State legislatures have always balked at appropriating funds for new construction inside prisons (with the single exception of new gun towers), and make do is still the rule.

Inmate teachers are still the rule as well. There are at least three things wrong with using inmates as teachers. First, most of them have had no training as teachers and are given no training. Second, the old "you got a number on your shirttail too" syndrome always appears and affects the learner and the learning situation. Three, too many prison teachers drop the entire teaching load on the inmates and are in effect nothing but high-priced babysitters and guards in civilian dress.

A few years ago, the Illinois State Prison had five qualified teachers in its education department and not one of them taught classes. They were used as supervisory personnel, and all actual teaching was done by inmates. The Southern Michigan Prison had four "outside" teachers in its academic school and all were in supervisory capacity. Inmates did all the classroom teaching.

An exception to this rule is the Indiana State Prison, where the seven professionally qualified teachers, including the principal, actually teach in the classrooms. But this is an exception to the general condition.

If an inmate happens to *be* a schoolteacher, he is not going to be able to teach when he gets out with a criminal record. He should therefore be trained for something else and not used for the selfish purposes of the institution. It also follows that inmates who have never been trained as teachers in the free community are not going to enter the teaching profession when released. They should be trained for something they *can* do upon release.

Much more to the point is the role of the teacher in modifying or changing attitudes and value systems. The "outside" man who is a teacher can have some effect in this direction, but the inmate teacher is seriously handicapped. He finds it difficult—even if motivated to do so—to introduce such subjects as moral values, ethics, or proper attitudes into the classroom. The inmate students will promptly tell him to shut his goddamn mouth because he is just another con and has no business "preaching" to them. With a number on his shirttail, he can't reach his students by attempting such feats in the classroom.

Most prison schools operate on supershort budgets and do not have adequate textbooks or materials to do a decent job of education. Since legislatures have steadfastly refused to appropriate monies for the purchase of such material, other means have had to be relied upon to obtain it. In some prison systems the money for textbooks, workbooks, pencils, and paper must be obtained from inmate funds—usually the profit from the inmate store. In other states the begging and bumming system is used almost exclusively, and the inmate clerk in the prison school spends a large part of his time typing and mailing out letters to school districts, libraries, and textbook companies, asking for donations. What they get in return may be without covers and have pages torn out, and the copyright dates may read 1920 or 1930. But it is better than nothing at all.

Illinois uses a combination system. Some money is supplied by the state, some comes from profits earned in the inmate store. A fertile source of financial aid overlooked by most prison schools is grants from private foundations and from the federal government, through the U.S. Department of Labor, and the Department of Health, Education, and Welfare. In Illinois, I offered to do all the paperwork involved in obtaining such financial aid, and the then director of education turned down my suggestion. He could not be bothered.

Walk into the typical prison school classroom and, if you ignore the way the "students" are dressed, you would think you were in the traditional one-room classroom of a half-century ago. The teaching is being done by an inmate, of course, who just might be a high school graduate, his one and only qualification for the job.

None of the teaching tools, methodology, or techniques developed over the last fifty years seems to have seeped in over or under the gray stone walls. Often a book is shared by two students; they sit in old-fashioned wooden desks designed for the frame of a ten-year-old; and they get one pencil a month (which had better last them a month).

There are no visual aids in use, unless you include the old, faded National Geographic map pasted up in one dusty corner of the room. The teacher sits behind a desk, listening to the students as they recite from the textbook. That's it. No homework, no book reports, no class or group projects, no tape recordings, no phonograph, no films or film strips, no workbooks. There is no real involvement in the learning process by either students or teacher. No meaningful discussions of material in the books, and no enrichment of the learning process by a teacher who can make a dull, dry textbook come alive. This is the way it is in nine out of ten prison classrooms—recitation and rote learning in parrot-like fashion out of puerile textbooks. Thank God for the other one tenth, but it just is not enough.

There is a real problem with the textbooks themselves. I was in a classroom recently where eight men, ranging in age from twenty-five to sixty years, were reading. The book was designed for third- and fourth-grade children and contained passages like the following:

> Mary and Jane were playing with a big red rubber ball. Carol saw them playing and asked Mary and Jane if she could play with them. Mary and Jane said yes and all three girls played with the big red rubber ball. . . .

That's enough. Can you imagine a forty- or fifty-year-old man attempting to relate to that kind of material? Five days a week for a whole semester? The book may be just right for seven- and eight-year-olds, but for the men in that classroom, it was pure agony.

Prison schools slavishly attach themselves to the organizational procedures and curriculum techniques used in school systems in the free community. No one is willing to experiment or break new ground or try new ideas. They should make extensive use of ungraded classrooms and allow the men to move freely within an achievement-interest-ability framework. The men should be given the time they need to master the necessary skills. Then let them move on. There is no reason why a man in a prison school has to spend four years getting his high school education if he is capable of getting it in two.

It is necessary to teach courses which prepare the man for the life he is going to lead once released. This means a curriculum set up for the world of work, for adequate functioning as a citizen and member of the community. Too often correctional educators seem to think they are teaching a college prep course. They overemphasize knowledge and skills that the men do not need. Precious time is spent in diagramming complex sentences or studying the Latin and Greek roots of verbs, when what the men want and need are such basics as how to get and hold a job, how to read and write clear and simple English on a par with his fellow man, and how to begin to understand himself and his society.

In the area of vocational education and training we find, on paper, a number of prisons offering courses in printing, automotive body work, automotive mechanics, drafting, electricity, welding, sign painting, refrigeration, bricklaying, plastering, carpentry, radio and television repair, typewriter repair, and machine shop.

All well and good. But . . . in the three institutions I

have been in, every course was being taught by an inmate, and most of them knew little about the trade they were assigned to teach. Carpentry was not taught by a carpenter but by a man who had "fooled around" with building construction as a day laborer. Brickmasonry was taught, not by a brickmason, but by an inmate who had never had a brick in his hand until he came to prison.

The instruction is terrible, but that is only part of the story. The material and tools used in prison vocational education are stuff that the prison maintenance department no longer regards as reliable or satisfactory. The lathes and drill presses are the kind that have been dumped in an alley somewhere. Whenever some shop in the vicinity of the prison wants junk hauled away without paying cartage costs, they just call the prison to come and get it for salvage. Not that this practice should be condemned. If it were not for donations of obsolete materials there would not be a vocational education department in most U.S. prisons.

However, what prison vocational training departments do have will train few men for skilled jobs in industry. Most training and education for the world of work which takes place in prison is unrealistic. It does not take into consideration changes in the world of work which have taken place during the last three decades. Nor is it training of a formalized nature. Rather, it is a sort of "poke around and see if you can fix it, Mac," type of training. There are no modern techniques or equipment and seldom are working conditions like those actually required in the free community.

The function of the classification committee in the prison is normally subverted from its original purpose—the adequate case study, analysis, and planning of a full institutional rehabilitation program for the individual. Consequently, men are thrown helter-skelter wherever needed to plug up a gap in a work roster. Thus, when it comes to setting up training programs, rarely has a classification committee or the vocational education supervisor raised the question of just what *are* the opportunities available in the community to which the men will eventually be released. Men are packed off to learn glazing when there is no demand for glazers in the regional job community, or taught bricklaying when the local unions won't let the men join it, or given training in wood turning when the nearest furniture factory is six hundred miles away in the next state.

A Michigan prison installed a bunch of little cubbyholes to teach welding during the Second World War when there was a terrific demand for welders. Fifteen years later the holes were still there and they were still turning out welders, although welders were now a glut on the job market. The men get out, cannot find a welding job, and wind up in a carwash at ten dollars a day.

This kind of unrealistic training is all too prevalent in prison vocational schools. And it is even worse when prison officials classify working in the prison license plate factory or twine mill as "vocational training." There are a lot of people in society who regard prison industries as an adjunct to the vocational training program in that they train men for the world of work. Nothing could be farther from the truth. Prison industries have two main purposes. First, to make money for the state, and second, to keep the cons busy, since even the most somnolent warden knows that idle men are a source of trouble. Making brooms and mops is not training men for the world of work. Making license plates or stuffing mattresses is not doing the job either.

In the cotton textile mill, the furniture factory, the shoe shop, the box factory, the mattress shop, men may spend years working on one minor detail of production in a job that takes an hour to learn and a day to master. These jobs, by the farthest stretch of the Labor Department's imagination, would not be classified as even "semiskilled." Nearly all the equipment utilized in prison industry is old, obsolete, worn-out junk. If a man learned the use of every piece of machinery in the shop, he still couldn't work on a similar job on the streets, since they don't use such equipment anymore, and have not used it for twenty or thirty years.

Many prison administrators agree apologetically that all of this is true and say there is nothing they can do about it because they cannot get money from the legislatures. This is true. They cannot get the money for an adequate program if they try, which most of them don't. But then they go on to say that *at least* the men are being taught good work habits. This is not true. Men in prison return to the community with poorer work habits, not better ones. Prison job assignments call for about five hours of work a day, and most assignments have at least twice as many men as they need. Nobody does much work. If a man does not feel like working, he goes on sick call and kills half a day. Then he arranges to be called off his assignment on various passes for the whole afternoon. He will go see the chaplain or the counselor or the recreation director or what have you, and then go back to his cell. Time on the job—zero hours.

Walk through a prison shop and watch the men at work. Let us go into the prison electrical maintenance shop and look around. We see fourteen men sitting around playing checkers or sleeping on benches. We walk into the office and ask the inmate clerk how many men are on the assignment. Sixteen men, he says. Where are the other two? Out replacing a light bulb in one of the cellhouses. How long have they been gone? Four hours.

The jobs are filled to overflow with men because the prison administrations don't know what else to do with them. And the average prison day of work is set up something like this:

> 8:00 A.M.—arrive at work
> 8:30 A.M.—begin work
> 10:30 A.M.—clean up for lunch

11:00 A.M.—lunch
12:00 P.M.—go back to work
12:30 P.M.—begin work
 3:00 P.M.—clean up for the day
 3:30 P.M.—go back to the cell

If you can get more than five and a half hours of work out of that schedule, you are doing better than I. Couple this with the coffee breaks (yes, they have them in prison too) and the fact that there are so many men on a job that they are stumbling over one another—and you see what the job picture is like. The work supervisors don't push the men. They can't. And I certainly don't blame the men working in prison industries for not pushing themselves. They get twenty-five cents a day for heavy industrial work which would net them about three dollars an hour in the free community. They are fed a diet consisting almost entirely of starches—bread, macaroni, spaghetti, noodles, rice, and beans—and if a man is injured or maimed for life by one of the big presses or stamping dies, he is covered by no insurance or compensation. He gets only the privilege of going to the local prison hospital—usually referred to as the butcher palace—where he stands a good chance of getting murdered just by walking in the door. The man with three fingers on his right hand or his arm gone up to the elbows is given a nice easy menial job, like dusting window-sills, for the rest of his stay in the institution. But he's just about guaranteed not to get *any* kind of job when released.

Finally, the civilian and guard work supervisors are the laziest people on the face of the earth. They usually drift into prison work because they can't compete with their fellow citizens in the free community and see prison work as an easy berth. They set a beautiful example to the men. So much for prison industries and vocational education and how they give a man "good work habits."

Men who do leave prison with a trade almost invariably possessed that trade when they entered. Very few men actually acquire one inside the walls, and less than 10 per cent of released prisoners can be classified as anything but unskilled labor.

And, of course, the same thing can be said of vocational education as has been said of academic education. Learning to be a bricklayer or a sign painter is no guarantee that the individual will not eventually fall back on the same old behavior pattern which got him into trouble in the first place. Providing the necessary skills to compete in the job world and thus fulfill needs in a socially acceptable manner is only half the job. The other half is the more difficult task. It is to alter attitudes and behavior patterns. Only when correctional educators and prison administrators are doing both these jobs adequately will they be doing the job that society asks them to do. At the present time they are not doing either, and the outlook for the future is bleak.

In the last decade a few prisons in this country have introduced prisoners to higher education with some rather startling results. Qualified prisoners make superior college students. Prior to the 1950's an inmate could take a college-level course only by correspondence. But since that time regular college-level programs have been started in Illinois, Michigan, California, Washington, and several other states.

In 1967 there were eight prison systems, exclusive of the federal system, which offered live instruction in college-level courses. One prison offered both live instruction and televised instruction, and three systems offered what is termed "furlough instruction." In the majority of systems which offer live instruction, the procedure is for the college or university to send professors down to the prison to teach the classes inside the walls. In the institution where televised instruction is provided, the students watch the lectures on the television screen and the instructors come down to the prison periodically for conferences with the men. In the furlough system, the men are permitted to leave the prison on pass and go to the campus for regular classroom instruction.

The School of Criminology of the University of California estimated that in 1968 about two thousand inmates of penal institutions would be enrolled in college-level work, exclusive of correspondence study. That is about one half of 1 per cent of the men incarcerated during that year.

Under a grant from the Ford Foundation, the California correctional system began to set up a program two years ago which will eventually allow qualified men to complete four years of college while confined. When this event does take place, it will be a major first in the history of U.S. education and corrections.

The system I am most intimately acquainted with is that of Illinois. Now the Illinois prison system does not have much going for it. It is antiquated and severely over regimented. Ironically, it has been a pioneer in the field of college-level education for its charges.

Starting in 1958 the prison at Stateville, Illinois, in cooperation with the Chicago City College and Chicago's television station WTTW, began a two-year liberal arts program which led to the Associate of Arts degree. In the eleven years since its inauguration, the program has been extremely successful and the program has been expanded to include a third-year program through the cooperation of Northern Illinois University, in DeKalb, Illinois. For the past five years N.I.U. professors have been driving the 120 miles down to the prison and back to teach classes.

Three evaluative studies have been done on the Stateville program, one by the Chicago City College, one by Joseph Scime, a school guidance counselor and administrator, and one by Michael Cromley, former director and coordinator of the college-level program at Stateville. All three studies show the program to be beneficial to the prisoners, the prison, and the community. Many graduates of the program are now holding down well-paying jobs in business and industry. Two graduates are employed by the city of Chicago, and two by the federal government in its OEO program.

The men in the college-level program have the lowest disciplinary and institutional court record of any group in the prison. The prison students, as a group, have academic records and grade-point averages exceeding that of the general student body of the Chicago City College. Many of the men in the program have been on the dean's list for academic honors during the whole two years of their study, and four men have been either valedictorian or salutatorian of their graduating class, placing first or second in academic honors among all the students of the Chicago City College system.

All of this is not to say that a college education is what every prisoner needs. Obviously the bulk of prisoners will not qualify for such a program. Of those who do qualify, a large percentage will not greatly benefit from it. But for those who can benefit, prison education on the college level is a genuine rehabilitative tool.

Nor is this to say that such an education will keep all the men who are exposed to it from coming back to prison. But parole violation and recidivism statistics in the state of Illinois provide conclusive evidence that the program is affecting the men's value system and does bring about permanent attitudinal changes.

The reason for the high caliber of the college-level programs in the few prisons which have them is that the programs are directed by "outsiders" from the colleges and universities. In contrast, the internally controlled programs in the same institutions, directed by prison staff at the elementary and high school levels, are awfully shabby affairs.

It seems to me that the only realistic solution to the problem of prison education is to do one of two things. Either put an awful lot of money into the programs, hire adequate teaching staffs, buy up-to-date equipment . . . or rely much more heavily on the community. Of the two solutions, the obviously superior one is the latter: take the bulk of education out of the prison milieu entirely and send these men into the community within the framework of work-release and educational-release programs, many of which could be fully or partially financed by the federal government under existing laws.

Educational and vocational training are not the "open sesame" to the restoration process called rehabilitation. It is only part of the answer. In the last analysis, keeping out of prison begins and ends with attitudinal changes within the individual. Today, prison education is only doing a half-job of providing necessary skill tools, and no job at all in changing attitudes.

—E.T.

8
Sports

A good sport don't win games.
—AN ANONYMOUS BLUNDERBIRD

The members of a visiting team that come to the Indiana State Prison to oppose the cons for the first time are often surprised to find that most of the inmate spectators cheer for the outside players instead of their fellow inmates. The outsiders often attribute this surprising display to "good sportsmanship" or simply courtesy shown to the visiting team. The fact is, good sportsmanship and courtesy have little to do with it.

Unlike a college or professional athlete who is exposed to the fans only on game day, the prison athlete argues with, borrows from, steals from, and snitches on his "fans" every day, and vice versa. The star and the fan eat and work together and sometimes sleep together at night. The fans know that the third baseman on the softball team is the pitcher's "kid," that last year he snitched-out that escape attempt from the powerhouse, and that he is a prison politician with a big-shot complex. That third baseman is going to have to come up with one hell of a play before the fans will cheer him.

Then, too, it's sometimes hard for a fan to accept a prison team as his "home team." Many cons automatically resist associating the term "home" with prison.

But the fans turn out to watch the game; many of them hoping to see their enemy break his leg, some of them to watch an athletic contest with no concern about who wins—plus a few supporters of the home team (mostly ex-team members). All of them boo and cheer and tell the guy sitting next to them how much better they could have done on that particular play, second-guessing every play and every call made by the umpire and screaming their angry defiance when a player looks to the bleachers. Then, their catharsis complete, the fans march to the messhall, eat half-raw beans, thin cold cuts, and complacently go to their cell.

A devoted prison sports fan is rewarded with antics that go unseen in any other arena. During last year's baseball season, an out-of-condition pitcher, fresh out of "lock-up," took the mound during an intramural game. He reared back to fire his first curve ball, snapping his wrist in the manner of all good curve ball pitchers. His arm also snapped. The bone in his upper arm broke completely. The x-rays showed a fracture only a fraction of an inch from protruding through the skin.

That was some curve ball though.

I remember one occasion when our football team was playing a team of toughs from the Calumet Harbor League in Chicago, whom we had beaten in a close game earlier that season. They had tried to leave a collection of money to be divided among us as they left the institution. The prison officials wouldn't allow this, but we learned of the gesture and appreciated it. Not to be thwarted by prison regulations, the Chicago team smuggled cash in with them on their next trip and slipped it to us as we played.

The same middle guard I had faced in the previous game told me as we came to the line of scrimmage for the first play, "Say, Big Man, I got five dollars for you." As our quarterback barked out the signals, I thanked my opponent and wondered when he would give me the money. The instant before I snapped the ball from my position at center, the opposing guard opened his clenched fist and let a wadded-up bill fall in front of me. I got the snap off, but was so concerned with picking up the money that I gave the defensive guard little resistance and he dropped our ball carrier for a loss.

Back in our huddle, I ignored the dirty look I got from the ball carrier as I stashed the bill (which turned out to be a one) in my sock. As the game progressed, I received the full five dollars, one bill at a time. Up and down our offensive line other players were busy picking up dollar bills while the defensive lineman charged by unmolested. I don't think it was a coincidence that we got our money one bill at a time, one player at a time, and didn't make a first down during the entire first half.

During the second half our defensive linemen got their money the same way, one bill at a time, one player at a time, while the Chicago team's backfield ran on and on and on. We couldn't understand how they beat us so badly until we compared notes (bank and mental) in the locker room after the game.

Several years later I had the dubious pleasure of coaching this prison's football team. It was a real fiasco.

Our baseball-oriented athletic director stalled until seven days before the opening game. Only then did he accept football again in spite of his annual request to cancel the sport. In seven days we tried to draw up, mimeograph, and learn plays, get in condition, and form an offensive and defensive team.

We did get the plays drawn up and mimeographed, but our other goals fell somewhat short of realization. In fact, we played most of that first game with a defensive team comprising anywhere from eight to twelve men, depending on who was too tired to play. In the offensive huddle, instead of a "28 power sweep" or a "35 cutback," the quarterback would point at the man he wanted to carry the ball and say something like, "You! Take a pitchout around the right end."

By mid-season, when the plays had been learned and the men had worked themselves into some kind of condition, we had enough injuries (because of our original poor condition) to qualify the playing field as a disaster area. It was about then, too, that we realized we had men playing first string that knew their plays, holes, and running assignments but didn't know the fundamentals of blocking and tackling or even the rules of the game.

We had a mammoth, Neanderthal type middle guard who would, when told to "submarine," flop flat on his huge belly and lay there while the other team literally ran over him. Though I hate to admit it, it didn't come to my attention until one day when he showed me cleat marks all over his back and complained that everyone stepped on him when he submarined.

Once, early in the season when I told a guard to "pull" on a certain play, he went back in the game and grabbed the defensive lineman playing in front of him by the jersey and "pulled" him right out of the play. Unfortunately, the referee took exception to our version of the pulling guard.

We had a second-string quarterback who was an excellent play maker and a fair ball handler but could not complete a pass except to the other team. It wasn't until the week before the last game that I found out what the trouble was. During a light passing practice this quarterback was still being intercepted even though no one was rushing him. After watching him throw three straight passes to defensive players, even though his own receiver was open, I angrily asked him what was wrong. With his head hanging, he finally admitted that without his glasses, anything or anyone over fifteen yards away was just a blur. And even the color of the uniforms made no difference because he was color-blind too. He had not told me before because he was afraid I wouldn't let him play.

Would you believe that I didn't get to coach the team the following year?

Even though I was coaching the team, I was asked by the sports editor of the prison newspaper to write stories of the games we played. (Writing wasn't this guy's long suit, just as coaching wasn't mine.) I agreed, on the condition that my name not be used and that no players be told who was writing the stories. In these stories, I castigated the players (and the coach) to such an extent that many of the players came to me and expressed their concern-unconcern, disgust-disdain, regarding the articles.

I sat in the messhall one afternoon and listened to two men behind me laugh about the articles, the general ineptness of the team, and the incompetence of the coach. They loudly voiced the opinion that the "newspaper guy" really had that raggedy team pegged. Then one of them noticed that I was sitting in front of them and whispered to the other, "Cool it." I laughed so hard I *almost* couldn't finish my meal.

Since it is unlikely that you will ever read similar stories in the sports section of your local newspaper, I'll include a few excerpts:

Sept. 17 . . . If the Thunderbird offensive team would stop letting the other team score, our defense could probably score enough points to win a game.

Sound backwards? You say that the offensive team is

the one that runs the ball and not the one that gives up points? Brother, you haven't been watching the T-Birds play the game.

The T-Birds lost their second game of the season to Bonivir, 18 to 7, but the "Blunderbird" offense gave up 12 of those 18 points.

. . . Jack Oliver intercepted a pass on the T-Bird 18 and again waltzed *unmolested* into the end zone. (One good thing can be said for the Blunderbird offense: In spite of those 11 men being in prison for a variety of crimes, the squad is notoriously short of molesters.)

The Blunderbird offense hasn't been effective in either of its games this season, but it has shown potential. Quarterback Cobb Williams has learned to eat the ball so well that he can stay out of the messhall for three days after each game. Ed Denton has had his right hand broken so many times in the two games he's played that he finally had to quit hitting guys on the other team with it. He is developing a nice left hook though, and intends to prove that a handicap can't stop a guy "What's got guts!"

Split-end Harmon Gray can leap up and grab a ball that is ten or twelve feet in the air. Unfortunately, he hasn't had a chance to demonstrate this in a game yet because he keeps getting knocked down at the line of scrimmage. Joe Hamilton, the center, is a vicious blocker and has proven it by cutting his own fullback down on two pass plays.

The Coach obviously supports "Hire the Handicapped" week because he sends more cripples into the game than you could find in a VA hospital. To make sure he didn't take advantage of the other team, he used only eight or nine men on defense for most of the second half. Maybe the coach should try that on offense too. It couldn't be any worse.

. . . Jim "Chink" Harriman, a T-Bird linebacker who has been compared to Dick Butkus (they both have the same color eyes), played his usual aggressive game. He was in the game less than a quarter and made four tackles, had two fights, and stomped on seven prostrate Colts before getting caught and thrown out of the game. Chink claims someone snitched on him. Harriman has been thrown out of the game early so many times he doesn't know about the second half.

More than one player threatened to assault whoever was writing the articles. I always agreed.

The average prison athlete would be hard-pressed to make the varsity on a high school team, but there are a few exceptions in most prisons. Here at ISP, Donald Hooks would have to be labeled one of the exceptions.

Hooks won the 1968 Indiana State Golden Gloves Heavyweight Championship while serving his sixth year of a one-to-ten year sentence for Entering to Commit a Felony. He traveled under guard from the prison at Michigan City to the arena at Indianapolis and won a three-round decision over Ronald Garrett. This made Hooks eligible to go to Salt Lake City and fight for the national title, but the prison officials would not sanction the out-of-state trip.

Hooks fought for many years before he ever put on a pair of boxing gloves. He fought poverty, the System, and his Blackness. Naturally he wound up in prison, where he fought guards, other inmates, and the System. He was a proud man full of self-doubt, an angry man who wanted to be respected. Boxing let Hooks be proud and respected. His championship bout in Indianapolis attracted the attention of Hiawatha Gray, the man who had trained Archie Moore. Gray agreed to work with Hooks when he was released and was, in fact, training him when last heard from.

Traveling was always a big incentive for a prison athlete under Warden Lane's administration from 1961 until 1969. Men competed earnestly to make the varsity teams in baseball, softball, basketball, boxing, wrestling, weightlifting, and even chess—because all of these teams traveled to cities all over the state to compete against outside competition.

The football team is the only major sport team that

didn't compete outside the walls. Although it was never admitted by the administration, I felt that there was no great security problem involved in football. The administration was just afraid of being embarrassed by the fumbling, bumbling, raggedy Blunderbirds.

When we were competing outside the walls, the cons' behavior was generally good, and we were usually well received by the outside teams and spectators. There was one small group of us, however, who always received a hostile reaction from the crowd—the wrestling team.

We wrestled under professional rules (as opposed to collegiate), and our matches were much the same as you have watched on television when Dick the Bruiser and Killer Kowalski were performing. I have been cursed, booed, threatened, and even attacked with a chair, but it had nothing to do with my being a convict. The fact that I wore a choir robe, a beard and shades and at every opportunity stuck my fingers in my opponent's eyes probably influenced the crowd somewhat.

Once at the South Bend armory, Warden Lane climbed into the ring and gave a stirring, somber ten-minute speech about the goodness that is in every man regardless of what he has done in the past. Lane closed his speech by expressing the hope that the inmates who were to perform in the boxing and wrestling matches would be viewed and appreciated as athletes rather than inmates.

My partner and I were scheduled to open the evening's entertainment with a tag team match. Lane's closing remarks were greeted with loud applause that turned into boos and jeers as he stepped through the ropes to leave the ring. He halted abruptly on the ring apron and stared in wonderment at the audience, trying to understand why he was being booed. Finally he spotted "Sailor Boy" Page and myself swaggering toward the ring in full costume, glaring insolently at the audience. Obviously relieved, but also piqued at the timing of our entrance on the heels of his inspirational speech about inmates, Lane sadly shook his head and left the ring.

With the exception of the crumbling forty-foot wall that surrounds it, ISP's recreation area is a beautiful place. It contains two ball diamonds, three miniature golf courses, two tennis courts, two *boccie* ball courts, an outdoor basketball court, four horseshoe pits, a volleyball court, two shuffleboard courts, two handball courts, plus a fieldhouse with an indoor basketball court, a weightlifting area, a ping-pong table, a shuffleboard table, five television sets, a score of tables for dominoes, checkers, and chess, and two shower rooms. (Think we ain't coddled?)

The equipment for all these activities is paid for not by the taxpayer but by the inmates. Profits from the money we spend at the prison commissary go into the recreation fund, which pays for our movies as well as the athletic equipment.

The population of this prison is almost two thousand, and about fifteen hundred of us are inside the walls. Nevertheless, I think a generous estimate of the number of men who even occasionally use some piece of athletic equipment would be five hundred. No more than three hundred would be regularly involved with competitive sports. Many cons are firmly opposed to spending money and using space for baseball bats and basketballs when no new books have been purchased for the prison library in years, beans are being rationed because of a budget deficit, and a con leaving on parole or discharge gets only twenty-five dollars gate money. Non-athletes especially resent paying exorbitantly high commissary prices in order to buy those bats.

When he learned that I was doing an article on prison sports, one such non-athlete (and a co-author of this book) gave a disgusted grunt and sat down at his typewriter. Ten minutes later he handed me the following one-page tirade:

SPORTS BEHIND THE CONCRETE CURTAIN

Snorting, farting, and screaming, the Michigan City All-American Boccie Ball Club of fierce, fascist protagonists burst onto the playing field, ready for all comers.

Of course Boccie Ball is just one of the many recreational activities of the Cons of the Indiana State Prison. Such American apple pie games as tiddlywinks with manhole covers and "shuffle and dribble" are also favorite sports for the boys.

Actually, the favorite sports of these misled boys are more of an indoor nature. Sodomy, gambling, drinking and playing the dirty dozens for example. But the boys put on a good show at anything they do. For example, when the institution's fightin' team is behind 8 or 10 touchdowns, they atavistically revert to their beast-like nature and begin pummeling and kicking the opposing team, since they know in their little hearts that what the spectators really want is some blood anyway.

I wouldn't say the prison's recreation department is exactly a joke. No, I wouldn't come on *that* strong. But I would say that it is a pretty sick affair. But then the whole joint is pretty sick and the recreation system fits in beautifully.

Supported by funds earned as profit from the inmate store (less what the officials steal) the sports program is less well-rounded than it is square. It kind of grabs you right here to see two grown-up and grizzly baby-rapers playing a game of jacks with all the intensity and emotion that most people give to more serious things, like the pitching averages of the Toledo Mud Hens or the Turkey Creek Tigers.

A recreation program serves an important function in any prison. Along with fish clubs, record clubs, and leatherworking, recreation is a privilege that is held out like a piece of candy to the cons who do not violate the rules. It is one of the many pacification programs that are lumped together and called "rehabilitation" by the prison administration.

The fact is, however, that baseball has very little rehabilitatory value in spite of such terms as "team play," "responsibility," and "discipline." What it does do is give some degree of badly needed emotional release, burn up energy that might otherwise be used destructively, and provide both the fan and the player with hours of simple pleasure. But it has damn little to do with transforming a criminal into a law-abiding citizen.

—M.M.

9

The Prison Artist

Art is one of the means whereby man seeks to redeem a
life which is experienced as chaotic, senseless and largely
evil.

—ALDOUS HUXLEY
Themes and Variations

Long before the first pages of this book were written,
my co-authors and I discussed those ingredients which give
impetus to creative and artistic endeavor in prison. The
subject came up often, and our bull sessions became a running discussion all through one winter and into early
spring. It seemed that almost daily some convict was at-
tracting "outside" attention by painting or by marketing a
literary manuscript.

In my job on the prison newspaper, I had the opportunity to chat with many of these convicts who were, in
prison vernacular, "doing something." I met painters, writers, musicians, and dozens of hobbyists. They proved to
be as varied in temperament and artistic ability as the wide
range of criminal vagaries which had thrown them together
in confinement.

There were some good guys among them, and—again to use the vernacular—there were some dirty dogs. Meeting these creative people early taught me that simply because a person had a developed sense of artistic expression he was not magically endowed with any saintly or puritanical qualities. No, every single prison artist I met remained, for the most part, a murderer, a rapist, a thief, or a drug addict. Some, in fact, retained the very essence of their artistry in the dark nature of their criminal urgings: the murderer often stroked his canvas in a white hot rage against himself, or stole from his fellow convicts the tools to paint.

The desire for self-expression is intense in prison, perhaps because it is inherent in man to fight against what he feels is a stifling of his Self, a repression of his artistic sense. Man's insignificance is nowhere brought home to him more forcefully than in prison.

I don't believe any administrator in the entire history of Indiana State Prison realized this need for self-expression more than Warden Ward Lane when he took over control early in 1961. For he immediately allowed about a dozen "self-help" or therapy groups inside the prison—and at one time these groups represented about 45 per cent of the total prison population. Convicts had art clubs, stamp clubs, aquarists clubs, chess clubs, Dale Carnegie clubs—you name it, the convicts had it.

Lane knew instinctively that one factor which weighs heavily against any "change for the better" in a man is the low self-esteem in which he holds himself after only a short time in lock-up. He knew that the barren, dismal environment, the atmosphere of utter dismay, cynicism, and futility, simply confirms in the convict's mind that he is, indeed, evil, the very personification of what is socially wrong. Lane often said that these things made a man a convict in every sense.

I should say that many convicts are motivated to

strive artistically for purely selfish reasons. Some are motivated to "create" solely for money, not exactly an addle-
headed idea since most have no source of income other
than meager prison wages. And my commitment extends to
saying that among these men you will usually find the crass
bastards who will go to any means to sell a painting or
market their plagiarized literary efforts.

Some convicts begin their artistic endeavors as a
hobby; some begin out of relief from the sheer, screaming
boredom of prison. But the point is that artists, writers, and
musicians—the primary prison art colony—abound, and
out of the many are those outstanding figures who instantly
strike the spark of true artistic creativeness from the moment they take up the instrument of their craft. In prison
you never have to walk far or look long to find this man.
Etheridge Knight, a black poet, perhaps serves best my purpose of drawing a composite of the true prison-born artist.

Knight was a contemporary of mine on the prison
newspaper for almost a year. When I got to know him, he
was well along with his writing career, having already published in *Negro Digest* and *Golliard's Poetry Magazine*. He
had also published a volume of his collected poems and
was halfway through a definitive work on Denmark Vesey,
a Negro who led a slave uprising in pre-Civil War South
Carolina.

Etheridge found his way to Indiana State Prison by
virtue of a ten-to-twenty-five-year robbery sentence. A confirmed drug addict, he grabbed an old woman's purse,
nearly crippling her in the process, to get some money for
his habit. He was unfortunate to have been caught at a time
when public sentiment in Indianapolis (the place of the
"happening," as he for years referred to his crime) was running high against such crimes. Two elderly women had
been similarly robbed and beaten shortly before, and the
police were running around in circles scratching their

collective ass trying to seize a suspect upon whom the out-
raged community could justly vent its frustrations.

When Knight fell into the police net he fitted the bill
nicely. He lay in jail for more than a year angling for a
short sentence, but the police, the judge, the newspapers,
and the public were insistent that only by meting out the
full measure of "justice"—a ten-to-twenty-five-year term
—could the best interests of society be served, although
Knight complained to me many times that "they sure as
hell never convinced me that they were acting in my best
interests with a sentence like that."

All things considered, Knight did have some justification for his attitude. Many times he told me that day after
day while he lay in jail waiting trial, he saw men return
from court with light sentences for crimes worse than his.
"I was a junkie, a petty thief, and a drifter," he used to say,
"and when the detective told me, 'Nigger, you're goin' to
prison!' I believed him."

He didn't have much going for him in confinement. His
work record was spotty; he had a limited education; and his
outlook on life was blackened by his sense of injustice. He
was assigned to menial jobs and was in and out of the hole
for refusing to work. His friends called him a "low rider," a
real sonofabitch. And so Knight, like countless thousands of
convicts before him, wallowed in a haze of red anger and
self-pity.

It wasn't long before officials transferred him from
State Reformatory to the prison as an incorrigible, which
amounted to stamping his packet with the recommendation
that he "serve his maximum sentence." Consequently, his
first look at Indiana State Prison scared the hell out of him.

We talked often, Etheridge and I, of our first impressions
of prison and the effect it had upon our thinking. He told
me time and time again that he had almost no recollection
of his first few months in the reformatory, he was so angry.

Not until months later would he be suddenly overwhelmed with the utter hopelessness and futility of his situation.

Of that time he said, "I knew goddamn well that there had to be something better for me in life than a ten-to-twenty-five-year sentence stretched endlessly before me."

From that day, Knight devoted every ounce of his energies toward getting out of prison. He read books like they were going out of style and applied himself in many areas —philosophy, art, science, and religion. In five years he covered a wide field, and he found a bit of Etheridge Knight in all of them. He found a sense of worth, a yardstick of measurement for himself. In his discovery he became an articulate spokesman for the prison Negro population. He gained a reputation, which, in an unguarded moment, he let slip that he valued highly. He became the Negro voice for "telling it like it is."

From the beginning of his artistic awakening, Knight's medium for "telling it like it is" was poetry, sweet, flowing, rhythmical, but at times harsh and bitter, at times ironic and snickering, at times plaintive and sad—but always truthful and exact, his soul expression, as he called it.

I watched him furtively, many times, a gaunt hulk of a man with hamhock hands and stubby fingers, hunched over his typewriter digging at the keys in utter consternation, and I thought, "If that bastard is creating something, I'll eat my hat." He never voluntarily offered any of his finished material for my inspection; I had to dig it out of him. And every time I did, there it was, a thing of perfection. I knew it. And I knew, too, from the first day I experienced this knowledge, that goddamn convict or not, anyone with such a keenly attuned sense of esthetic expression had to be more than just the sum total of a long prison sentence.

"I died in Korea from a shrapnel wound," Knight told me once in conversation summing up his life, "and narcotics resurrected me. I died in 1960 from a prison sentence, and poetry brought me back to life."

I know that at heart Knight was always a poet, gentle and easygoing, his brutish crime notwithstanding. It only remained for the proper circumstances to awaken his dormant, untapped poetic talent. He told me often that he disliked writing about prison and prisoners, but paradoxically those stories he wrote of his fellow convicts were consistently his best literary efforts—the ones he marketed. He had much to say about prison, about social injustice to his race, and about himself. A constant theme, predominant and unashamed, ran throughout all his writings: he emphasized the lengths to which men are driven in seeking their identity.

Knight found through writing what he had been searching for through narcotics, a way to express, a way to be himself without violating the social restraints of his fellow men. When he writes, then, he is functioning, and he likes the feeling.

Knight did have his rebirth, but up close he remained the same Etheridge he had always been. It was generally conceded among intimate friends that he was still pretty much the arrogant sonofabitch he had always been. But I, for one, never saw his complexion as all that warty. He could indeed be mean and petty at times, out of sorts with everyone and everything around him, but the evidence of his change in value priorities was plain enough: he preferred discussions on philosophy to crime. As he said many times, "My interest now is in Kant, not cunt."

His rebirth, then, was that through poetry he made others aware of Etheridge Knight as a person measuring his worth against theirs. Gwendolyn Brooks—poet laureate of Illinois and his close friend and adviser—said in her preface to his volume of poetry: "Here is a work of major pronouncement." As his prolificacy grew and his sophistication increased, he became aware of his responsibility to his fellow convicts, not just as any kind of spokesman for them, a term he disliked—"I speak only for Etheridge Knight!"—but a responsibility not to use his newly found prestige for self-aggrandizement.

He had been a bastard straightaway most of his life—thief, pimp, hustler, dope addict—and his personal philosophy when he entered prison naturally reflected the acculturation of his environment. Therefore, his soul struggle became a beautiful thing, a triumph greater than his emergence as a major literary voice.

Now Knight becomes the pure composite of the prison-born artist, the personification of the embryo-birth and subsequent flowering of creativeness in barren circumstances. For above all else, Knight was a rock-ribbed realist. "How in hell can we escape into dreams and soft words in prison?" he asked a thousand times. "Each day there is enough harshness manifest here to shatter the dreams of an opium eater and snatch him back to the hard realities of high walls."

Knight's prison-born poetic existence, then, transcends that of the composite "art group"—the hobby clubs—of which I spoke earlier, organized by an understanding warden with good intentions but wherein soon were to be found the wise guys, the angle shooters. The clubs soon became meaningless collectives, pocked and festered with jealousy and pettiness that rotted out the core of potential good. In the prison art clubs creative expression became a screaming message in its negativeness, an inarticulate posturing—hollow, phony.

Why? Because convicts, as a group, are notoriously shallow; they are full of natural pretense and rationalization. How easy it becomes for some idiot to call himself an artist, to dare suppose he has given meaningful direction to some creative urge, when, secretly, alone with himself, he nakedly steals another's literary or artistic ideas. His thievery is simply the means to an end: inwardly he is strangling in his ineptness. His shouting and posturing about his newfound talent is often a disguised cry for rescue from himself.

One convict told me he joined the prison art clubs "because the parole board denied me parole until I learned a trade!" It never occurred to him to further his formal education and prod himself into an awareness of what was going on around him. Instead he magnified his gray discontent by giving way in his helpless misery to the comfort of the herd—the prison "self-help" club. His artistic ability, if indeed he had any, could never have been anything but crass and commercialized.

It's to these underhanded bastards that Knight's artistry becomes a fair-game, "up-for-grabs" meal rich in caloric value to their ego. One plagiarist convict told me, referring obliquely to Knight's being a Negro, "If he can do it [write], I can, too." But he never did.

Once I read about an art show held in Illinois Statesville Penitentiary. At a single exhibition, more than 380 inmate artists exhibited a total of 2,675 paintings. Not surprisingly, the exhibit drew an estimated crowd of around 20,000 in something less than a week. Not bad for the public image, and not bad for the convict artist's image, usually held at ground level. But after reading the account of the exhibit, I had the uneasy sense of something wrong, that I was being put on.

"Not only is this a profitable pastime for inmates, but it also develops hidden talents that may be used professionally and profitably when they are released from prison," said the editor of the prison newspaper. Here was a man, by the very implication of his prison position, himself an artisan, perpetuating the myth that anyone can become creative in ten easy lessons—especially if he is a convict, in prison, and applies himself. (Another opium eater?) Prison-born artists? Perhaps. But 380 of them from a prison population of 5,000? Hardly, baby. I never met a single man who exhibited in that show; I didn't have to in order to know that the figure was a gross misrepresentation of the esthetic haves to the have-nots in prison.

My heartfelt sympathies went out to the Etheridge Knights of Statesville Prison, because I knew that of 380 "convict artists" exhibited, nine tenths of them were feeding on the real talents. (Not bad feeding, either, for in their eagerness to satisfy their obligatory feelings of "helping the convicts," the public bought $20,286.50 worth of paintings!)

I knew Albert Drucker only from reading about him in a prison newspaper. Drucker became prison "copy" when he wrote a novel in the unbelievably short span of seventy-one days. A New York publisher signed Drucker to a contract, advanced him $1250 royalties against advance sales, and told him he would like first crack at anything else he wrote. Drucker has since written and published two other novels.

Like many aspiring prison novelists, Drucker began from scratch. His education, like Knight's, was limited, and he had never written a line for publication before he came to prison. He joined a writers' group not, as he said, "to make my sentence easier, but to satisfy an inner urge that kept telling me I could write."

Drucker, like Knight, found within himself a means of expressing his esoteric life style. He was more fortunate in ways than Knight: he had a shorter stay in prison, he was younger; but his expression, like Knight's, freed him forever from the restraints of physical prison.

He may very well credit his initial success to the Ink

Weavers, the prison literary club in Minnesota Prison to which he once belonged. But only Albert Drucker, not the Ink Weavers, can reflect the artistic and esthetic meaning of the man. These Minnesota Ink Weavers can also boast graduate authors Frank Elli (*The Riot*), Dave Hill (children's books), and Emil Johnson (who recently won the "Edgar" Award for one of his mystery novels).

No analysis of the prison-born artist can be complete without the presentation of the enigma of the self-destructiveness inherent in the creative convict. Just as we stand angrily before the corrupt judge who sentences us to prison in righteous indignation; just as we choke back our humiliation at the very castration of imprisonment; just as we are humbled in the presence of the malignant illness in an old friend; so are we helpless to understand the contemptuous waste with which an occasional magnificent talent will dissipate itself in silliness.

Francisco Gomez was such a person. Something good happened to Gomez during one of his many trips to prison, and into his life there came a sort of hopeful waiting. He dared to hope, cautiously. For the first time in his stormy life, he found a peg upon which to hang his future.

I first met Gomez in the prison art club, a quiet, introverted Mexican-American. He was thirty-five years old, a veteran of many prisons and of twenty years' drug addiction. At first acquaintance Alfaro impressed me as being much, much more than an unfortunate drug addict who had for more than two decades been kicked from pillar to post, from prison to prison. Gomez was more fortunate than most convicts, if you can call convicts fortunate, in that some years earlier in State Reformatory he had fallen in love with painting. Now, in prison again, he had won the respect and admiration of the civilian art instructor, who saw a wellspring of artistic expression hidden within

Gomez. Gradually, slowly, Gomez was finding a way to rise above his prison surroundings. He was becoming more than Francisco Gomez, convict.

"Gomez is a true artist, and a fine talent," the art instructor told me. "There is nothing I can teach him. The truth is, he should be giving me instructions, for he has a rare, God-given talent."

A quick look at Gomez's canvas could dispel any doubts about his ability. The air of the competent, sure artisan was unmistakable in his work. He was good.

Later, I found that his self-possession hadn't come easy. In his manner there were reflections of past jail sentences and hospital stays and lengthy prison terms. Fighting off the monkey, he called it, trying to seek out his rightful place. In the end, Gomez always became a helpless victim of the frustrations and pressures of his search.

When I met him, he was nearing the end of a ten-year sentence. He swore that he had developed a tolerance and understanding of his weaknesses that had for so long kept him bound to narcotics, thievery, and prison. And I believed him; he spoke often of his limitations with a humbleness short of self-deprecation. He convinced me that he had rebuilt a new Francisco Gomez through his self-searching. And the search had left its scars. "I don't want to be unjustly criticized or stereotyped as a Mexican junkie," he often told me. Still, he wasn't above commercializing his art in prison: he repeatedly sold insipidly done paintings to the prison officials.

I suspected that even as he told me all this he knew that one day his art, like his reborn Self, would have to stand alone on its merits. He insisted on the sharp line separating compromise from surrender.

The promise of his new beginning wasn't long in coming. Shortly after I last talked with him in the summer of 1967, he was granted a parole and went to a city near the prison. His art instructor found him a job in an art gallery and acted as his parole sponsor. In less than two months, he was arrested for possession of dope and was thrown in jail. End the story of Francisco Gomez.

Despite the terrible lessons, the hard knocks, the agony and the frustrations, Gomez went right back to being a simpering bitch, whining and ignorant. Life, too, like paintings, has its art style.

He will never cease to pay for his mistakes. His backsliding return to drug addiction was a contradiction of his prison-expressed philosophy that he would never prostitute his art. The real significance of the contradiction was that, in effect, it did far worse than cheapen his art: it cheapened the man.

I cannot say in summing up Knight, Gomez, and Drucker that prison was the hothouse for their mental aberrations or even that in prison they held to a set of values not in keeping with the mores of open society. But I can say with a certainty as rooted in fact as the prison wall that surrounds me that the impetus for their energies (with the exception, possibly, of Gomez) has been hatred for the baseness of prison, and prisoners.

In *The Song of the Lark,* Willa Cather has suggested that " . . . art is but a mold in which to imprison for a time . . . the elusive element which is life . . . too strong to stop, too sweet to lose."

As a measure of his worth, then, the prison-born artist must make all his barren yesterdays into articulate tomorrows. Only then will his substance have meaning, his art value.

—A.P.

10
Religion

If God made us in His image, we have certainly returned the compliment.

—VOLTAIRE
Le Sottisier, XXXII

I have no idea what percentage of the people in "free" society attend church regularly. It probably isn't much higher than 5 per cent, about what it is in prison. And certainly there must be those in both instances who actually believe in their God and are genuinely dedicated to their church.

Yet I've often heard that many people "outside" look upon their church affiliation as a status symbol (the wealthier the church the more valuable the symbol). I've heard that they attend church to impress others with their piety and/or to salve their guilt-ridden consciences. If this be true, then here, it would seem to me, is where the comparison between "outside" and "inside" church-goers must end.

This isn't to say that there aren't also a lot of phonies in prison church congregations. On the contrary, there are men in prison who see their church attendance as a means to some end other than spending eternity in Heaven.

The prison chapel is considered by some cons for example, an ideal rendezvous for lovers—especially in the wintertime when it's too cold to go to the recreation yard. And it is said that they do something more than merely hold hands. Of course, I've never thought of "The Old Rugged Cross" as music to make love by, but it might be groovy. What's the saying: "If you haven't tried it, don't knock it"?

Then, too, there are those cons who think that by going to church regularly they may favorably impress the parole board and thereby gain an early release. On the face of it, this may not sound like a bad idea. The only thing, it doesn't work. I know. I tried it.

It is also a well-known fact in prison circles that a portion—sometimes as much as 40 per cent—of church congregations in prison are made up of sex offenders—especially child molesters. I have no idea why this is so, but I would guess that it has something to do with their immaturity and the fact that they view the minister as a father figure. In any event, it's their concern, so I'll leave it at that.

In any event, a book about prison without a chapter on religion would be somewhat like a loaf of bread without leavening. Therefore, I've interviewed both Father Joseph Sedlak, the Catholic priest here at the prison, and Reverend Russell E. Daubert, the Protestant chaplain. Both men were most cooperative, and the following two interviews resulted. These, then, should give you some insight into what organized religion *is* or *is not* doing to rehabilitate the convicted felon.

The chill wind sweeping in from Lake Michigan carried the threat of rain as six grim-faced men trudged slowly toward a newly opened grave. Their burden—a coffin containing the remains of a man completely unknown to them.

Only hours before, these six prison trusties, assigned to the greenhouse detail just outside the prison walls, had been informed by their superior that they were to open a new grave and act as pallbearers for a prisoner whose corpse had gone unclaimed by the next of kin.

As they approached the edge of the mound of freshly turned earth and the gaping hole that would soon close on this all but anonymous man, the Reverend Russell E. Daubert, the Protestant chaplain here at the Indiana State Prison, stepped forward. At his side was a uniformed prison guard—a lieutenant—who, in accordance with state law, would compare the face of the corpse with a mug shot he held in his hand.

This done, the coffin was closed for the last time and placed on the bier. Then, as the dark clouds overhead released only a few drops of rain, as if even they were reluctant to mourn the passing of this forgotten man, Reverend Daubert began to pray: "Man that is born of woman has but a short time to live here on earth and is full of misery . . . he cometh up and is shortly cut down as a flower . . . unto Thee Almighty God we commend the soul of our departed brother, and we commit his body to the ground: ashes to ashes, dust to dust. . . ."

As Reverend Daubert continued to pray, the winds from the north increased in velocity and brought with them torrential rainfall. With this, he ended his prayer and gave the pallbearers a nod, their cue to place bouquets of cut flowers on the coffin.

Except for some variations in the weather, this might well have been any one of the thirty-six graveside services Reverend Daubert has conducted in what the prisoners refer to as "Boot Hill" since he became the Protestant chaplain at the prison in December of 1961. .

According to him, these prison burials are the most

difficult part of his duties as chaplain here. "I usually feel," said Reverend Daubert, "a sense of awkwardness while conducting a funeral in the prison cemetery, for rarely do I know the deceased, and in some cases I've never set eyes on the man before. When he is a total stranger to me, I always think: If only I'd had an opportunity to speak with him about the Christian faith and his beliefs. It's a little like calling a doctor after the patient has died."

Reverend Daubert feels differently, however, when the deceased is one of his congregation. "We are assured by the Word of God that all true believers will meet in Heaven and be with God forever," he said. "Therefore, when a Christian man dies here, I don't have this awful feeling that another man has died without a saving faith in Christ."

The brighter side of Reverend Daubert's prison ministry is the regular Sunday morning services he conducts inside the prison and at the minimum security building just outside the towering walls of the prison. The inside service includes the singing of the Protestant chapel choir under the direction of Chester Schlegal. This all-male choir is made up of more than twenty prisoners, who can also be heard every Saturday between 12:30 and 1:00 P.M. over radio station WIMS, Michigan City, Indiana.

In addition to his regular Sunday morning services, Reverend Daubert does personal counseling, encouraging those men who come to him for advice to seek spiritual solutions to their everyday problems. "This way," he said, "I can sometimes help a man resolve a personal problem that might otherwise get out of hand."

He also conducts Christian group therapy sessions every Thursday afternoon in which Christian men can share discussion and fellowship with one another. He considers these group discussions an invaluable extension of his regular services.

Standing more than six feet tall, Reverend Daubert is

a man whose sense of purpose is as sharply defined as the dark suits he wears; and, as he approaches the pulpit in the prison's chapel-auditorium each Sunday morning to offer the invocation, a hush falls over the congregation. It's obvious then that the prisoners gathered there to worship God respect this stern-faced man of God.

A 1943 graduate of Eastern Baptist College in his home town of Philadelphia, Reverend Daubert had three regular pastorates and for nine years represented a group of Baptist churches in Pennsylvania before coming to the Indiana State Prison in 1961. He feels the years from 1943 to 1961 prepared him for his present assignment, which in some ways he considers the most challenging of his career.

Another pleasant aspect of his work is his Tuesday afternoon Bible-study classes. For those inmates wanting to study the Word of God in depth and prepare themselves for a life of Christian work and devotion, this systematic study of the Bible is a godsend. To date, more than two hundred men have completed this course and have received certificates of achievement.

Reverend Daubert likes to maintain a flexible schedule, allowing himself time to make periodic visits to the prison hospital, seclusion units, and death row. This isn't always possible, however, because in addition to all of his aforementioned duties he must also find time for his voluminous correspondence and interviews with prisoners' families and pastors. And as if all of this weren't enough, he is frequently called upon by the prison Alcoholics Anonymous group and Jaycee chapter to officiate at their open-house meetings and installation banquets.

According to Reverend Daubert, a prison chaplain has many obstacles to overcome before he can reach an imprisoned man with the Word of God. Said Reverend Daubert, "I must first overcome the prisoner's general distrust of other human beings. Then, when this is accomplished, I must convince the man who would accept Christ as his personal Saviour that he can, with God's help, ignore the abuse that will be heaped upon him by nonbelievers. It's an uphill struggle all the way, but the prize of life beyond the grave for the Christian convert is worth every sacrifice. Unfortunately, only about 5 per cent of the prisoners avail themselves of Christian teachings."

Reverend Daubert thinks that a man converted to Christianity while in prison is a better parole risk than one who fails, for whatever reason, to take up his cross and follow Jesus. And, according to the chaplain's clerk, Jack Giselbach, who watches such things closely, of all the men who return to the Michigan City, Indiana, prison either as parole violators or on new commitments, less than 5 per cent of them are men who had previously taken part in the religious programs in the prison.

Reverend Daubert would like to lead every one of the nineteen hundred men in the Indiana State Prison to a saving faith in Christ; but alas! he must face the harsh fact that most prisoners—like most outsiders—would rather feast the flesh than cast their lot with Christ.

Said Reverend Daubert, "Most men live only for today, and all too often death finds them unprepared. As a result, they'll eventually be like the rich man in hell, who cried out for Abraham to send Lazarus to dip his fingers in water and cool his tongue to ease the pain."

Reverend Daubert doesn't know at what hour he will be informed of the death of another prisoner whose body will go unclaimed by the next of kin. He would hope, of course, that he will never be called upon to perform another burial in the prison cemetery; but being a realist, he knows differently. All he can do is pray that the next . . . and next . . . and . . . will be men who have made their peace with the Lord and will not, therefore, go unclaimed by God also.

Father Joseph F. Sedlak believes he has one of the most interesting and challenging jobs in the world. He's the Catholic priest here at the Indiana State Prison. And judging from his open-minded enthusiasm for his work, he is indeed equal to the challenge.

Just as a woman's home tells a great deal about her character, so does a man's office reveal many things about the inner workings of his mind. When you get to know Father Sedlak well, you're not surprised to find his prison office and library richly furnished yet unpretentious, his bookcases brimful with well-thumbed, contemporary books instead of dust-catching, archaic tomes.

Transferred from the Blessed Sacrament parish in Gary, Indiana, to the prison in July, 1968, the thirty-seven-year-old priest let it be known that he was available to Catholics and non-Catholics alike for personal counseling. In addition, he has since instituted a series of group counseling sessions for the benefit of those cons interested in discussing such things as psychology, criminology, and penology. "These group discussions," says Father Sedlak, "take some interesting turns and serve to ventilate the prisoners' frustrations and anxieties resulting from their being separated from their families. We discuss such things as religion, family, and civic responsibility and yes, even sex and homosexuality."

Asked if he favors conjugal visits or temporary paroles for men serving long prison terms, Father Sedlak said that some means of allowing a married man to be with his wife occasionally must be found. "Everything within reason should be done to safeguard and strengthen emotional ties between the imprisoned man and his family," he said.

His personal counseling also serves as an emotional outlet for those cons who from time to time find themselves unable to cope with problems of a personal nature. It isn't unusual, therefore, for a con who has received a "Dear

John" letter to seek out Father Sedlak for advice and consolation. Too, an occasional con pushed to the limits of his tolerance by a maze of petty rules and regulations will go to him for help.

"Some of them," said the priest, "use me as their whipping boy to rid themselves of their anger. Fact is, some of them even curse me. But I don't mind. I'd rather have them release a barrage of verbal invectives at me than see them strike out with physical violence against the prison officials." He was quick to add that the percentage of prisoners who lose control of their emotions is comparatively small considering the claustrophobic frustration inherent in prison living.

Violence—the bedmate of fear and anxiety—is not unusual in prison. As a result, Father Sedlak's ability to remain cool under stress is an asset. Perhaps this explains why the atmosphere in his office is so serene—an oasis of brotherly love midst the burning sands of ignorance and misunderstanding.

In addition to conducting Mass each Sunday morning in the chapel-auditorium, Father Sedlak holds a Friday afternoon liturgical Mass in the John F. Kennedy Memorial Library. This room, adjacent to his offices located in a remote corner of the prison, was remodeled and decorated by the cons themselves. Because fewer men attend these services than the Sunday Mass, they are able to take a more active part in the dialogue which aids them immeasurably in understanding just what their responsibilities are to the Church and to one another. Newcomers to Catholicism receive instructions on Mondays and Tuesdays.

Having found the barnlike chapel-auditorium in the prison unsuitable for religious services, Father Sedlak and others at the prison have asked the budget committee of the Indiana legislative body to appropriate funds for the construction of a new "Faith Center" to be used exclusively for religious purposes—chapel, offices, and classrooms. However, because newly elected Governor Edgar Whitcomb has asked for "less government spending," it isn't likely that such funds will be forthcoming.

Realizing that the American people tend to look on crime in only one dimension—focusing on the *chase* and *capture* of the criminal instead of thinking in terms of what causes crime—Father Sedlak welcomes the opportunity to speak to club groups and fraternal organizations in nearby cities about the causes of crime and what he thinks can be done to ameliorate its fantastic rate of increase.

"These audiences are delighted to hear about a notorious convict who has escaped," he said to me. "But they begin to squirm when I start talking about the economic and legislative needs of our prisons. They don't want to hear it. Yet they must. They must be convinced that a prisoner is a human being with hopes, dreams, and aspirations not unlike their own. They must understand that a so-called criminal has behaved antisocially in one area of his life only after society has been *anti-him*. In other words, at some point in the 'criminal's life,' one or more of our social institutions have failed him. Therefore, we—the more fortunate members of society—are obligated to help him; and we can't do this by locking him up and throwing away the key. He must be given the chance to earn his way back."

After a pause to relight his cigar, Father Sedlak continued: "Men in prison don't need repression, nor do they need sentimental treatment, but rather opportunity for restitution. The key to resocializing prisoners is to allow them to earn self-respect. Prisons are full of men who above all else need a chance to serve society in order to respect themselves. When the public accepts this fact, we will be on the road to genuine rehabilitation. Without this acceptance, rehabilitation will continue to be merely a word in the penal dictionary."

Feeling that our so-called corrections systems in this country are corrupt and archaic, Father Sedlak would like to see the Church play a more active role in putting the finger on the corruption and calling for updated treatment programs for social outcasts. He isn't sure just how this could be done, but he feels the need of such involvement of the Church. "Whenever human rights are affronted, the Church as a social institution—that is, the Vatican, the diocese, the parish, the local Catholic school and other such divisions of the organizational chart—must respond with all of its strength and vigor."

Of one thing he is certain, however, and that is that too few of our tax dollars go for alleviating our domestic social problems and too many to waging an "evil" war in Vietnam. "As a people, we're *good* at waging wars," he says, "but very *bad* at finding the root causes of and solving our social problems. There's a contradiction here someplace."

Being deeply concerned about juvenile delinquency, Father Sedlak likes nothing better than a verbal confrontation on the subject. And his adversary had better be up-to-date and well informed. Otherwise he will be found wanting when faced with Father Sedlak's youthful wit and sagelike wisdom.

When asked to comment on the causes of juvenile delinquency, Father Sedlak adjusted his black horn-rimmed glasses and said, "This is difficult . . . obviously juvenile delinquency has its origin in a problem family. Not necessarily the economically deprived or broken home—although many of our troubled children come from such an environment—but rather a problem family in which there are double standards at work. That is, many families confuse young people by preaching one thing and practicing another—by telling them to live honestly and then demonstrating to them that it pays to be dishonest. And, too, our society's reluctance to change anachronistic structures that are invalid has *turned off* today's young people. They're rebelling against our immorality, and we call them delinquents."

Believing that man should clean his own house first, Father Sedlak is critical of the Church. He would put much of the blame for juvenile delinquency and crime squarely at the door of the Church. He justifies this by stating emphatically that the Church is guilty of "saying" one thing and "doing" another. "The Church," said Father Sedlak, "acquiesces to society's way of life and plays little theological and religious games to compensate for its lack of relevance to life's problems and more specifically to youth's concerns and problems.

"My experience with youth and youth leaders has shown me that the young people in this country see very clearly the double standard expressed by the Church's behavior. Religion is not related to life, and for this generation of young people anything not related to life—here and now—must be rejected as meaningless. The Church is often more out of touch with the times than politics and economics and certainly way out of focus with science and technology," he said.

"Today's kids," Father Sedlak continued, "are *turned on* by the latter two sources of strength. The Church thus contributes ideologically to delinquency and youthful crime. Of course, we do have youth programs; but like so many other things in the Church, we concentrate on saving the saved and eliminate the problem child—thus contradicting the very essence of Christianity, which is to concern ourselves with those most in need."

Father Sedlak doesn't proselytize in the sense of going around the prison trying to convert the cons to his religious persuasion, but the very fact that he *practices* what he *preaches* when dealing with the guys has won him a few converts and many friends within the walls.

"The Church has been too concerned with getting people into a *box*," he says, "but when you look at this *box*, you can ask: Is there religion there, or are they merely going through a ritual? The essence of religion is to love, understand, and help our fellow man in all of our daily contacts.

"This business of putting people into a *box*," he said, lighting his cigar again, "is a hang-up with the Church. That's why young people—and prisoners too—shy away from the Church."

When asked what Christians can do to help reduce juvenile delinquency and crime in this country, Father Sedlak replied, "They can become concerned—honestly and deeply—about their families and about their communities. Too many Christians consider Christianity a personal matter. It is that, but it is also a social matter. Helping to break down the structures of prejudice and hatred in society is the task of society itself. Christians should be at the front of any action that promises to improve our culture, and viewing the so-called criminal and the imprisoned man as a brother who has stumbled and fallen by the wayside and is in need of our help would enhance the entire fabric of our society. Then to actually extend him a helping hand in the form of legislative appropriations to improve his lot would be to weave the social fabric of our society even tighter."

—H.J.G.

11
The Penal Press

A censor pretending to protect morality is like a child pushing the cushions of a railway carriage to give itself the sensation of making the train travel at sixty miles an hour.

—GEORGE BERNARD SHAW
The Shewing Up of Blanco Posnet

More than two hundred separate publications—newspapers and magazines—roll off the penal presses in this country on a weekly, biweekly, monthly, bimonthly, and quarterly basis. Their combined circulation exceeds 250,000—nearly half of which are mailed to "outside" subscribers. Well over a half-million readers are exposed to what prison editors and writers are saying about such things as the causes of crime and juvenile delinquency. These men —and women—also have their own opinions about what could be done to improve penal conditions in this country.

Owing to lack of formal journalistic training on the part of personnel and a shortage of modern printing equipment, many of the periodicals on the penal press circuit leave something to be desired in content, layout, and production. Yet despite these drawbacks, a few of these little newspapers and magazines literally sparkle.

Because of my close proximity to the *Lake Shore Outlook* (I'm the editor), I can't swear that our monthly, eight-page tabloid "sparkles," but it does occasionally ignite a spark of interest in some of our sixteen hundred outside readers.

For instance: In August of 1968 I wrote an editorial in which I shocked a few of Indiana's leading newspaper editors by charging them with using sensationalism to sell newspapers. I'm still hearing their static. Thankfully, most of it is positive.

Since its birth on September 1, 1949, the *Lake Shore Outlook* has increased its circulation from less than five hundred (all of which were distributed within the walls) to more than thirty-eight hundred. It is now read in all fifty states plus several foreign countries.

In addition to being awarded prizes by the Northwestern and Indiana university schools of journalism, the *Outlook* has been named one of the top ten penal publications in the nation by *The Saturday Review* magazine—and all of this has been accomplished with printing and typesetting equipment that should long since have been relegated to the junk heap.

Unlike "outside" newspapers and magazines, the penal press members are not in business to make money. Rather, the goal of most prison periodicals is to "bridge the gap between prisons and society." Only a handful of them charge for subscriptions, and only one or two sell advertising. And it's doubtful that even they support themselves entirely.

Rather than being money-making operations, most prison publications are considered a part of the prison's education system. As such, they are thought of as learning programs. The *Lake Shore Outlook* is no exception in this regard. But because we are forced to work with outdated typesetting and printing equipment and function under the cumbersome hand of untrained supervision, it isn't likely that anyone trained here in the fields of journalism or printing could hope to qualify for such work upon his release from prison. In this respect, the state is missing a good bet. For it is altogether possible that if men leaving prison possessed the proper vocational skills more of them would find it possible to remain out of prison.

As editor of the *Outlook,* it is my responsibility to decide who will write what and when—but preferably not how. I would prefer (except in straight news stories) for the writer to express himself in his own way, emphasizing what he considers important. Once a writer has gained my confidence and has earned column space, I let him choose his topic as well as his style.

Censorship, the sword of Damocles to all prison editors, is a two-edged threat—first, because he has to live in close proximity to the very people about whom he is writing, and second, because he is to a great extent beholden to the officials who censor his copy. Consequently, he must mellow his criticisms of institution policies.

As George Bernard Shaw once said, "All censorships exist to prevent anyone from challenging current conceptions and existing institutions . . . the first condition of progress is the removal of censorships." It is doubtful that he had prison journalism in mind when he made this statement, but I can think of nothing more *apropos* to describe the present state of the penal press: it serves only to preserve the status quo, and the status quo in penology is backward and vile.

Our normal copy deadline is the fifteenth of the month; however, because of voluminous institution "job work" (printed forms) that must also be set and printed in our "back shop," it sometimes takes us as much as two weeks to get our copy set on one of the two M-14 (1915 vintage) linotype machines. When we have finished the compositing, we can get on the Miehle (1909 model) flatbed press. Here again, however, I am often told by the print shop supervisor (in view of his blue uniform, he outranks me considerably) that there are a number of "rush" orders ahead of us. There is little we can do but gnash our teeth while our brain children grow whiskers. I hasten to add that this shortage of updated print shop equipment results from the "penny-pinching" penal philosophy espoused by state legislators who year after year refuse to make funds available to update antiquated prison facilities in the state of Indiana.

When the newspapers have finally been printed and trimmed on the model 37 Chandler & Scott hydraulic cutter (the only reasonably up-to-date piece of equipment in the print shop), they are carted to the "fish tank" (receiving department where new arrivals at the prison are housed) and folded by hand.

Following this, the four of us on the *Outlook* staff hand mail sixteen hundred copies and distribute the remaining nineteen hundred throughout the prison.

It is a rather well-known fact among the inmates in many prisons that the officials do little or nothing to encourage the printing of an inmate newspaper or magazine. I sometimes wonder if some officials don't do everything possible to sabotage them.

There are exceptions. Officials sometimes prevail upon inmates to produce "official organs." In instances where this is done, the editor can count on the full cooperation of the officials in question. For my part, however, I want none of it. I'd prefer to go my own way—even if this does make the going a little rough at times. Because despite all the setbacks and frustrations experienced in producing our little tabloid, we continue to grow in circulation and improve in style and content. This fact alone is ample compensation for our work and worry.

A study conducted by Professor Joseph K. Balogh of Bowling Green University showed that most inmate writers felt that only under the most enlightened penal administrators could prison journalists produce anything either of literary value or accurate information concerning prison life. Unfortunately, there are few such prison administrators on the scene today. Certainly, when a man can't be sure that what he is writing—regardless of its merit—will ever see the light of day, he isn't apt to do his best work. Yet, despite this obvious handicap, a few prison journalists have managed to distinguish themselves. One such man who comes immediately to mind is Don Reed, who, prior to his release from San Quentin, wrote for the newspaper there. He is now a well-known journalist in California.

As long ago as 1955, Nina Mermey, while writing for the *American Mercury* magazine, stated that riots and other prison disturbances occur because prison inmates are not allowed to relate true prison conditions to the outside public.

While prison editors agree generally that prison publications justify their existence only when they cultivate freedom of expression and thereby increase communication between the prison population and society, their approaches to this end are as diverse as their individual personalities.

I personally use my office to enlist the aid of "outside" editors and publishers in my campaign to focus attention on the existing evils of the antiquated penal thinking in this nation. Although I haven't been as successful in this respect as I would like, I have created a little interest here and there in the academic community and will continue to try to reach what appears to me to be a "we don't give a damn" public.

Writing in the *Ohio Prison News* (Ohio State Prison), Dr. Florence S. Randall said, "The penal institutions belong to society, and what they do is everyone's responsibility and concern. The prison press not only has an obligation with the general public but a vital need to reach the outside. The people need to know something about these inmates. They are not only one's fellow mortals but are also often one's relatives or friends, and could easily be oneself."

The following selections taken from past issues of the *Lake Shore Outlook* illustrate rather well, I think, what the penal press is all about.

Prior to his release from the Indiana State Prison in late November of 1968, Etheridge Knight served on the staff of the *Lake Shore Outlook* and, in addition to his job as circulation manager, wrote a column entitled Lend Me Your Ear. The one that follows was his way of handling an anonymous writer who sent a *hate* letter to our office complaining that we were being partial to Negroes. (Etheridge himself is black.)

To The Man Who Writes Unsigned Hate Letters

Dear sir/man/human/being:

Your letter of hate was received and read with great interest. If you intended for it to shake us up, you will be happy to learn that it did just that. It embarrassed us all and filled the air with un/cool/nervous laughter. (Incidentally, the magic word is spelled with two "g's" instead of one.) You will also be happy to know that your letter was the first of its kind that we have ever received (knock-knock), so that "first" should be proudly listed among your accomplishments.

Your letter not only shook me, man, it started me to thinking: now why would a guy take the time and energy to write an unsigned (or even a signed) hate letter? And I've come to the conclusion that you must be hurting something terrible. And I can dig that, man, cause I'm hurting too. But I happen to know that you are not the cause of my pain, and you ought to know that I am not the cause of yours. I also know that if I am to rid myself of my pain I will have to seek out its source, which I believe to lie partly within myself but mostly within those nebulous forces called society. And so will you. You cannot ease your pain by trying to project it onto me; and even if you could, I would not accept it. You've got to bear your own cross, baby.

I realize that I am the perfect mark, am a highly visible and real target, and that it is easier to vent green anger and frustration upon me than it is to face the frightening intangibles of your own mind and the awesome, and capricious, realities of so/ci/ety. But face them you must, cause air bubbles burst. Since I refuse to be your easy mark, the docile target, the slings and arrows you hurl at me will turn into boomerangs.

At night the cell doors clang shut on me, too. And so, I'm hip that when they do,—that the heart and mind become lonely hunters, frightened hunters. Like two lost children following the faint voice of their mother, the heart and mind sees the haunting cry of the fretful soul —the hungry soul. Roam, they do, thru the midnight alleys, sifting thru heaps of refuse, chasing after dark phantoms and purple demons that quiver and shimmer and disappear like figures in a fog. But the hungry soul will not be caught and stilled. I'm hip that sometimes when the searchlight of the imagination sweeps thru the dark night and falls upon the pillars of fact that they seem to be distorted, grotesque piles of fiction. I'm hip to all of that. But the soul cannot be fed the food of fiction, nor will it be stilled by another man's pain. Your own/will/ only/grow/more/intense. So you see, you can't feed off me; I ain't got enough food for myself. You dig it?

It would seem that the misery of prison existence would form a common bond, would provide an atmosphere of tolerance. But the eyes are shut tight in exquisite pain. Open them and look around you, man. Ain't nobody here but us poor folks. Now don't that tell you something?

It has been suggested to me that I, too, am wasting

time and energy by responding to your hate letter. But I
don't think so; I think you're worth it. Plus, it got my column filled. *E.K.*

The following story appeared in the February, 1969,
issue of the *Outlook*. It concerns the formation of a "help-
ing-hand" organization by "exconvict" Paul Couch and
therefore represents one of the few instances where a released
prisoner has done something constructive to help those he
left behind the walls. Understandably, I headlined the
story:

A RAY OF HOPE

An Indianapolis-based organization called "Volunteer Parents of Prisoners Association Incorporated," or
VOL-PAR, has recently been organized to assist inmates
of state penal institutions through the involvement of the
inmate's family, relatives, and friends.

Formed by Paul E. Couch, Coordinator of Correctional Training at Indiana Vocational College in Fort
Wayne, Ind., VOL-PAR is an attempt to break down the
communications barrier between inmate and citizen, a
barrier which is higher than any stone wall. VOL-PAR
hopes to organize a citizen's Task Force of over 100,000
people in the state to maintain lines of communication,
and in so doing, help prevent crime and lower the rate of
recidivism. It hopes to do this by:

1. Educating the general public concerning the function
of their prisons.
2. Telling the relatives of prisoners of the need for regular communication.
3. Conducting seminars and workshops throughout the
state, called "Where did we go wrong" sessions.
4. Publishing a newspaper to provide up-to-date information about VOL-PAR and the field of corrections.
5. Proposing and supporting legislation favorable to good
prisoner public relations and opposing legislation considered detrimental to such relations.

Anyone at all familiar with prisons knows that many
inmates in any penal institution live a life of total isola-

tion and alienation from the "free world." Often the prisoner will not initiate communication with friends and relatives because of shame, fear, bitterness, or a feeling of hopelessness. He may feel that he has been deserted by people because he broke the law.

Any prison contains men who have never received a letter or a visit since they have been there. Too, all prisons hold men who receive mail and visits when they first arrive, only to find that after a year or two they are forgotten men and almost all commnication has ceased, leaving them isolated and bitter.

With initial membership of about 150, VOL-PAR hopes to attract the interest and participation of the parents, relatives, children, friends, and former employers of the 7500-plus prisoners now confined in Indiana. The stress is on "involvement" and "commitment" on the part of these people in order to assist in the preservation of family ties and the resocialization of the prisoner.

VOL-PAR is a long overdue and obviously necessary step in the right direction. We should all, therefore, give it our wholehearted support.

Anyone wishing more detailed information concerning this organization may write to Paul E. Couch, President, Volunteer Parents of Prisoners Association Incorporated, P.O. Box 300, Indianapolis, Indiana 46360.

In August of 1968, two inmates—while armed with homemade knives—locked up two officers in one of the cellhouses in the Indiana State Prison and demanded that newspaperman Al Spiers be present while they aired complaints about the parole board and living conditions in the prison.

As I mentioned earlier, some of Indiana's leading newspapers referred to that incident as a "Prison Revolt" or "Riot"; and I—in turn—wrote the following editorial in the *Outlook:*

"It was a little tense and sticky—but no big deal," was the way Al Spiers, editorial director for the Nixon newspaper chain, described the altercation that occurred here at the prison on Sunday, August 11. And this, mind you, was the newspaperman who was here on the scene and was partially responsible for the release of the two hostages.

On the other hand, the Indianapolis *News,* which had no reporter on the scene and therefore possessed no first hand knowledge of the incident, referred to it in their headline as a "Prison Revolt." Also, in the story covering the incident, the *News* called it "a cell block uprising by about 150 State Prison inmates," when, in fact, only a few men voiced complaints—and even they, according to Al Spiers, were orderly and gentlemanly.

There were other newspapers in the area who also tried to capitalize on this unfortunate situation as a means of . . . selling newspapers? Oh well, whatever their motives for doing so, they should refrain from playing up the "sensational" aspects of disruptive incidents of this nature and use their vast news gathering and disseminating facilities to dig beneath the surface of the news and try to determine the causes of these social "revolts." They could in this way arouse their readers' intellectual interest instead of provoking their emotional feelings.

Corrections Commissioner Anthony S. Kuharich and Warden Ward Lane have said repeatedly that the penal institutions in this state are in deplorable condition and that they need legislative funds to correct the situation. Yet, have the Indianapolis *Star* and *News* supported them in any meaningful way? Have these and other newspapers in the state of Indiana, with the exception of the Gary *Herald,* the *News-Dispatch* and the Hammond *Times,* expended any real energy to find out what is needed in this state in the way of penal reform and then reported this to their readers?

This past spring both Commissioner Kuharich and Warden Lane tried everything short of standing on street corners and begging for handouts to finance a college program here at the prison. Were any headlines written about that? Did any of Indiana's fine newspapers come forth and support this program and say that 150 prison inmates wished to take part in a college program? The answer is, of course, that they did not and, as a result, the program had to be shelved until the next regular session of the State Legislature, when Kuharich will ask for funds with which to finance a college program. And, will he get the funds even then?

What really occurred here on Sunday, August 11, was that two men (ringleaders, they were called) sacrificed themselves in order to draw attention to what is wrong here and what is needed to rectify the situation. And, while everyone may not agree with their method of doing this, no one can deny that they accomplished their purpose.

Now—the question is—what will be done about it? Or better yet, what will you—the taxpaying public—permit Commissioner Kuharich and Warden Lane to do to improve conditions at this institution and elsewhere in the state?

Yes, it will cost money . . . and a lot of it; but wouldn't it be wiser and more humane to spend (invest) extra dollars (dollars that should have been spent years ago) now and prevent other altercations that could indeed justify the headline "PRISON REVOLT"?

As an individual (yes, a prison inmate) and the editor of this periodical, I plead for your understanding and hope that each reader of this editorial will actively support any state official who will stand up and be counted in favor of penal reform in this state.

What can you do? You can write your state legislator and demand that the penal institutions in this state and the conditions therein be brought up to date.

Since I wrote the above editorial, the Indiana General Assembly has met, but no worthwhile penal reform bills were passed into law. Nor were any funds allocated for a college program here. To make matters worse, both Commissioner Anthony Kuharich and Warden Ward Lane, who were at least trying to improve conditions, have been replaced with hard-line, custody-oriented men. The prospects for anything better in the foreseeable future are, at the moment, quite dim.

—H.J.G.

12

Medical Facilities

A moral expression at the close of a lewd play is much like a pious expression in the mouth of a dying man. . . . The doctor comes too late for the disease and the antidote is much too weak for the poison.

—LEWIS CARROLL
Alice in Wonderland

Shortly after being confined in the Menard branch of the Illinois State Prison in August of 1962 for robbing the Commonwealth Loan Company in Rockford, Illinois, I fell from a loading platform and dislocated my right shoulder.

I was working in the rock quarry at the time. And because I couldn't go to the hospital without a lieutenant, I had to wait for a half-hour in the hot sun—it was nearly a hundred that day—until one could be summoned.

By the time he arrived, I was nearly out of my skull with pain and could hardly believe it when he said that I would have to get to the hospital under my own steam. The hospital was the equivalent of two city blocks away. I couldn't straighten up: when I tried my shoulder muscles spasmed and the pain became unbearable. I doubted I could make it. But necessity being the hardhearted whore that can move mountains, I did . . . cursing every step of the way.

I told the lieutenant about his baby sister being a slut and conjectured that he had fucked his mother on numerous occasions and then refused to pay her. Being the low-grade moron he was, he merely showed his tobacco-stained teeth in a crooked grin and kept saying, "Come on, boy, keep movin'. I ain't got all day."

When we arrived at the hospital, a seventy-year-old brick structure bearing a large white cross over its front entrance, I was taken by a con into the first-aid room. There were three other cons there, but the doctor could not be found. I later learned that he had left for the day without telling anyone.

Finally, one of the cons, a grotesque fat man wearing a dirty T-shirt, offered to *try* to get my shoulder back where it belonged. His appearance and acrid odor didn't do much to bolster my confidence in his ability, but something had to be done, so I told him to do what he could.

After another con, who looked like a weightlifter, caught me in a bear hug from the rear, the fat man placed both his hamlike hands on my forearm and jerked like hell. I started to scream and then blacked out.

When I came to I was lying on the floor and my arm was still separated from the shoulder socket. I rolled onto my back and, with the help of the fat man who had hooked both his hands beneath my upper arm, attempted to stand. At that instant my shoulder literally jumped in place. We both learned something: he how to reset a separated shoulder and I to steer clear of the hospital there.

After swallowing two aspirins, I was returned to the quarry and the heat. The lieutenant's parting shot to the guard in the quarry was, "Put the bastard on a sledge hammer. He's jest tryin' to get outa work." I had hoped that he would throw my ass in the hole for "putting him in the dozens," but he didn't. In retrospect, maybe he was really a high-grade moron. In any event, the guard, who said he didn't "cotton to brass," let me take it easy the rest of the afternoon.

I relate this story because in many respects it is representative of the quality of medical attention given to convicts in this nation's prisons. Indeed, there may be exceptions, but generally speaking, a con is accorded little more in the way of medical care than were the Jews in Nazi concentration camps just prior to and during World War II.

If the above incident were the sum total of my experience with prison medical facilities, I would not level such a charge. But because I later worked in that same hospital for more than three years, I feel qualified to make these comments.

After three months in the quarry, I was transferred to the prison's main barbershop and from there to the hospital barbershop. And that was when I began to see what was taking place in that cockroach-, rat-infested edifice that the officials there had the balls to call a hospital.

After becoming well acquainted with a few of the con nurses, I learned that it was not uncommon for them to prescribe medicine—yes, even narcotics. And, what was worse, that much of the Demerol, Darvon, Nembutal, and other such medications they prescribed for their patients were in fact used by the nurses themselves.

One old man, a terminal cancer patient just down the hall from my one-chair barbershop, rarely got more than a shot of distilled water to quiet his pain. This was, of course, only one of hundreds of such cases that I learned about during those three years.

The cons used a simple but effective dodge to "beat" the screws who were required to watch them inject Demerol into post operative and cancer patients.

The con nurse about to order a hundred milligrams of Demerol would fill a syringe with distilled water and lay it under one end of a three-way-folded face towel. Then, when the screw brought the container of Demerol, the nurse would draw it into another syringe, and, in full view of the screw, lay it atop one end of the folded towel that concealed the water-filled syringe. After that, it was simply a matter of flipping the center flap of the folded towel, which exposed the water-filled syringe and concealed the one containing what the cons called "the good shit." This last deft little maneuver was usually effected while another con—the nurse's confederate—attracted the screw's attention briefly with an inane question or off-the-wall remark about the weather.

When the nurse left to give the shot, the confederate removed the towel and the Demerol-filled syringe from the scene. Later, he and the nurse would share the "stuff" and brag to one another about their cunning while the patient suffered from lack of medication. Cold-blooded? Decidedly so . . .

I wondered then, as you probably are now, who authorized those cons to prescribe medicine—especially prescription drugs—for their patients. The answer, I learned, was that the doctor, who couldn't, of course, be there around the clock, had left orders for the con nurses to administer the drugs he himself had ordered. And he had given the nurses permission to prescribe and administer such emergency pain-killing drugs they deemed necessary in his absence.

When the nurses did in fact do such prescribing—and it was often—the doctor would later sign the "narcotics book" that was stamped with his register number.

After working for several months as the hospital barber, I was asked by one of the cons from the dental department if I would like to work there.

"Doing what?" I asked.

"Pulling and filling teeth," he said.

"You've got to be joking," I said.

"No, I'm not," he said. "I've already talked to the outside dentist about you, and he thinks that because of your barber experience you'd make a good dentist."

"Well, in that case, why not?" I said.

Thus, I became one of the two convict dentists at Menard in the spring of 1964, and remained on that job—job hell, a position—until March of 1967, when I was transferred under guard back to the Indiana State Prison, from which I had escaped in June of 1962.

During my first day in the dental office, I extracted two upper bicuspids with what I learned were called dental forceps instead of a pair of pliers. Within two weeks I was also drilling and filling teeth, taking and reading x-rays, and making impressions and bites for dentures.

In all I extracted in excess of eight thousand teeth and filled hundreds of others in the three years that I made like a dentist. If I do say so myself, I developed some expertise and something of a following. Many of the cons wouldn't think of letting anyone else touch their teeth.

There were two dental chairs in the office. The other con dentist and I ran the regular morning sick-call lines on Monday, Wednesday, and Friday of each week.

Because I became rather adept with a scalpel, it fell to me to remove all impacted molars and perform such other oral surgery as was required. And because I had to learn by the trial-and-error method, my operations weren't something you'd want to watch just before lunch—especially when I first began doing such work. But, as I said before, I eventually developed a smidgen of technique and quite a following. And it beat hell out of the rock quarry or the barbershop.

I should explain that the institution had an outside

dentist on the payroll who visited the prison dental office each Tuesday morning and remained there long enough to drink a cup of coffee, read the newspaper, and get his shoes shined by one of the hospital porters. He never made his appearance before 9 A.M. and was always gone by 11 A.M. In his defense, however, I would add that he was a fairly decent fellow.

The only time the dentist did any work was when he was called in to set a broken jaw. On these few occasions, I merely assisted. Although after assisting him in a couple of these operations, I felt certain that I could have done a better job myself. Professional jealousy—huh?

Because of the prestige of my position—remember now, I was a convicted thief serving five to fifteen years for armed robbery—and the fact that I was subject to call around the clock, I was given a room on the third floor of the hospital in which to sleep (much better than a cell). The bed had an innerspring mattress; there was a huge floor-model radio instead of a set of earphones; and there were no bars on the windows. In addition, I was given special food and preferential treatment by everyone concerned. And why not: besides saving the state at least fifteen thousand dollars annually, I was also doing dental work—under cover, of course—for some of the prison personnel.

The part-time dentist wasn't the only official member of the hospital staff in Menard who neglected his duty and was guilty of malpractice.

The resident physician, who made no secret of the fact that he held all convicts in utter contempt, was at the top of the list of those who didn't seem to give a damn what happened so long as he drew his pay. I never did learn just how much he was paid; but whatever it was, it was much more than he was worth.

The doctor—a hatchet-faced man with beady eyes—made his appearance there five days a week. But his clerk,

Jimmy LeBanes, and I often speculated that his time there was a waste for the doctor and a burden for those who worked around him. At that, we were being kind to the man.

Perhaps because all of us are to some extent afflicted with laziness and no little procrastination, it is understandable that employees in public institutions may to some extent become immune to human suffering—both physical and mental. But for a medical doctor to completely ignore his Hippocratic oath to "maintain the utmost respect for human life" and to fail to consider the health of his patients his most important responsibility—even if they are social outcasts—is negligence in the extreme. But that is exactly what that particular "good" doctor did.

Not only did he consistently fail to make regular rounds in the hospital to see the patients that either he or his convict nurses—usually the latter—had checked into the hospital; when he did occasionally get around to see the patients, his manner was supercilious and disrespectful.

It wasn't unusual for a con to be checked into the hospital, stay a week or so, and check out without ever seeing the doctor. I knew of several cases where a man spent more than a month there without seeing him. Little wonder then that minor ailments often got out of hand because of lack of proper medical care and became major afflictions. Unquestionably, some of the instances of non- or malpractice resulted in death.

There have been many patients who, after spending weeks and months in the hospital, died without ever having their afflictions diagnosed. And if they died during the night—as was often the case—the con nurse would call the doctor on the telephone to inform him that such-and-such a patient had expired. The doctor would then almost invariably instruct the nurse to release the body to a mortuary in the nearby town of Chester, Illinois. In these instances the doctor would sign the death certificates on the following mornings. Therefore, the records show that an inordinate number of men there died of cardiac arrest or pneumonia.

On the lighter side, but nonetheless unpardonable in the realm of medical care for human beings in any situation, were the cases involving cons assigned to the hospital staff as nurses who hadn't as much as an eighth-grade education and no medical experience at all. Some such individuals were so dense as to be incapable of taking a patient's temperature or properly operating a blood-pressure cup— even after months on the job. Yet, there they were, walking the wards in white clothing with clipboards in their hands, as if they knew what the hell they were about.

In one case involving such a nurse, when the doctor, while examining a heart patient, said, "This man has got to have oxygen," the con nurse present walked briskly to the nearest window and threw it open. "There you are, Doc," he said, "that should help him."

Then there's the case of the moronic nurse who kept giving a patient a suppository each morning along with a glass of water. Finally, the patient rebelled, saying that "them big pills hurt my throat when I swallow them. I ain't taking any more of them."

Thus far I've confined my remarks to what is referred to as the general division of the Menard Prison. But because it relates to the subject at hand, I will now relate to you a little about the psychiatric division.

This part of the prison is separated from the general division by what the cons there call the "blue wall." And although it is but an extension to the prison, it is said to be a hospital for the criminally insane; that is, the men who break under the harsh discipline in all of the other state penal institutions are sent there for "treatment."

I visited the psychiatric division many times to exchange supplies with the men working in the dental laboratory there. I know, as a matter of fact, that the only "treatments" available to the cons there were shock therapy, ice-water baths, and massive doses of tranquilizers. And more often than not, these things were used as a means of punishment instead of a way of treating mentally deranged patients.

If a patient refused any of these "treatments," he was literally bludgeoned to the floor, stripped of his clothing, and thrown into one of a long line of cells that were devoid of a bed, a table, a chair, or a toilet. The only thing I saw while walking along in front of those cells were naked, emaciated bodies of men who were obviously in the clutches of some powerful tranquilizing drug. They were incapable of coherent speech and were almost always in a supine position. All that separated their naked bodies from the cold concrete were a few strands of straw and their own excrement.

The air there was foul, the light poor, and the atmosphere maddening. Every time I saw the goddamn place I felt like running into the warden's office and shouting, "Listen here, you freak sonofabitch, turn those men loose and begin treating them like the human beings they are!" But, perhaps because cowardice is the better part of self-preservation, I—like others before and after me—swallowed my indignation and went *my* way.

One New Year's Eve a con in the general division who, by virtue of his having done some book transcribing for the blind students at nearby Southern Illinois University, had a tape recorder in his cell. So when the fellows in his cellhouse began hollering and catcalling by way of ushering in the New Year, this con thought it might be fun to record the noise.

Well, no sooner had he started the recorder when a screw happened by his cell and, on seeing what he was doing, reported him to the captain's office. And within a matter of minutes this con was on his way to the hole and the next day was transferred—in handcuffs—to the psychiatric division for "treatment."

I made a special trip there to see him two days later and there he was in one of those stripped cells getting his "treatment." He was so thoroughly tranquilized that he was completely incoherent and didn't even recognize me.

On many occasions while I worked in the general division hospital, dead men were brought there from the psychiatric division—always at night. And even though many of the bodies were badly marked and bruised, invariably the records were made to show that they had died in the general division hospital of natural causes—again, usually of heart trouble or pneumonia.

As I have indicated in the chapter dealing with prison riots, in the fall of 1965 six cons—two of whom I knew well —staged a bloody revolt in the dining hall at Menard. Three guards were killed and five others were seriously injured in that altercation. And during their trial, which was held in Springfield several months later, many of the witnesses testified as to the deplorable conditions in the prison —especially the medical facilities and treatment. As a result, the hospital received a paint job, curtains were placed on the windows and a real live female nurse was hired by then Director of Public Safety Ross V. Randolph.

At first most of the custodial personnel predicted that she would be raped and possibly killed within a month. But they were wrong. She was still there more than a year later when I left, and she still hadn't been violated or, to my knowledge, even seduced.

What the custodial people obviously failed to realize was that had some fool tried to molest her, he would have been set upon and torn limb from limb by the other cons. Yes, Marie, a lovely flower among nineteen hundred weeds, was held in very high esteem by all the men. One sharp little word or look from her was enough to discipline the most wayward patient or hospital worker—myself included. And her smile—well, her smile was radiantly warm and very engaging. How we would vie for a smile or a small bit of praise from her.

Despite Marie's warm personality and tireless efforts to improve things, the place still wasn't nearly up to par when I left Menard in March of 1967. After all, there is only so much one person can do—even a beautiful, hardworking, registered nurse—to update facilities and care in a money-starved, archaic prison hospital without help from prison officials, state legislators, or yes, even the governor's office.

Upon my return to this prison in 1967, I found things had changed little in my five years' absence. I was taken for a physical examination which consisted of having my pulse, blood pressure, and temperature taken.

Of course, I didn't see a doctor: you rarely do in prison, even when you're sick. Rather, after the physical by a first-aid man, a con nurse not too unlike the ones I described earlier, looked me over for crabs and lice and, finding none, authorized my release into population.

I had no other contact with the hospital until about a year later when my right shoulder—yes, the same one again—separated while I was working in the print shop.

On this occasion I was wheeled to the hospital and into the presence of Doctor David Brown. But he too was at a loss about what to do. I knew this as soon as he began pulling on my arm as had the obese fellow in Menard.

"Wait a minute, Doc," I said. "Have you ever had a case like this before?"

"No," he said expansively. "In all my years of practice, I've never before been confronted with a dislocated shoulder. But with your cooperation, I feel certain that I may be able to help you."

"Damn!" I thought. "Not again. Can't I ever run onto someone who knows what the hell he's doing?"

"Doctor Brown," one of the convict nurses said, interrupting my thoughts. "Doctor Stark is here today. I just saw him down the hall."

"Very good," said Doctor Brown, obviously much relieved. "He's a bone specialist and will know exactly what to do."

Doctor Stark, a visiting specialist from Michigan City's St. Anthony Hospital, was summoned. After one look at my shoulder, he gave me a shot of Demerol in the main line and, after a couple of minutes, during which I was placed in a prone position, he deftly steered my shoulder back into place. And he did it with a smile on his face. Now I know what people mean when they say they "felt like kissing his feet." For that's exactly the way I felt at that moment.

Prior to this incident I had heard a number of cons complain about Doctor Brown's incompetence, and following that incident, I was ready to believe much of what they had said. But had I needed more convincing, the following would have done the trick.

A patient, who obviously felt that he might soon die, asked that Father Joseph Sedlak, the Catholic priest here, be called to administer last rites. The priest did as he was asked, then telephoned the man's relatives and informed them that if they wished to see their loved one while he was still alive, that they should visit him very soon.

At that point, Warden George Phend, who for reasons of his own doesn't encourage outsiders to visit the prison, got word of what the priest had done. He checked with Doctor Brown, who assured him that the patient was not in critical condition, then called the priest on the carpet and chewed him out royally.

As it turned out, however, the patient died that night.

Since he had called the con's relatives to assure them that they need not visit the prison immediately, the Warden found himself in an embarrassing position. As a result, Dr. Brown was dismissed.

Doctor Joseph R. Hopkins is now in charge of the hospital here. And although he himself is physically handicapped—he is a post-operative epileptic and therefore incapable of holding down an outside practice—he is nonetheless much respected by most of the cons for his compassion and understanding. But he has a couple of problems: One, he is forced by the warden to carry a small piece of paper signed by a deputy warden which authorizes him to carry his own medication; Two, he is severely censored by the hospital administrator.

According to Doctor Hopkins, the hospital administrator, Ira Parkman, cuts or sometimes cancels his prescriptions—especially where narcotics are involved.

When I asked him how Parkman could get away with such a thing, he closed his eyes in disgust and said, "I suppose because he is so close to the warden. They see eye to eye."

"Why can't you go to the local medical society and contest this?" I asked.

"Because," he said, "I'm a coward. I have a family to feed and I need this job. I couldn't begin to hold down a full-time practice outside these walls."

Parkman, who is one of the most despised officials in this prison, justifies his interference with the doctor's practice of medicine simply by saying that expenses must be curtailed and that security must be emphasized. This is strange indeed coming from a man who was once fired from his present job for trafficking with convicts. He later appealed and got his dismissal reversed; but, the state also appealed to an even higher tribunal and got a reversal of Parkman's reversal. The only reason he is still here at all is that the state's political machinery changed hands. Dear old politics!

Another area where security takes precedence over the health and welfare of the cons results from Parkman's insistence that the heavy steel doors to all the wards be locked around the clock. Unquestionably, this procedure will eventually cost some con his life.

For example, a patient in the cardiac ward recently had an attack and called for the nurse. The nurse in turn called for the guard in charge of the hospital that day. When he eventually got to the door where the nurse was waiting, this guard had left the key at his desk near the front entrance. Finally the door was unlocked, but the nurse discovered that the oxygen tank was in another locked room across the hall. When this door was unlocked, it was learned that the oxygen tank was empty. In all, it took more than twenty minutes to get an oxygen mask on the patient. It's a miracle he's still alive.

Some efficiency, huh? And some hospital! But not, I dare say, a place in which you would care to be taken for medical treatment the next time an accident or ill health befalls you. That's the way we feel, too.

—H.J.G.

13
Sex

By virtue of my grace, he was a kind of jewel. . . . His
tears and sobs on my neck proved my virility. I was his
man.

—JEAN GENÊT
The Thief's Journal

He murdered at least four people while committing
robberies. Usually he shot them in the head at close range
from behind. It took a nationwide manhunt to capture him.
Sentenced to life in the Indiana State Prison, he appealed
and, while back in jail awaiting a new trial, escaped. He
was again apprehended, and, back at ISP, he again attempted to escape, taking a guard hostage in the process.
We'll call him Charlie.

Another Hoosier—we'll call him Don—was paroled
from ISP. A short time later, brandishing a pistol, he entered a county jail and helped a friend of his to escape. A
few weeks after that, he disarmed a policeman and stole his
car, gun, coat, and hat. When Don was finally caught, the
police chief called him a "tough cookie" and immediately
sent him back to ISP for safekeeping while he was awaiting

trial. The prison authorities labeled him a "constant disciplinary problem."

Green was an armed robber who fought his case in the appeal courts while confined at ISP. The courts ordered him freed. Within thirty days he had robbed a bank and soon after that he was placed on the FBI's "Ten Most Wanted" list. He was to be considered "extremely dangerous." Green was an avid weightlifter and student of karate.

These three men would certainly be considered dangerous in most situations. They are not the type you would ask to baby-sit for you. But what if you were sentenced to prison and found one of them was your cell partner? How would you get along with Charlie? What if an argument started between you during your first night in the cell? How would you handle it? Remember, he killed four people in cold blood.

The best way to handle "tough guys" like the three whose case histories I outlined accurately except for the names, is to blow in their ear or kiss them behind the neck! The three of them are "penitentiary punks" who will purr like a kitten for the right "jocker."

In the prisons throughout this country, you just can't tell who the real tough guys are without a scorecard!

On April 12, 1930, the Indiana State Prison's most famous alumnus was "written up" for being "in another prisoner's cell in bed." His name was John Dillinger. Two old-timers who should know swear that he was "catching" rather than "pitching." That is, he was the passive partner in a homosexual relationship. He certainly wasn't a homosexual outside (although, had he survived the fatal treachery of the "Lady in Red," he may have considered giving up women) but evidently wasn't above obtaining sexual gratification from another man when there was no woman available. He has a lot of company.

Most convicts do not abandon their sex life at the

front gate of the prison. Our natural biological urges remain with us, but we must find so-called unnatural outlets. That outlet takes many forms, all of which are socially unacceptable, some of which are harmless and some of which are not so harmless.

For those who cannot make the transition from the soft, feminine graces of the free world to the hard, hairy swishes of the tag shop, masturbation is the most frequent outlet. In most prisons it is a violation of the rules, as is any form of sexual outlet other than a nocturnal emission. In fact, prison regulations concerning sex could have been taken straight from my old Boy Scout manual, which told me that a "wet dream" was the only acceptable sexual outlet other than intercourse between husband and wife.

Behind prison walls, masturbation does not carry the same social stigma that it does outside. A con is often heard to proclaim, "Tonight is 'Jack' night, baby!" It is said in a tone that both condemns the system that forces him to perform this act and praises "self" for using this outlet rather than one of the other more (to him) unnatural outlets.

The frustration of life without women has accentuated the ingenuity of many a convict. Cons have been known to find sexual gratification in objects so strange as to make Portnoy's antics seem routine.

One amorous prison baker was observed behind the large prison ovens "making love" to a hot loaf of bread. His co-workers persuaded him to transfer from the bakery mainly because they weren't sure what the rascal had been doing with the loaves after he had satisfied himself. A routine shakedown of another con's cell produced a large slab of fatback that had been carved into the desired shape and inserted into a hole in the con's mattress. Another lonesome soul made a life-size dummy, complete with a simulated vagina. The loving couple was caught by an officer in a tag shop shower stall while the other cons were in the messhall eating lunch.

For those who had rather not do it themselves, there is no shortage of cooperative partners even though the number of true homosexuals in most prisons is small. (For instance, in this prison of nineteen hundred inmates, the actual homosexuals number less than twenty although the number of men engaging in some form of homosexual activity would run well into three figures.)

The "activists" can be classified into three general categories—(1) the couples, (2) the opportunists, (3) the prostitutes.

Either of the first two categories could account for the largest number of participants, depending on which prison you are in, but the third category will always be in a minority.

The Couples

The "fun couples" can be seen holding hands in the rear of the chapel auditorium while a movie is being shown or even while religious services are being conducted. They have been observed in passionate embraces in supposedly secluded spots in the shops and shelters.

Their "affair" is usually general knowledge among the other inmates and any officers who might be interested enough to investigate. Once a couple has actually been caught and "written up" for sodomy, the officials try to discourage the affair by placing the offenders in different job locations and shelters. Occasionally, however, true love will outlast the diligent perseverance of the staff and the couple will manage to effect a reconciliation.

The sexual pleasure that #40650 and #45515 might obtain from each other harms no one—unless, of course, the knowledge that someone is engaging in acts that you disapprove of makes you *angry*. But then, that's your hang-up, isn't it? Nevertheless, most prison officials, no matter how enlightened, frown on it, even when the relations are between consenting cons, because of the trouble and violence and even death that sometimes result. For #40650 and #45515 might swing together nicely, but when #27320 decides he wants a piece of the action, peaceful arbitration is unlikely. At this writing, the concept of "free love" hasn't penetrated the gray, greedy world of prison. A con who has been starving for affection and finally finds it in the person of the burglar right in the next cell is not open to suggestions of communal living.

An example of the type of violence that can erupt occurred recently in this prison. While watching television in the prison fieldhouse, the passive partner in a "couples" relationship left his "man" in the bleachers to go to the toilet. There a remark was made to him by an ex-mental patient who happened to be a Negro. Shortly thereafter the Negro was stabbed in the stomach. As many of his black friends watched him being placed on the stretcher, he suddenly sat up, and while holding his intestines in with one hand, pointed at the white man and accused him of the stabbing. As the victim growled and threatened, he was again stabbed (in the back this time), allegedly by the passive partner. The victim's black friends then attacked the couple with baseball bats. The fight that followed resembled a mixture of the White Sox' spring training camp and Custer's last stand. That the couple is alive today is due mainly to the lack of batting practice. They took healthy enough swings; only their timing was off.

Marriage ceremonies between a "punk" and his "jocker" are still performed occasionally in some prisons but not so often as in the past.

Recently a couple in this prison had a document pre-

pared that read: "I _____ and I _____ agree
to join in sexual congress on a trial basis for a period of
thirty (30) days from this date forward. During this period
of thirty days, neither person will cohabitate with any other
person lest they be punished with severe injury. Either
party may, however, withdraw from this contract of his
own free will upon finding the other party unsatisfactory."

Both men had signed it in complete sincerity and
below their signatures, beneath a line that read, "Sworn before me this day of_____," was a beautiful forgery
of the warden's signature.

In February of this year (1969), two sixteen-year-old
escapees from the Indiana Girls' School were picked up by
the police. The girls requested and received an audience
with a reporter from the Indianapolis *Star*. They told him
of the "marriages" that took place between inmates of the
school who were engaging in abnormal sex practices. The
escapees went on to say that they had been propositioned
about "100 times." The superintendent of the school, Mrs.
Dorothy Van Brunt, stated that she was aware of the marriage ceremonies but claimed that they had no sexual over-
tones, that the girls merely participated in this kind of thing
in order to create an artificial family type of life. She went
on to claim that the girls' imaginations were working over-
time.

Two months later a fourteen-year-old girl escaped and
was quickly caught. She told similar stories and added that
male and female employees were also engaging in sexual
acts on the school grounds. She was given a lie detector
test, which indicated that she was telling the truth. Again
the superintendent scoffed at any suggestions of illicit sexual conduct. She stated that girls of that age often engage
in "sexual fantasies."

Couples are looked upon by the rest of the inmate
body in a number of different ways. The liberal con who

believes in doing his own time couldn't care less. The bigot
white and Muslim black will condemn a racially mixed
couple. Some cons complain that the "fags" make it hard
on the rest of the inmates by causing tighter rules. There
are a few inmates who have sincere moral objections and
fewer still who resent the couple's pleasure on the same
ground that an old maid would resent Elizabeth Taylor's
husbands. Generally the participant's personality will be the
most important factor involved in his being accepted or rejected by the rest of the inmates.

The Opportunists

The opportunists are those who have no full time
"punk" or "man" but prefer to play the field. This is done
in some cases to avoid the risk and reputation that go with
a steady affair and in some cases because the need for companionship is not as great. Others simply cannot find the
right companion.

Those who have limited sexual encounters during their
incarceration could also be included in this category. On
my range in I-Cellhouse is a young man who has been here
fourteen years. For over thirteen of those years he had no
sexual relations with another inmate. He is a musician and
artist and has developed an excellent physique through ex-
ercise and horizontal bar work. The most sought-after
"queen" in the prison, a practicing homosexual outside, finally seduced him after almost a month of flirting. Their affair lasted a few months. Then they parted peacefully and
remained friends.

While involved with the "queen," the young man's
dulled emotions came alive. He composed beautiful, me-
lodic ballads, wrote poems of love, and drew an excellent
portrait of "her." He lost no friends because of the relation-

ship, and he remains glad for the experience even though he doubts that he will ever again partake of the charms available.

The Prostitutes

One morning a friend of mine standing in the messhall breakfast line felt a tug on his sleeve. He sleepily turned toward his accoster and was asked in a desperate whisper, "Man, I need two packs! You want some head?"

The "punk" was, of course, offering to commit oral sodomy. It was 6 A.M.

My friend grumpily declined. We watched the "punk" proposition several more cons before he finally found a customer. They slipped out into the morning darkness of "Bean Alley," where the enterprising young salesman no doubt earned his two packs.

This incident is unusual only in regard to time and place. It is repeated many times with variations of time and place, characters, and price. Three "reelers" or two "Big D's" (pills) might be the price rather than coffee or cigarettes. More often than not, the customer will be the one to propose the transaction.

An outside reader might be appalled that a man can sell himself to another man for two packages of cigarettes. I am not qualified to analyze such a man's psychosexual motivation, but I think I can comment on some of the factors that contribute to his "need."

A man in this prison earns about four dollars a month. Out of that amount he must purchase his own toothpaste, razor blades, hair tonic, deodorant—in fact, all his toilet articles with the exception of soap. None of these items may be sent in from outside. (Some prisons allow this to be done, but not this one.) That leaves little money for coffee, cigarettes, envelopes, food, etc. Very few cons try to make it on that four dollars. Most cons hustle. A few, such as the writers, leatherworkers, and crossword-puzzle makers, do it legally. Others gamble, sell food, do laundry, cut hair, sell pills, fix radios or sell clothes. And some sell sexual satisfaction.

In my opinion, the prison prostitutes' "need" goes beyond the cigarettes or coffee. It includes the need of sexual experience. Why they choose this method of obtaining the experience would probably vary with each individual. I have said earlier that I'm not qualified to analyze their motivation, so you'll have to form your own opinions.

A few inmates are sometimes more or less forced into prostitution. There was a notorious penitentiary pimp here who had a regular "harem" where, for a price, you could obtain any kind of sexual gratification that one man can provide for another. Eventually some of his "stable boys" went to the man (informed) on him and his playhouse was broken up. Most of his former employees then went into business for themselves.

Rape

It's a safe bet that, on a *per capita* basis, there are more rapes committed inside the county jail of any large city than are committed in the community outside the jail. (There may be a few jails where diligent supervision and the physical structure of the jail prevent this, but I haven't heard of them yet.) Any young boy is easy prey for an experienced con who may be in jail waiting trial for his fourth felony (and who may have been "turned out" himself when he was young).

The young ones being jailed for the first time come in scared. They may swagger and talk tough, but they're *scared!* They have reason to be. Never mind that they are being thrown in close confinement with thieves, murderers, and burglars. It could as well be forgers, embezzlers, and income-tax evaders. The thing is, they are being placed in close confinement with men who don't have access to women. As I pointed out, a man doesn't leave his sexual desires outside the barred door.

Judge Alexander F. Barbiere, Jr., of Philadelphia recently released a twenty-year-old car thief from jail even though the youth couldn't raise the required eight hundred dollars bail. The young man had already been homosexually raped several times during pretrial custody in county jail. The enlightened judge said, "Even if he's guilty, it would be a greater crime to keep him in prison than to allow him to repeat his offense."

An investigation showed that there were two thousand sexual assaults in two years in the Philadelphia prison system.

Judge John Beauchamp of Wabash, Indiana, sentenced a seventeen-year-old boy to the Indiana Reformatory at Pendleton. Aware of the conditions there, Judge Beauchamp said, "I hate to send the boy there because, frankly, they'll make a girl out of him the first night he is there."

Rape in prison is not so common as in jails, but it does happen frequently. It seems to flourish in direct proportion to the permissiveness of the administration. I mean "permissiveness" in the sense of allowing this to happen, not in the sense of progressiveness.

Under a previous administration, gang rapes were not infrequent here at ISP. The major contributing factor to these rapes was tolerance on the part of the officials. The offenders were given a slap on the wrist and placed back in the population while, in some cases, the victim was kept locked up "for his own protection." During that administration, a very few men accounted for quite a few rapes.

Here again, the attitude of the general population was mixed. Most cons have a thing about getting involved in something that isn't their business. So unless a rape victim happened to be their friend, they stayed out of it. On the other hand, most of the rapists were Negro and most of the victims white, and all the bigots were *mad!* And, of course, anytime a victim had one or more good friends, there was the danger of retaliation. Most victims, though, were "raped" without a struggle and without even a show of resistance. It is often contended that any con, no matter how young and how "pretty," can protect himself if he is willing to pick up an iron bar or chair. It is one thing to rape a young boy who will break open like a shotgun the first time you growl at him and quite another to know that you are going to have to fight him first. And to carry this one step further, even if the boy loses his virginity and the fight, *retaliation is hell!* Size is never a barrier if you decide to hurt someone and don't care how.

During the ten years that I have been in this prison, I have seen only one youngster protected by the administration when he first entered the prison. This sixteen-year-old, whom we will call David, was kept in the Admission and Orientation section of the prison for almost a year and then went to work in the Seclusion Unit for a few more months. In both places he was separated from the general population. Then he was placed in the Education Department but still kept under official surveillance. From there he was assigned to the Warden's residence. Finally, after almost two years, he came back inside to finish his schooling and was placed in the general population. By this time David was able to take care of himself and the "wolves" had gotten the administration's message of "hands off!"

David was not a homosexual who needed protection from his own emotions. He was a young, good-looking boy who needed protection from other cons' uninhibited emotions. He got this protection—but why him and not others who came in as young?

David came from a middle-class family. His parents were intelligent people who were concerned about what might happen when he entered prison. Concerned enough to come here and talk to the warden before David even arrived. One visit from two concerned middle-class parents was enough to insure this boy's protection. Unfortunately, most young cons' parents are neither intelligent nor middle class.

Homosexual rapes can be kept at a minimum by diligent administration. Conjugal visits would certainly reduce the need of homosexual relations for some. The work release program could be expanded to include a periodic "home leave" for those who qualify. But these simple measures have been needed for a long time now, and there is no indication that they will be implemented in the near future.

Meanwhile, make certain that your young son doesn't get jammed up with the law and sent to this prison. For a carton of cigarettes, I can get him moved right into my cell, and I've been ten years without a woman.

There are many men like me in all of the prisons of the United States.

—M.M.

14

Capital Punishment

> When the state itself kills, the mandate "thou shalt
> not kill" loses the force of the absolute.
> —(FORMER) U.S. ATTORNEY GENERAL RAMSEY CLARK
> SPEAKING TO THE SUBCOMMITTEE ON CRIMINAL
> LAWS AND PROCEDURES OF THE SENATE JUDIC-
> IARY COMMITTEE

Death row in the Indiana State Prison houses five men
who are awaiting execution; yet not one of them—it would
seem—*really* expects to die in the electric chair. Or at least
this is the impression I get from hearing them talk among
themselves each evening. For as often as not, their conversation centers around what the White Sox did the day before
or what is on the menu for the following morning.

I should perhaps explain at this point that my cell is
separated from death row (called "X-row" by the guards
who keep vigil there) by no more than ten feet and a set of
steel bars.

To be sure, when one of them comes within hours of
paying the ultimate price before learning that he has been
granted a stay of execution, the others rib him about his

"close call." And on such occasions, their voices are high-pitched and nervous. But even then, their *sang-froid* leads me to believe that they actually thought that someone or something would intervene. And when, in fact, another one of them has been snatched from the clutches of premeditated death, they are obviously that much more convinced that humankind has, at long last, reached maturity—a maturity that precludes such a monstrous thing as socially condoned (legal) murder. And statistics would seem to bear them out.

While the population in this country has nearly doubled since 1930, the number of executions in the same length of time has fallen from 155 in 1930 to none in 1968. Indiana has not executed anyone since 1961. No wonder then that these men feel they may never die in the electric chair.

Of course, unless the capital punishment statutes in the forty-one states that still have such laws on their books are revoked, some of the hundreds of men now awaiting execution in prisons across the country will have to die the horribly cruel death of capital punishment because some people still think that it serves as a deterrent to crime.

As reported in the October 1968 issue of *Esquire* magazine, special agent Alvin Dewey of the Kansas Bureau of Investigation feels that the nine states that have abolished capital punishment have made grave errors. He seems to feel that capital punishment does deter others from committing capital offenses. Yet he fails to say just how this deterrent works. Nor does he support his contentions with any data. He—like J. Edgar Hoover and other "get tough" advocates—relies on the emotional approach by arousing *fear* and *hatred* in his listening audiences.

On the other hand, Edward Bennett Williams, one of the nation's most distinguished trial lawyers, feels that capital punishment is purely vindictive and, therefore, serves no legitimate end in the criminal process in this country.

According to Williams, homicides are committed by men who act out of impulse in the clutches of anger or some other passion and by men who calculate their criminal acts carefully. The former, he feels, act with reckless abandon and never consider the consequences, and the latter act deliberately and believe they will escape detection and thus any form of punishment for their misdeeds.

Despite these and the many other opinions for and against capital punishment, Professor Ernest Van Den Haag of New York University feels that there is no proof that the capital penalty has been or is effective in reducing crime. He bases his opinion on an exhaustive study conducted by Thorsten Sellin. "Sometimes," says Professor Van Den Haag, "without the death penalty the homicide rate increases and sometimes it even decreases."

My own feeling, which is based on fifteen years lived in various prisons with many men who have been convicted of murder, is that capital punishment serves no other purpose than to state in gruesome terms that human life is not, after all, so very precious and that the taking of it is indeed justifiable under certain circumstances.

I have never heard a convicted killer (during unguarded moments) say other than that he was sorry for having taken another person's life and that he would do anything to undo his act of violence.

Certainly, executing a killer can never restore the life of his victim, nor can killing him improve the fiber of our society. On the contrary, capital punishment is nothing more than legal murder, which of necessity casts a specter on the whole of society and cheapens human life.

True, our flaming emotions may cry for vengeance in the wake of a horrible crime such as Richard Speck is said to have committed in Chicago a few years back. But reason and experience tell us that killing the criminal will not prevent other crimes or bring justice to the victim, the criminal, or society. As George Bernard Shaw said, "Murder and capital punishment are not opposites that cancel one another, but similars that breed their kind."

Indeed, there may have been a time in the dark reaches of man's recorded history when self-preservation necessitated the capital penalty for such crimes as murder and treason; and I would even admit that, at a somewhat later date, the isolation of dangerous persons may have required inordinate sacrifices on the part of innocent, law-abiding people. But, our present civilization can claim no such excuses.

Some recent polls would indicate that more Americans now want capital punishment wiped from the law books than there are those who still favor this grisly, inhuman practice. Of course, in the wake of the assassinations of Martin Luther King and Robert F. Kennedy, this sentiment has temporarily reversed itself. But the trend is for the good, and perhaps, therefore, it is not too much to expect to see capital punishment become a thing of the past in this country in the next ten to fifteen years. I hope this proves to be the case.

In any event, it is almost a certainty that the next few years will see capital punishment challenged in the United States Supreme Court. And although those who oppose the capital penalty think it unlikely that this high court will "strike it" from the books in all states, they do nonetheless hope that a succession of high-court rulings will challenge concepts and raise issues that, in effect, will further divert judges and juries from imposing the capital sentence.

One such concept—the question of "standards"— surfaced in California in the early part of 1969. On this question, anti-capital punishment jurists say the penal code fails to spell out specific "standards" to determine when one defendant should be executed and another one should escape such punishment. This question of "standards" has, of course, long been a touchy one and must eventually be answered satisfactorily.

In the past, it has generally been the indigent person who has had to "dance" at the end of a rope or "fry" in the electric chair. As a matter of fact, of all the men condemned to die in the prisons where I was (am) serving time, not one of them had even a middle-class background, and certainly none of them were from the upper echelons of society. The reason for this state of affairs is obvious: the man who can afford expensive lawyers to defend him and a battery of psychologists and psychiatrists to testify in his behalf is seldom if ever required to walk that "last mile." Rather, he will frequently be given life in prison (if he's convicted at all). Then, after a few years have elapsed and the public has lost interest in his case, he receives executive clemency and is released from prison.

The most celebrated case in recent history in which a man from "the wrong side of the tracks" had to suffer the supreme penalty for his crimes involved a young rebel by the name of Caryl Chessman. God, how he must have suffered as he watched more than ninety condemned convicts, over a twelve-year period, pass grim-faced by his cell on their way to the fate which, in the end, was to be his own.

In his writings, Chessman attempted to salvage something of significance from his past life, which held none. It became his personal realization that gas chambers make sense only when the life of the condemned man does not.

Certainly Chessman's life prior to his long stay in San Quentin's death row was little more than a series of rebellious, antisocial acts that earned him the wrath of his fellow human beings. But the nearly thirteen years he languished in the shadow of death transformed him into a thoughtful man with something worthwhile to offer his society. Yet despite this fact, the executioner was not to be denied, and Chessman walked quietly—almost sedately—to his death.

For too long now, state executions have been condoned in a manner revealing "situational ethics": here we take a life, there a life is spared, which reduces punishment for capital crimes to a numbers game in which only the wealthy can play and hope to win. For it has been the weak, the poor, the ignorant, and the hated who were executed. And—time and again—racial discrimination has occurred in the administration of capital punishment. Speaking before the Sub-Committee on Criminal Laws and Procedures of the Senate Judiciary Committee, former U.S. Attorney General Ramsey Clark said, "Since we have been keeping records, there have been 2,066 Negroes and 1,751 white persons put to death, although Negroes made up only one-eighth of our population. And of the 455 men executed for rape, 405 were Negroes. If we can't devise a system under which all men are treated equally under the law relative to capital punishment, then obviously, for this reason alone, we should abolish capital punishment for all time."

"If a civilized society cannot say why one man should pay the supreme penalty and why another one should not, it does not rationally, logically apply such punishment," said one state supreme court jurist.

A spokesman for the American Civil Liberties Union has stated that he thinks the federal courts will set rigid "standards" to determine why and under what circumstances a man can be executed. If it turns out that he is right, this will indeed be another step toward the abolition of capital punishment in this country.

Should this come about—and again I believe that it will—the electric chair here at the Indiana State Prison, which was constructed from parts taken from the defunct hangman's scaffold that preceded it as a means of extinguishing human life, should be preserved and displayed publicly as a symbol of our having at last learned to "turn the other cheek" and as a reminder that we, as a people, have finally determined that we can and must live up to our cherished ideals.

—H.J.G.

15

Riots

Vengeance is in my heart, death in my hand, and blood and revenge are hammering in my head.

— SHAKESPEARE
Titus Andronicus

Cut the motherfucker's head off . . . Shut up, punk, this is my show . . . If you don't kill the motherfucker I will . . . Please, boys, don't . . . Shut up . . . Oh please God don't . . . Let me do it, Red . . . I said this is my show . . . Please, boys, I'll do any . . . I'll do it slow and easy . . . This'll teach you, you lousy mother . . . Oh, no . . . Please . . .

At this point I descended the few remaining steps leading to the locker room in the basement of the prison's powerhouse and saw a sight that both frightened and angered me. There, kneeling before two knife-wielding cons, was a sixty-year-old guard literally begging for his life. And the cons, who I knew were capable of such an act, looked as though they were about to offer a sacrificial lamb to the gods.

Being unarmed and knowing by the fixed expressions

on their faces that I had to act fast, I blurted out, "You guys want some pussy?"

"Some pussy?" Red repeated, turning slowly to look at me. His eyes, flecked with tiny yellow spots, were fierce and cruel.

"Yes," I hurried on. "That tall, good-looking kid that was here last night is upstairs again looking for more dick."

"My God!" Red said, a smirk breaking the frozen mask that had been his face. "Didn't she get enough last night?"

"Red, you let that bitch alone," hissed the smaller of the two cons as he stepped between Red and me.

"You don't tell me what to do, punk," Red said from the corner of his mouth, his smile disappearing. "If I want to fuck the broad again, I will."

"Not when I get through with her, you won't," the smaller con said, dashing for the stairs.

"Jesus Christ! Look what you started," Red said, taking off after his kid.

This episode transpired in the Washington State Prison during what was not only my first prison riot but also during my first prison term; otherwise, I would have better sense than to interrupt what, in their minds, would have been a revenge killing. Fortunately though, my little lie saved the day for the guard but unfortunately, not his life: he died two days later of a heart attack.

When they had gone, I helped the old man to his feet, led him to a nearby wooden bench, and helped him search his pockets for his glycerine tablets.

I know you're wondering if Red's kid caught up with the other faggot before Red could stop him. The answer is no. You see, the tall, good-looking kid wasn't even in the building. And because the powerhouse was locked from the outside by the ringleaders of the riot, there was no danger that Red's kid could get at his competitor.

Yes, I had some explaining to do to Red and his kid when I got back upstairs, but with the aid of a gallon jug of raisin jack, I didn't have too much trouble. Fact is, the last I saw of them that day, they were in the shower together cavorting like newlyweds. By then they had forgotten about killing—they were thinking more in terms of making love . . .

Actually the riot had started the day before when, just after the breakfast hour, a half-dozen cons in the detention cellhouse (hole) overpowered their guard, took his key, and unlocked the door leading to the prison's control room. Once there, one of the smaller, more agile men dove through a small opening in the heavy mesh wire across the front of the control-room cage, and with a makeshift knife forced two other guards to lie on the floor. Then, after he had unlocked the door from the inside to let his comrades in, they all proceeded to Deputy Warden Al Rimbolt's office and made him their fourth—and most important—hostage.

From there the six ringleaders, led by a lifer they called Big Jim, took their hostages to the steward's office at the back of and overlooking the kitchen. And because this office was adjacent to the food supply room and had a telephone, hot plate, coffee pot, and other conveniences, it proved to be an ideal place from which to issue orders (demands) and control the institution. Also, because this stronghold could be reached only by a narrow, steep flight of stairs, it afforded maximum security against anyone who might try to storm it. So, with the ever-present threat that the hostages would surely die violent deaths at the hands of the captors should the governor's representative refuse to meet their demands, Big Jim and his wild-eyed crew of power-mad convicts reigned supreme in the Washington State Prison for two days.

During that forty-eight-hour period the hands of the clock stopped, and incidents—some funny, others tragic—

became superimposed on a background of timelessness. In some instances casual acquaintances became close friends, and in others, men who had previously been close friends became dreaded enemies.

As I write these lines I can once again smell the damp, pungent odor of the tear gas and hear the wails of fear. I can once again see men brandishing butcher knives and meat cleavers while swaggering under the dual influence of prison-made hooch and fear-triggered adrenalin.

This then was the riot on which Frank Elli later based his best-selling novel. And if those who read his fictional account *Riot* (which actually occurred in the summer of 1955) thought it had a touch of authenticity, they should not be too surprised to learn that Frank was there in person. Just prior to the riot, Frank was one of the ticket runners (bagmen) for a gambling ring I operated—oddly enough—from the same steward's office. This had been the ideal spot for my operation, since it was in the center of the prison. But enough of this digression. Several months before this riot—which was, in the final analysis, the granddaddy of several such altercations—all of us joined forces to stage a sit-down strike for a period of two days, during which we refused to eat or work.

Without question, it was the best organized effort of its kind. The governor sent a state representative from the state capital in Olympia to Walla Walla to discuss our grievances. Because those of us most involved did not want to be identified as ringleaders, we at first refused to meet with this man (who shall remain nameless) until we had been assured by a guard who was sympathetic with our cause that the governor's representative would meet with as many as fifty of us. This agreed upon, we assembled in the prison chapel at the rear of 7 wing and presented a detailed list of demands which included the replacement of the warden and a more liberal parole-board policy. After much haggling, the state representative agreed to do everything in his power to persuade the governor to meet these demands. Under the circumstances, of course, he could do little more.

Following this there was an air of expectancy in the prison. Most of the cons—myself included—thought things would get better; but unfortunately, that didn't prove to be the case. No official action was taken to improve either conditions in the prison or the actions of the parole board. The gloom that had pervaded the prison before the sit-down strike returned. So, as might be expected, the cons reacted—this time violently.

It began in the tag shop. Someone left the burning nozzle of a blow torch up against the side of a large oxygen tank in the vicinity of the highly inflammable paint department. Soon afterward, a gigantic explosion that shook the prison to its century-old foundations was followed by a number of secondary explosions (paint drums popping off). In a matter of minutes the entire tag shop was a flaming inferno. Needless to say, this was all it took to send many of the cons into a window-breaking, mattress-burning frenzy. And although not everyone in the prison was involved, we were all summarily gassed and looked upon with suspicion. Funny thing . . . we never did find out who left that blow torch next to the oxygen tank.

As I recall it, the loss resulting from that fire was estimated at between two and three million dollars by the local newspapers. Certainly enough, one would think, to impress upon both the state officials and the taxpaying public that something was radically wrong behind those high gray walls. But, it obviously wasn't . . . for little in the way of improvement occurred. Rather, more guards were hired and the convict's row became increasing harder to hoe.

There were, to be sure, a few other scattered incidents in the prison: disgruntled cons threw trays in the dining hall or punches at the screws, but the next real flare-up was *the riot.*

Because I worked nights in the powerhouse (from 3 P.M. to 11 P.M.), I was still sleeping on the morning it began. But shortly thereafter news reached the small dormitory at the rear of 8 wing where I and the other powerhouse workers slept. I was awakened by the guy in the next bunk and told that "the shit had hit the fan" once again. He was jubilant at hearing the news until I pointed out that because of his reputation as a snitch plus the fact that he operated an inmate store (selling cigarettes, instant coffee, and candy bars at exorbitant prices) he might not fare so well without a policeman around to look after him. I had seen one such individual during a shit storm in the county jail. His complexion turned from a healthy pink to a waxylike gray. His eyes took on a ferret-like sheen. The last I saw him that day he was looking for a place to hide. But, his efforts were apparently in vain, for someone caught up with him, kicked in his teeth, and gouged out one of his eyes.

After learning that all was well with my partner in 6 wing, I walked on to the powerhouse and headed for my stash. I had hidden five one-gallon jugs of raisin jack the night before.

I was soon joined by several other powerhouse workers, two of whom produced guitars seemingly from thin air, and the party got underway. It had always been necessary to sneak around when making and drinking homemade hooch, but with the cons in control of the joint, the sky was the limit. At some point that afternoon, the tall, good-looking kid referred to earlier joined the party, and the powerhouse crew was transformed into a group of debonair bachelors vying for the hand of a princess. Even the oldtimers in the crowd stretched their gaunt frames and rolled their fading eyes.

Although tipsy by that time, I was still sober enough to appreciate my immediate surroundings. Two of the guys were singing an old country and western ballad—"You Are

My Sunshine," I think it was. Their voices blended in perfect harmony as they sang, cheek to cheek. The plaintive, melodious words of the song released nearly forgotten memories of boyhood and young love . . . of better days
. . .

Yes, that day and evening of singing and laughing and remembering was a brief respite from the numbing, humdrum existence that is prison living. Our hearts and minds were open as we drank in the joy of those few stolen hours.

Finally, I tired of the revelry, found myself a cozy perch atop the number one boiler, which wasn't then in use, and crapped out. It was following that snooze on my way to the basement for a shower next morning when I encountered Red and his kid about to commit what they no doubt would have considered a revenge murder.

Some weeks prior to that day, this same guard had found a large sack of raisins and sugar which were to have been used to make booze by Red and his kid. To make matters worse, the guard had assigned the raisins and sugar to the fiery furnace in their presence—then laughed about it. It was a great loss to them, for sugar and raisins are hard to come by in prison. But it was still hardly grounds for murder.

But this trivial incident merely served as an excuse for Red and the kid to rid themselves of frustrations born of their grudging homosexuality. That is, they were both cowards who during the early part of their prison experiences had been forced at knife point (this is fact, not conjecture) to give up some hips and/or lips. This then was their way of striking back, their misdirected way to assert their manhood—or what was left of it.

During the two days it took Big Jim and the other ringleaders of the riot to reach an agreement with the officials, there was a great deal of petty grumbling between different cliques in the prison, fistfights, and a few minor cutting scrapes. But surprisingly, there was no actual loss of life other than the old guard who died of the heart attack.

The reason was that Big Jim—an intellectual killer —organized a group of ball-bat-carrying cons who were ordered to hold down the fighting, stealing, and raping. And these men—all hard-rock cons—did their work well.

After the hostages had been released, we were all forced at gunpoint to go to the big yard—an open field surrounded by high walls and four gun towers—and there we remained, sans coats or blankets, until the next morning. We were then told to strip naked and one by one were allowed to pass through an inspection gate and return to our respective shelters. While this was going on, newsreel cameramen were shooting like mad from atop the walls. I later saw one of these photographs in *Life* magazine. It showed a long line of bare-assed cons reluctantly returning home after a long, wild weekend on the town.

This time the official promises from Olympia were kept—all, that is, except the one about granting the ringleaders amnesty. They were each given an additional ten-year sentence. But a new warden was appointed, and all the parole board members were replaced. Following this, the governor called a special session of the state legislature, which in turn passed what was to be called House Bill 12, which gave the new parole board the authority to review the case of every man in the prison. As a result, many of those whom the board felt had already been imprisoned too long were released almost immediately. Others were given time cuts.

In my own case, I neither gained nor lost any time as a result of the riot. But because Big Jim and the others were friends of mine, I regretted seeing them pay such a severe penalty for their part in the trouble. After all, what they actually had done was sacrifice themselves in order to call attention to existing evils in the prison. And they had managed to do it with no loss of life.

Of course, all prison disturbances aren't as bloodless

as was the riot. The one in the Menard Branch of the Illinois Penitentiary in the fall of 1965 (I was there also) cost the lives of three guards. They died almost immediately of wounds inflicted by four knife-wielding cons who had obviously cracked under the strain of what was then an unbearable reign of official oppression. In addition, five other guards were seriously injured in that incident, which Warden Max Fry refused to call a riot. Instead he referred to it as "an isolated altercation involving four deranged inmates." Despite his opinion, however, three of them were sentenced to death and are now awaiting electrocution in Statesville's death row. The other one received a life term. I knew two of these men well, and it was obvious to "old dumb convict" me that these men needed professional help. Yet they received no such treatment.

During their trial in Springfield, Illinois, several months later, more than a dozen cons testified as to the unresponsiveness of the Illinois parole board and of the lack of suitable medical and mental-health facilities. They also pointed out that the cellhouses, kitchen, and hospital at Menard were infested with rats and cockroaches and that the food was not fit for hogs. But was anything done—even then—to correct these conditions? The answer is no.

Another—and more recent—example where pleas for updated facilities and a meaningful "rehabilitation" program fell on deaf ears was in the Ohio Penitentiary. And once again, this somnolence on the part of state officials and the public resulted in violence on two different occasions in 1968.

The first of these two uprisings occurred in June, when more than six hundred cons burst from their cells and set fire to five buildings inside the walls. Before the National Guard and State Police could restore order, ten guards and twenty-five convicts had been injured and more than a million dollars' worth of property destroyed.

Ray Walker, a prison social worker at Ohio, who was later fired because of his public candor, said that official indifference to "rehabilitation" programs caused the trouble. Because of that indifference, the second riot—which proved to be even more violent than the first—erupted in the Ohio Penitentiary in August of the same year.

In this instance three hundred cons captured one of the cellhouses, took nine guards as hostages, and threatened to kill them unless authorities submitted to a list of six demands. At the top of that list was a demand that federal authorities be called in to investigate conditions in the century-old prison.

All Warden Marion Koloski would agree to was that after the hostages were released unharmed, he would give his full attention to improving conditions. But fearing the warden might fail to keep his word, the cons refused to release their hostages on those terms. Finally, after two days, the stalemate was broken when Ohio National Guardsmen blew holes in the cellhouse wall and roof to allow police to charge through the breach. When the shooting was over five convicts lay dead on the floor.

We could go on and on describing various riots in our nation's prisons that have resulted from public apathy and official indifference to antiquated prison facilities and anachronistic penal practices. But I seriously question the value of such a chronicle. People just don't seem to give a damn! Yet, they should—and must! For there is something more at stake here than the loss of property (real estate) and human life. For every building burned down or man killed during a prison riot, there are thousands of minds twisted, spirits crushed, and bodies broken. This is the greater loss.

Each time another young person enters one of this nation's so-called correctional institutions, he passes through what Karl Menninger has called the "heartless jaws of a creaking, groaning monster" to be maimed and embittered so that he emerges an implacable enemy of our social order. He has then been confirmed in his criminality. There are, of course, a few exceptions—but only a few . . .

Yet despite the gloom that shrouds our penal institutions, the mental anguish and despair that defeats any attempt at rehabilitation of the men therein, they—the hated and much maligned convicts—resort to violence only when all other methods have failed.

Unlike the college kid who joins a campus disturbance or a peace march knowing that, at worst, such involvement may cost him a cracked head or a few days in jail, the con knows that his involvement in a prison riot may cost him many additional years in confinement, possibly his life. Therefore he pursues such a course of action only when he's "driven to the wall."

In the final analysis then, prison riots don't just happen, but are preceded by weeks, months, or even years of suppression on the part of officials in the face of much needed change.

Even as I write these lines, I sense a tension in the atmosphere of this prison, and according to the grapevine, the same tension exists in the Indiana State Reformatory at Pendleton. I hope that nothing develops from it. I've seen more than my share of prison violence.

—H.J.G.

16

For Your
Natural Life

The jury, passing on the prisoner's life, may in the sworn twelve have a thief or two guiltier than him they try.

—SHAKESPEARE
Measure for Measure

It has been more than twenty years since I stood in San Quentin's big yard and watched an old man with more than thirty-five years behind walls bid his fellow convicts a nervous farewell. I never forgot the sight: here was a man with more years behind bars than I was old, about to reenter the outside world.

The old man served as an object lesson for me, too, even if the significance escaped me at the time. (I was twenty-one years old and serving my first prison sentence.) His circumstances pointed out more than any single thing I've since encountered to what lengths arrogant and indifferent men may be driven to manifest cruelty and vindictiveness over those upon whom they are empowered to pass judgment.

The man was seventy years old, I discovered later, and a "lifer." He had killed a man in a tavern fight. As I recall from newspaper accounts of his release, relatives of the victim were protesting the convict's parole even after thirty-five years. Three prisons and ten miserable years of hindsight later, I know their protests accounted for at least fifteen of the thirty-five years the man spent behind bars. And the hindsight has also shown me that this is but one aspect of the brutish, inhumane indifference shown toward all convicts.

More than any other type of prisoner, the lifer is completely at the mercy of his keepers. In Indiana for example, these officials act out of a vague sense of obscure rules, regulations, tradition, court rulings, and general indifference —not to mention some occasional skulduggery.

The Indiana lifer's term is not clearly defined by legal statutes. His fate rests largely in the hands of an all-powerful clemency commission. In some states life terms are designated as "natural life" or "life without possibility of pardon or parole" or as "x number of years." But Indiana statutes have no such clear-cut definitions. Instead, the parole board–clemency commission, one and the same body, can, if it so desires, keep a lifer imprisoned for his natural life.

The parole board may condemn the lifer behind bars for natural life for any infraction of prison rules. An institutional incorrigible would certainly never see the light of day in Indiana. Neither would the lifer escapee. One lifer died here recently after serving more than forty years. He escaped and was at large three months during the early 1930s. He sealed his doom by escaping. So have others.

According to *Burns Indiana Statutes, 1956, Annotated,* there are six criminal felonies for which a person may be sentenced to life imprisonment. They are murder

—first and second degree—kidnap, habitual criminal, rape of a child under twelve, and inflicting injury during the commission of a felony.

Aside from these felony definitions and penalties, nothing is specifically written out. Nowhere in *Burns* is life designated as a specific term of years behind bars. That prerogative is left to the parole board, a five-member body which sits monthly at the prison. Presently that august body has, by directive, stated that life imprisonment for first- and second-degree murder shall be punishable by no less than fifteen calendar years. That is, no lifer serving either of these sentences is eligible for parole or clemency consideration in less than fifteen years. But in actual practice the lifer in Indiana State Prison serves closer to twenty-five years than to fifteen.

Kidnapers, rapists, those who have inflicted injury during the commission of a felony, and habitual criminals must serve a minimum ten-year sentence, five less than the two murder/life categories. These lifers serve an average of fifteen to twenty years. And in all instances, the burden of initiating clemency hearings rests with the convict, not with the parole board or prison officials. Initiating these petitions does work a hardship on most lifers, especially those without outside help. They must secure signatures of sentencing judges and prosecutors, obtain sworn affidavits, and persuade witnesses and suppliants to appear before the hearing board.

All the statistical data originally planned for this article have not been obtained because I ran into an unusual amount of buck-passing and indifference. Even convict clerks, normally more than glad to conspire against their official supervisors, would not release what little information they had in their charge. To my surprise I found this reluctance stemmed not so much from a lack of official cooperation as from the fact that—unbelievably—almost no records were kept on lifers once they were paroled. What little information was available was pathetically useless.

Subsequent questioning of inmates and officials revealed that they were reluctant to be quoted on what few facts and figures were available. Most were ignorant of administrative procedures. Several lifers I questioned admitted they did not know whether their fifteen years minimum "board date" was stipulated by law statutes or by parole board decree. One custodial officer told me, "It has always been fifteen years for parole eligibility." (He had been employed at the prison less than three years.)

One lifer told me that one of the deputy wardens (we have several here) told him the ten and fifteen years' minimum parole eligibility dates derived from an executive decree of a former governor. But a quick check in *Burns* revealed that a preceding executive order is not binding upon following administrations. *Burns* says of life imprisonment only that, upon sentencing, a life-term prisoner shall be taken to state prison "for and during his or her life." (*Burns Statutes, 1956, Annotated,* 9-2207)

Nor is anyone able to account for the dual function of the parole-clemency board. Indiana statutes clearly provide for two separate and distinct bodies, yet the parole board also functions as the governor's clemency commission. The Hoosier legislature merely enlarged the parole board from three members to five in 1963 and stipulated that the board should not exceed a political imbalance of 3–2. This combined parole–clemency power makes the board the most powerful body in Hoosier corrections.

All felony offenses in Indiana provide for indeterminate sentences, and once the convicted person has been committed to prison, the length of his term is fixed by the parole board. (Several crimes in Indiana have both determinate and indeterminate penalties.) Hoosier parole boards have a notorious reputation for sensitivity to public criticism. By their actions in the past, "Nervous Nelly" parole boards have proved that no matter how deserving a lifer might be of parole, the slightest show of indignation from judges, prosecutors, or "interested citizens" is enough to cause them to deny parole. Several months ago the parole board granted release to an inmate, but when the sentencing judge and prosecutor raised a storm of protest, the board recalled the inmate and rescinded his parole. No explanation, no excuses, no public statements. They simply recalled the convict, who was, it would seem, a fit parole risk one month and a public menace the next. He is still with us.

Even with the odds so heavily against him, the short-term prisoner may "discharge out"—serve his maximum sentence—and leave prison free from parole supervision, not at all unusual under the present Hoosier hard-line philosophy. But discharging out is quite another matter for the lifer. Under department of corrections rulings there is no life-term discharge from parole. The lifer is under supervision for life. Recently, the lifer's status was further clouded when an Indianapolis parole office directive stated that lifers might, under certain "favorable circumstances," be discharged from supervision after ten years on parole. In rare instances, lifers who have served more than five years on parole may petition the department for annual reporting. But these are parole board options and subject to withdrawal at any time, certainly under "unfavorable circumstances."

In any event, lifers waiting for their first board appearance are unconcerned with the far future. At this writing there are 442 lifers in Indiana State Prison, nearly 150 of whom are outside the walls on trusty assignments. They come from all walks of life. Some are young; some are old. Some are fortunate and will one day be free men;

others will not be so fortunate—they will never walk the streets again. More real and pressing is the crushing weight of the sentences which set them apart from other convicts. Even hardened recidivists cluck in sympathy for the lifer —in any prison.

Every lifer's hopes are centered around serving his ten to fifteen years until his clemency hearing without incident, and his subsequent release. And the burden of initiating the proceedings which may bring about his freedom rests solely with him. No administrative function provides for his automatic board appearance in ten or fifteen years. If he does not file when he becomes eligible, he is not called. If he never files, he is never called. He could serve a hundred years, if he lived that long, without the board members being aware of his existence. Added to these woes, the lifer's clemency hearing, once it is underway, is a long, nerve-wracking, tedious process.

First, his record must be clear of rules infractions. When he meets this requirement, he files his opening petition with the sentencing judge and prosecutor. After duly noting their recommendations, these dignitaries file the papers with the clemency commission. The board then calls the lifer in for an interview. It lasts less than fifteen minutes (not much time in which to talk over ten or fifteen years with the body of men who hold your freedom in the palm of their hand).

The lifer leaves the hearing as befuddled about his status as when he entered the hearing room. He is told absolutely nothing other than that he will be hearing from the board. "We'll let you know." It may be a month; it may be six. "But in the meantime, you'll be here, won't you?" he is often facetiously asked. Next the board holds public hearings in Indianapolis. Here any "interested parties" may make known their wishes. No one, states the board, will be denied a chance to be heard.

I have yet to hear of a clemency hearing for a lifer

where at least one of these interested parties didn't show up. They make it their business, year after year, to be there. They have been known to file perpetuating written depositions against the lifer's release. (These are known as cases that "draw heat.") Then if every critical comment from judges and prosecutors hasn't been pacified, the lifer may as well try to sprout wings and fly out of prison. Clemency commissions are simply too spineless, too afraid of public criticism to consistently release lifers as they become eligible.

James Byrd, a twenty-six-year-old lifer from Salem, Indiana, is a case in point. Byrd was sentenced from a small town in southern Indiana for inflicting injury during the commission of a felony. Byrd was young; a semi-illiterate, a swaggering bully and extremely dangerous. At twenty-six he was already a two-time loser.

It was inevitable that Byrd's own stupidity would get him caught. While he was in jail awaiting transportation to prison, he attempted to saw out. The sheriff aborted the attempt and hustled Byrd off to prison. Anyone with half a mind, the sheriff noted later, could see that Byrd was a psychopath and in desperate need of psychiatric help—which, incidentally, has never been available in any Hoosier prison. As it developed, the sheriff proved a most astute judge of Byrd's character.

Six months after sentencing, Byrd escaped from his guard in an Indianapolis hospital where he had been taken for a minor operation. Taken into custody later, Byrd was brought back to prison in chains. Add to his already impressive crime total one attempted escape, one successful one. The only treatment Byrd got was, as he later told me, "an ass-kicking when the guards threw me in solitary."

Byrd next drew special attention when he and another prisoner escaped from a downtown Michigan City hospital by tying up their guard and stealing a car. Again Byrd was at large for a short time before he was caught. He had by now probably killed any chances for eventual parole he might have brought to prison with him. It is not too ridiculous to imagine that he might have been paroled after fifteen years had he settled into prison routine and shown, in the vernacular, an inclination to better himself. He could have had some years of his life outside prison. What is difficult to imagine is that with all things considered—his age, his sentence, his one attempted escape, and his two successful ones—not one single prison or hospital official thought to ask him "Why?"—didn't, in fact, think to do anything, except, as Byrd said, kick his ass. Less than a year later Byrd scaled the wall late at night, breaking his ankle as he dropped to the ground. Despite this serious handicap, he managed to get as far as Nashville, Tennessee, before he was apprehended. (He was returned in a hip-length cast, the only time during his imprisonment that he wasn't a serious escape threat.)

The cast was barely off before—yes!—he again scaled the wall with two companions and escaped. At long last the then Commissioner Anthony S. Kuharich broke his mysterious silence to announce that he was "quite disturbed about Byrd." But his disturbance was more with Warden Ward Lane, with whom he had been recently intensifying a running struggle for administrative control of the prison, than it was with Byrd. Kuharich had simply chosen Byrd's latest escape, which embarrassingly came at the very time Kuharich "experts" were at the prison explaining custody techniques to the staff, as an excuse to place a crony in the newly created assistant warden's post, thereby further undermining Lane's authority at the prison. (At the end of the governor's administration, the assistant warden was elevated to the ousted warden's post.)

Tragically, Byrd and his companions shot and killed a Lincoln, Nebraska, detective in a running gun battle when the detective stopped them in a stolen car. All three were subsequently brought to trial in Lincoln and are now serving life terms in Nebraska State Prison. Just as tragic was that Hoosier correction officials were not cognizant of the sorry state of affairs at the prison which the Byrd episodes pointed up. Byrd should have served as a classic demonstration that the prison system was ineffective and laughable. But even these lessons were lost in the resultant power struggle at the prison. What little face-saving efforts were made came in an attempt to tighten custodial rules, which later proved ineffective. Less than a year later two other men rode to freedom concealed in a trash truck. (One of them was a lifer.)

The "deepest concern" I heard expressed over Byrd and his pathetic fate was one custodial officer telling another: "Byrd was a wild sonofabitch."

Yes, he was that, and more. But who is to say that with the properly furnished motivation and guidance from professional help he might not have been as strongly inclined to apply his determination in constructive channels.

Predictably, each of Byrd's escapes made the parole board recede further into its conservative shell, manifesting its guilt complex more strongly with each monthly meeting, extracting still further punishment from those who had done nothing more unfortunate at the time than to fall into the category of lifer.

"We are taking a long look at our parole procedures," came the nervous pronouncement from on high. Nobody knew the reasoning behind this. Byrd certainly was many things, but not a parole violator! Past experience had taught prison officials that this was enough to cool the hot breath of public protest. (It did.) Byrd may also have inadvertently served to create a few more job classifications in the Hoosier department of corrections. Shortly after his fourth escape, the legislature, at the warden's insistence, appropriated additional money for an increased custodial staff, and Byrd's name is still mentioned occasionally in connection with "added security," "precautionary measures," and "maximum custody"—an indication that even though regulations prevent officials from literally kicking his ass, they are, indeed, still figuratively kicking him in another manner—as a political football.

Hoosier legislators have a miserable record of updating or modernizing their prisons. Salaries for career correction officers and for qualified personnel are at the bottom of the national scale. Prison help is transient. Except for the brief eight-year tenure of Warden Ward Lane from 1961 to 1969, prison programs have always been mired in a slough of indifference. The prison is a physically decayed plant. Buildings are peeled and rotted. The insides of most are jerry-built with cardboard room partitions. The entire prison is a giant fire hazard. Such is the atmosphere that once prompted Lane to announce: "We're all poor people here."

This is the atmosphere which legislators piously tell their constituencies is "good enough for hardened criminals." In reality, Hoosier prisons are unfit for caging wild animals, much less criminals.

This "penny wise" philosophy is a primary reason Hoosier prisons have such a proportionately high percentage of lifers. Add to this the fact that most ten-year lifers serve at least five years over their minimum sentence, and that most fifteen-year lifers serve in excess of twenty-five years (often thirty), and the picture is complete. Lifers simply are not as transient in the Hoosier prison population as they are in, say, California (where Carole Tregoff was recently released after serving ten years on a life sentence), or Nevada or Ohio or Kentucky—or a dozen other prisons. Lane perhaps most aptly labeled the Hoosier prison system when he called it "a monstrosity."

Under these pathetic circumstances then, Indiana lifers serve out their sentences. It is no surprise that prison officials cannot account for the optimism and hope most lifers maintain throughout their sentences. What, in effect, does give them the necessary will to struggle on instead of throwing up their hands in utter hopelessness?

Hope usually is there at the outset, after the trial itself. For after the guilty verdict there still remains a long series of court appeals. These begin shortly after the lifer gets to prison. If he cannot afford a lawyer, as most can't, he has a "jailhouse lawyer" file his rehearing petition. Court appeals take anywhere from two to five years to work their way up to the U.S. Supreme Court. Hope is high during this time.

One lifer I questioned told me, "I've been here ten years, and I've never set any long-range goals for myself. I set my sights on something only a few years away, like finishing high school. Then on perhaps learning a trade or vocation, depending upon what is available. In the meantime, I join intramural sports, form some friendships, and fill the time in between as best I can. This is my method of serving my time."

Lifers cause less disturbance and violate fewer rules than the short-term prisoners. Keeping clear disciplinary records becomes important to them as over the years they acquire a vested interest in the prison community. Lifers are more settled than short-term prisoners. They find their groove—some call it becoming institutionalized—and, as one lifer put it, "settle down to the board ten years away." Lifers, without fail, feel that escape, fighting officials, and other major prison transgressions would only add more years to their sentences.

During the eight years Lane was warden at the prison, lifers could look forward to outside-the-walls trusty assignments after five or six years. Lifers with clear prison records traveled into the community setting with ball teams, bands, chess teams, crime prevention skits. More than fifty lifers traveled with these groups. Only one escaped in more than one hundred trips. (And he escaped on Christmas Eve after he had been traveling for two years.) Now all such trips have been canceled. Lifer trusty assignments are much harder to come by now than under Lane's administration. Requirements are not so easily met. Consequently, fewer lifers are on trusty status.

To knowledgeable people, it is no surprise that lifers make good security and parole risks—better proportionately than other convicts. George Denton, once in Indiana Corrections and now head of Ohio's Adult Parole Authority, says of the lifer: "The parolee most likely to succeed in the outside world is the one who has committed the crime society regards as most heinous and the one for which it reserves its severest penalties, the murderer."

Denton is backed by statistics. He says that murder is an act that usually occurs in the heat of passion. In the majority of cases, the victim is someone in the killer's family. A murderer usually has a skill and is employable, he adds. Thus when he is paroled his chances of becoming self-sufficient are better than for any other group.

From 1945 to June, 1968, Ohio paroled 307 first-degree murderers, all of whom had served at least twenty years. Only twenty-two violated parole, and of the twenty-two, only three committed a new crime. To date, 166 of the lifers have been given a final release and discharged from parole.

Writing in the *Colony,* a prison newspaper, lifer Norman Porter cites Massachusetts prison statistics supporting at least two of Denton's contentions that lifers make good parole risks. Fewer than 81 per cent of Massachusetts lifers had less than five conduct reports, writes Porter, and 42.4 per cent had none at all. These proportions are impressive, considering the long period of imprisonment. The recidivism rate of lifers from 1943 to 1966 is less than 11 per cent of the over-all rate. The over-all rate of recidivism for other offenders is approximately six times higher than that of the lifers, writes Porter.

Unlike many states which have incentive programs for convicts, Indiana offers nothing to its lifers. There is no meritorious good-behavior time off their sentences. There are no work release programs or institutional rewards for exemplary conduct. The lifers are denied the token good time the short-termers are allowed. Lifers' terms are determinate inasmuch as they are for life, but there are no provisions for statutory good time for them. Hoosier citizens have a long history of get-tough attitudes where penology is concerned.

They have repeatedly defeated efforts in the legislature to abolish the death penalty. Nobody has died in Indiana's electric chair since 1961, but presently there are eight men awaiting the outcome of appeals from their death sentences. Community attitudes are reflected in the prison philosophy of hard labor, long sentences, and a dehumanized prison atmosphere. Hoosier criminal statutes are indicative of the public temper toward crime. That is why the state has more felonies which have life-imprisonment penalties than liberal states. That is also why lifers make up 22 per cent of the nineteen hundred convict population.

Bible Belt Indiana is old-line conservative, and Republican. The state budget reflects the austere philosophy of legislative leaders who have stood pat behind a hundred years of tired moralistic clichés on penal matters that propose "right is right and wrong is wrong" or "an eye for an eye, a tooth for a tooth." Such is the Simple Simon approach to Hoosier penology.

Indiana criminal statutes are a hodgepodge of patchwork applications, corrections, and amendments. Item: Criminal conspirators to a burglary receive a longer term, two to fourteen years, than the actual perpetrator of the burglary, two to five years. Item: Indiana's archaic and outmoded statutes provide for two robbery penalties. Unarmed, a purse snatcher or mugger is liable to an indeterminate term of ten to twenty-five years. The armed robber is subject to a determinate term of ten years, which can be served in six years, eight months.

This inept and fuzzy thinking settles into the prison atmosphere. Coupled with a lack of diagnostic facilities, counselors, and incentive programs, lifers are faced with insurmountable odds against ever being worth much to themselves, much less to society. In short, lifers are left to fend for themselves, to get along as best they can. I have talked with many lifers with ten, twelve, or fifteen years behind bars. Some didn't know how to reach the prison counselors available.

One lifer was recently continued for further parole hearings because "the board doesn't have adequate information on your criminal background." (This after ten years.) Parole board inadequacy is an open joke among prison officials.

Another lifer served more than four years on death row before his sentence was reversed to life imprisonment. His case had attracted considerable attention (heat) in the press. When his death sentence was reversed by an appellate court, he was once more under the jurisdiction of the parole board. They promptly called him for a hearing, wherein they affixed an added penalty of five years' parole violation to his life term. And the life term was held in abeyance until the five years were served. This despite the fact that the convict had two murder detainers on his record from Kentucky and would never in all likelihood leave prison. One newspaper which had earlier demanded his life as a "mad dog killer" softened its stand, allowing this might be called excessive punishment. Amen.

This inconsistency has proven embarrassing to Hoosier correction officials in the past. One ex-lifer showed up unexpectedly, walking the downtown streets of his home town after serving less than five years on his term. A surprised sheriff tried to arrest the man, thinking he had escaped from prison. When the ex-lifer produced a governor's commutation, amounting to a full pardon, the sheriff raced to phone Indianapolis for verification of the story.

The ex-lifer was telling the truth. He had been paroled because, according to the prison doctor, a woman, he was suffering from terminal cancer. Several days later, reporters smelled out the story, the prison doctor was contacted, and the circumstances of the ex-lifer's parole became a bit muddled when she denied she had recommended parole. Yes, she had examined the prisoner. No, he wasn't suffering from terminal cancer, only a few small ulcerated sores on his feet, certainly not a terminal illness by any stretch of the imagination. She had, she told newsmen, merely recommended treatment in an Indianapolis hospital—but certainly not clemency.

The mystery further deepened when reporters contacted clemency commission members and were told that the commission had merely made their recommendations to the governor on the basis of the doctor's report. (This is the only known case in Hoosier history where a doctor supposedly had a say in a clemency hearing.)

So many irregularities in the case cropped up that it became a standing joke among convicts, commentators, newsmen, the ex-lifer—everybody but the embarrassed correction officials. The sentencing judge and the prosecutor were incensed. Both threatened grand jury action in the matter and got as far as issuing a few subpoenas before Governor Matthew Welsh announced he was taking full responsibility for the ex-lifer's release and announced the matter was closed. But later, a surreptitiously conducted investigation revealed that as a lawyer some years before, Governor Welsh had defended the ex-lifer, a man of considerable means even then. (He got him off then, too!) It also developed that the ex-lifer had extensive land holdings almost adjoining property belonging to a highly placed correction official.

At last report, five years later, the "dying" ex-lifer was still walking the downtown streets of his home town. All other concerned parties have since departed the Hoosier prison scene, too—the governor, who cannot under any circumstances succeed himself in office, two highly placed correction officials prominent in the case, the chairman of the parole board and, of course, the lady doctor who never seemed willing to be the scapegoat officials wanted to make of her.

The dust from that fiasco had hardly settled when another lifer with more than twenty years behind bars escaped from a trusty assignment. He was heard from next when he sent a postcard greeting to the warden from Florida, not exactly wishing that the warden were there with him, but solicitous nonetheless that the warden should not worry about him. The escaped lifer informed the warden that he was on his way to join Castro's freedom fighters in Cuba, distinguish himself in battle, and prove to the world that he was more than just an escaped lifer.

Unfortunately, he did not get the chance to do any of these worthy things. He was arrested in short order and brought before a judge. Here things took a strange turn. To Indiana's chagrin, the Florida judge refused to extradite the lifer escapee. The hearing judge said that in excess of twenty years was enough time for a murder committed during the heat of a family quarrel. (The convict killed his cousin.)

Several months later the escapee made a trip to Tennessee to visit relatives, where through his lawyer he began negotiations with the parole board chairman to make his freedom legal. (Hoosiers still carried him on the prison count as an escapee.) Letters passed from Tennessee to Indiana authorities with the understanding that he would surrender to Tennessee authorities, waive extradition to Indiana, and serve a short sentence for escape and be released. The lifer agreed to this.

Once the lifer was back inside Indiana State Prison some unforeseen circumstances developed. The chairman of the parole board retired and the warden, who somehow had been on the outer fringes of the negotiations, confessed to the lifer that he had no power to effect his release with the present board chairman. At this writing, the befuddled lifer sits inside ISP destined to a long one-sided fight to regain the freedom he once had and negotiated away—a strange paradox compared to the official Hoosier attitude toward the ex-lifer who showed up in his home town after serving less than five years.

The incident is worthy of note also in that it points out the wide divergency in penal philosophy as to what constitutes proper and humane treatment. Florida obviously thought that in excess of twenty years for a crime was enough time behind bars. Indiana just as obviously thought not. Who is right? Is a man's life worth more in Indiana than it is in Florida? This is a point for Hoosier correction officials to think about in their spare time. Item: It was ascertained that during the lifer's brief fourteen months of freedom he had been gainfully employed every day.

Typical of the callous indifference to the welfare of Indiana prisoners is the case of Claude Morphew, ISP #22745. Morphew entered prison in June of 1944 with a life term. Under existing parole board ruling, he became eligible for parole in 1954. Unaccountably, Morphew didn't file when he became eligible. In fact, he sat out seven additional years before convict friends persuaded him to file. He filed in 1961 and was denied. Under parole board ruling, Morphew had been eligible to file every two years since 1954. After his first denial he waited another seven years, and again convict friends persuaded him to refile. In 1968, after serving almost twenty-four years to the day, Morphew was granted a parole. His charge was rape. And he served almost three times the equivalent of what a murderer would have served in Kentucky. The fact is that, if convict friends hadn't kept pestering him to file, he easily could have died in prison.

Denton says, "Murder is a one-time offense." There are, undeniably, vicious murders committed every day but, for the most part they are flash-fire murders, unlike a premeditated series of burglaries or robberies or auto thefts. Most lifers are, with the exception of a few habitual criminals, criminally naïve. Many never had so much as a traffic ticket before they committed their crimes. One lifer I know "kidnaped" his ex-wife, drove her home, and was arrested next morning on her complaint. They had argued violently, he told me, while they were driving around town. He slapped her. In a fit of pique the next morning, she talked the matter over with a city prosecutor who advised her to file kidnap and assault charges. (Twice before the trial, the husband told me, the ex-wife attempted to drop the charges, but the prosecution refused.) One "habitual criminal" I know received his life sentence after three convictions for auto theft, all for joy-riding in his home town. Public indignation at his trial was high because, while speeding through town to avoid arrest, he struck a young boy on a bicycle. The prosecutor filed habitual criminal charges with the explanation that, "I know you're not a bad guy, but the newspapers are yelling for your hide."

This "nailing the pelt" sometimes carries over to include the lifer's friends. One told me his mother was treated very disrespectfully by officials when she appeared in his behalf before the clemency commission. "They continually stressed my negative side to her," he said, "and told her that I was no good, didn't deserve her help and concern, and hadn't shown any signs of improvement since I had been in prison."

The lifer told me his mother came away from the hearing shocked and dismayed. She never appeared at another hearing. Contrary to what officials had told his mother, the lifer had participated in several of the more worthwhile programs then available, took scholastic correspondence courses, and kept his record free of infractions.

A lady friend of mine who appeared before the clemency board in my behalf had a similar experience. Commission members hinted at an illicit relationship between us—there had been none—made a pointed and derogatory remark about my personal character, and stressed my lengthy criminal history. They mentioned my broken marriage, questioned the woman's intentions, and generally stressed only my bad points.

Commission members deliberately led her to believe that they were well informed of my prison progress of which, to be sure, they knew nothing: they had some weeks before spoken to me for the first time, and not a single civilian employee of the prison, in fact, had ever taken the time to investigate my prison circumstances for a parole board report. Very often civilian supervisors have convict clerks fill out progress reports with the explanation that "you convicts know each other better than we civilians know you." One commission member told the lady he knew me personally. Another lie: He wouldn't have known me from Adam's house cat had I jumped in his lap.

When commission members asked the lady why she presumed I was worthy of clemency, she drew their wrath by stating that there was a large disparity between my sentence and that of my co-defendant (already paroled). One member slammed his palms down on the table and informed her that they were considering my clemency, not my co-defendant's, and that nothing which had happened to him was pertinent to my hearing. This same member, however, thought it pertinent, perhaps for shock effect, to inform her that my brother was also at that very minute serving a sentence in prison, and allowed that how several other members of my family had served prison sentences as well.

Item: One man here, Whitey Mosely, has served forty-five years on a life sentence. He has gained a measure of notoriety since becoming Indiana's number one prisoner. He has served more time than any other prisoner in Indiana prisons. Mosely is the victim of a strange set of ironic circumstances. His crime was particularly vicious. He shot and killed three people and wounded several others. Hoosier public outrage is such that after forty-five years Mosely has a standing protest from the prosecutor's office in his packet. This is enough to scare the parole board silly, as I've indicated. In Mosely's case it is more than enough. No parole board or governor would touch him with a ten-foot pole. Mosely knows he is not about to be paroled as long as there is a single protest against him, so he is, very literally, mired in hopelessness.

Still, Mosely has put his forty-five years' imprisonment to good use. He has worked hard to improve himself, mentally, morally, and scholastically. During those forty-five years he has held every key prison job of consequence. His record is without blemish. Every single official I have talked with agrees that Mosely could safely be released on parole.

Many influential people have been attracted to Mosely's case: newsmen—two from *Life* magazine—radio and TV people, former wardens, some of whom have made personal appeals on his behalf to parole board members, many prison supervisors, and a state psychiatrist. Mosely himself has written appeals for outside help and twice has laid his pleas for freedom before the governor. No dice. He has, it seems, by virtue of his status as Indiana's longest-term lifer, and the resultant publicity, diminished any slim chance for freedom he otherwise might have had.

Why a single lawman's protest should outweigh hundreds of recommendations for leniency is beyond comprehension. But it has been enough; and it will continue to be enough. Perhaps the explanation is in the fuzzy generality advanced by the clemency commission that "this man is a menace to society." End of official explanation. One cannot help but wonder when Mosely, a completely different individual from the one he was forty-five years ago, will stop being a menace to society. And, if he is indeed a menace, does he not stand as a chilling reminder of the utter inadequacies of Indiana's penal system? Who is supposed to have been converting Mosely to a useful, productive person all these years? The prosecutor?

If he truly has been such a threatening menace all these years it would have been more logical had somebody taken Mosely out and shot him. A state psychiatrist once appeared before the clemency commission for Mosely and told them he would not be hesitant to trust Mosely to baby-sit for his children. "There is not a whisper of doubt in my mind," the psychiatrist testified, "that Mosely would be a safe and successful parole risk in society." His testimony was discounted. Mosely told me that at one time or another every member of the board has told him that he has done enough time but that collectively they say otherwise.

Mosely's case raises one other question. Is parole determination made on the basis of the board's emotional reaction to the manner in which lifer crimes are committed?

It would certainly seem so. Rape on minor children is a despicable crime, in any state. It must be particularly odious to parole board members. But is it any more hateful than murder? Or kidnap? Or habitual crime? Or inflicting injury during the commission of a crime? No single man, regardless of the heinous crime he may have committed, has served more time in the state of Indiana without parole than Mosely. Is the taking of three lives, then, more dastardly than taking one, or raping a minor child?

If some omnipotent bureaucrat decrees raping a minor child is more heinous than shooting a common law wife in the head at close range, so be it. But pray don't let the decision be based on whether the child was eight or ten, or whether she was raped in the woodshed or in the back seat of an automobile. Establish instead a common sense logic, not for some political administration, like a common whore groveling to please her pimp, but for a prison system that, God help us, seems after a hundred years likely to remain with us.

There is an ongoing "in residence" confusion in Hoosier prisons. It is unique, unlike, say, in Illinois or California. The confusion of convicts stems from the indifference and official arrogance of the prison staff. And this indifference and arrogance come about because prison officials usually hold prisoners in extreme contempt. Unlike Quentin and Statesville, Indiana State Prison has no gang-connected or Mafia mobsters. There are fewer than five out of a hundred professional criminals in all of Hoosier jails and prisons. I'm red-faced to admit that my fellow convicts are for the most part petty- and nuisance-thieves. They commit felonies, and serious ones, as attested to by the four-hundred-plus lifers here. But the bulk are drug store robbers, filling station burglars, and purse snatchers. Even the few habitual criminals I know are serving time for three or four "lesser" felonies.

The conditions of which I write are not general or common to all prisons. A few, like Quentin in California and Waupan in Wisconsin, have meaningful programs for convicts. Conjugal visits, furloughs, and meritorious good time off sentences were pioneered in California several years ago—and are working. Halfway houses for parolees have been in use in some states for years. Hoosier prisons have none of these programs.

The single most important thing for a lifer is his outside ties. Lifers who receive mail, visits, and personal encouragement from their families are less likely to violate prison norms that would jeopardize their release. No lifer in his right mind would deliberately throw away his chances for early release. There is, however, not one single scrap of evidence to show that Hoosier prison officials encourage a prisoner's family and friends to maintain their ties. In fact, most prison programs are structured to discourage inside-outside ties: mail and visitors are thoroughly screened and drastically limited. Officials treat outsiders as meddlers and are hostile to (and deathly afraid of) the slightest bit of criticism of their prison, as though a prison is sacrosanct and above all reproach from those outside.

If you have read this dissertation as an angry subjective criticism of the Hoosier prison system, you have read correctly. That is exactly what I meant it to be. But if you presume to think that by the circumstances of my position as convict I am unqualified to criticize, then, my friend, you are wrong. For my position as an inmate, who for four years has breathed the corruptness and rottenness, gives me that right.

The miserable circumstances under which men are forced to live out their punishment is nowhere written in law statutes or executive decrees but in the hearts and minds of intelligent men. Prisons are very necessary. After ten years of having lived with men who have conceived and

carried out every abominable crime known to man, I would
be the last to say tear down the prisons. No. They are a sad
necessity.

But these prison circumstances, the bungling and ineptness, affect not only the lifer but all convicts, in all prisons. I merely chose the lifer who, by the nature of his sentence, is exposed to longer, harsher doses of prison
treatment than his short-term fellow convicts. He does, by
virtue of his being condemned to a lifetime of the miseries I
have described, epitomize the general character of convicts
in all prisons.

I chose the parole board as my chief villain. But it
does not stand alone in the injustices perpetrated. Every
single man who earns his bread by prison wages, from the
lowest prison guard to the administrative head, must share
the blame.

I believe that is why Mosely, with forty-five years behind bars, spoke for prisoners everywhere, long-termers and
short-termers, when he wrote in the prison newspaper, *Lake
Shore Outlook:*

> What effect does all this have on the lifer? It is
> doubtful that anybody knows, except the lifer himself. Of
> course, when he is told by board members that "life is life
> in Indiana," perhaps he is astounded by the inequity of
> the application of that dictum. Others get out. Why can't
> I? Who holds the key to the front gate, anyway?
>
> There never was a man sentenced to a life term who
> did not anticipate eventual release. Many don't make it.
> But this kind of situation need not be. Clemency is often
> referred to as an act of grace or mercy, or a privilege, but
> not a right. Whatever its name, it does exemplify some
> kind of faith in a human being as the giver.
>
> Every prison has its forgotten men. Indiana is no ex-
> ception. It may be rightfully said that any lifer serving
> over 20 years has become a forgotten man. And on the
> dollars and cents side, if you aren't squeamish at measur-
> ing a man's life in terms of dollars and cents, it costs

$1300 a year to support him in a Hoosier prison; twenty years penal servitude, then, is a taxpayer expenditure of $26,000.

There is another side to imprisonment other than the mere loss of liberty, and as brutally ugly as speaking in terms of man's imprisonment in dollars and cents savings to taxpayers. That is the side of protest of the convict's release from prison after he has served a reasonable portion of his official sentence.

Perhaps the explanation for the protest has its roots in another form of protest, one which exploded in angry confrontations on college campuses, and gave birth to this plaintive chalked scrawl: "I do not like thee, Dr. Fell. The reason why I cannot tell. But this I know all too well. I do not like thee, Dr. Fell."

Can we not attribute a more benevolent nature to man than this?

—A.P.

17
Politics

Probably the best way to illustrate the detrimental effect patronage politics has on state prison inmates would be for me to give the reader a running commentary on what occurred in Indiana just prior to, during, and after a recent change of administration.

During the latter part of 1968, when Republican Edgar Whitcomb was making his bid for the governor's mansion in Indianapolis, his campaign promises revolved around "law and order, less spending and lower taxes."

The moment the ballots were counted in November of 1968 and it was certain that Whitcomb had been elected, a shock wave of fear and apprehension descended from the apex of state government, filtering out and down through its various branches. The penal system was no exception.

Here at the Indiana State Prison there was much speculation between November and January on who would be selected to replace liberal Warden Ward Lane, who was then rounding out his eighth year. Many names were mentioned. All of them were of the "get tough" school of thought.

As the days and weeks passed, rumors ran rampant. Our newspaper office became a focal point for all those cons who considered themselves political pundits. One self-proclaimed clairvoyant named Tom Mays predicted that Commissioner Kuharich would be replaced but that Warden Lane would serve at least another four years as warden. Others, myself included, hoped that both Kuharich and Lane would remain in their respective positions; but I doubt that any of us really felt that our hopes would materialize. For, as PACE (Prisoners' Aid by Citizens' Effort), an Indianapolis-based citizens' group, said at the time: "Another Quadrennial Musical Chairs game has begun in the Indiana Department of Correction."

In a news release, this organization went on to say:

> Historically, traditionally there have been major shake-ups in the Department of Correction every four years when the state administration changes.
>
> Competent and able employees from the office of the commissioner down through the newest custodial officer, have had to be concerned with whether or not they will be promoted, demoted, or just ignored by the administration changes.
>
> This situation has existed for years and has occurred with such predictable regularity that even the inmates quite freely speculate about such changes.

The news release concluded by stating that "continuity of administration, proper planning and evaluation, and the effective treatment of criminal offenders cannot be achieved until a bipartisan approach to corrections is initiated and becomes operative."

Prior to the election in November of 1968, Anthony Kuharich, who had held his post little more than a year, made every effort to woo state legislators—particularly members of the Penal Benevolent Committee—in hopes that they might eventually place his job under the merit system. But his efforts failed. Shortly after January 1, 1969, he was relieved of his duties as commissioner and demoted to the position as superintendent of the State Farm at Putnamville, Indiana.

Shortly after Kuharich was replaced as commissioner by James E. McCart, the following UPI story was reprinted in many Indiana newspapers:

> *Greencastle, Ind.* (UPI)—James E. McCart, commissioner of the Indiana Department of Correction, and nine other men were indicted by a Putnam County Grand Jury Wednesday (May 21, 1969) in connection with the disappearance of nearly 125,000 pounds of choice meat from the Indiana State Farm at Putnamville.
>
> McCart, 46, a veteran penal official, was charged with the theft of beef, T-bone, sirloin and round meat from the farm which raises cattle to supply food to prisoners at Putnamville and other state penal institutions.
>
> Before the release of the grand jury report, which contained 17 indictments, Governor Whitcomb announced he had asked McCart to resign from his $20,160 a year job.

Others indicted with McCart were Albert Ellis, a former superintendent of the State Farm at Putnamville, physician Louis Advincula, chief supervisory engineer Roy Martin, brickmason Stanley Helliger, former correction officer Howard Jessup, guard captain Robert Garrison, preventive maintenance supervisor Michael Frost, and slaughterhouse supervisor Michael Vietti.

A bit of comic opera occurred when Governor Whitcomb publicly asked for McCart's resignation. McCart, who had at one time in his life studied for the ministry and is well known for his dogmatic pronouncements and self-righteous beliefs, refused to be fired and continued to report to his Indianapolis office for work. In an article in the Michigan City *News-Dispatch,* McCart was quoted as saying that the form letter of resignation he signed when accepting the post was invalid. In another (AP) story McCart said:

I'm going to work. I'm fighting for my integrity. And I intend to serve my term unless I become convinced by something other than public attacks and unfounded accusations that my services are not in the best interest of the state of Indiana.

The Governor, on the other hand, maintained that McCart had definitely been fired and, to add substance to his remarks, Whitcomb announced that he had temporarily appointed then Assistant Commissioner Robert Hardin to replace McCart. But because Hardin had originally been appointed as assistant commissioner by McCart and apparently felt some loyalty to him, Hardin continued to look upon McCart as his boss.

At that point, the Governor's administrative assistant, William Sharp, personally visited McCart's office and asked him to vacate. But McCart still refused to leave. There was then speculation that Whitcomb might use force to eject McCart, but when Sharp was asked about this, he was noncommittal.

To the Governor's extreme embarrassment, this situation remained unresolved for two weeks. Finally, the Governor called McCart to his office and somehow convinced him to leave quietly. And it's also interesting to note that eventually all charges against McCart, Ellis, Advincula, Martin, Helliger, Jessup, Garrison, Frost and Vietti were dropped completely.

During this period, there was much speculation here in the prison about who was actually the commissioner. Some said McCart and others said Hardin, while still others said both and others said neither. Oh, well, such is the life of a poor convicted criminal: he just never knows where his next commissioner is coming from—or where he's going.
. . .
During the six months that McCart served as Indiana's commissioner of correction and was having his afore-

mentioned troubles, the man he had chosen to succeed Ward Lane as warden here at the state prison in January was also meeting with difficulties. In truth, George Phend's troubles actually began when he arrived here in September, 1967, to become Warden Lane's assistant.

Some years before, Phend had served as superintendent of Indiana's Boys' School at Plainfield and, while there, he acquired the reputation as a stern disciplinarian and "a layer on of hands and feet."

Perhaps the most receptive and certainly the most instrumental of our official allies here was the Catholic priest, Father Joseph Sedlak. He was quick to assess the problem and immediately went to work on its solution. To do this, he rallied the support of numerous guards and a few of the more liberal-minded officials, then asked them to meet as a group with State Representative (D) Dean Bolerjack of nearby Mishawaka, Indiana. Bolerjack, in turn, took the information this group had given him to the press and charged that Warden Phend's unwarranted "get tough" policies would surely cause a bloodbath in the prison.

To counter these charges, Phend suggested that Bolerjack would do better to come to the prison and "see for himself" instead of accepting the word of disgruntled employees. Following this, Bolerjack did indeed visit the prison—accompanied by three other state representatives, two of whom were Republicans. But instead of taking a guided tour and talking with only those inmates selected by Phend and his few trusted staff members, Bolerjack and company insisted that they be given free access to the prison grounds and allowed to talk with anyone they chose. As a result, they talked to more than a hundred cons, most of whom told it like it was. Bolerjack became even more convinced that Phend should be replaced as warden.

As a result of that investigation by Bolerjack and the other three members of the Indiana General Assembly plus subsequent pressures that were applied on Governor Whitcomb, Phend was transferred from the prison here and named as Superintendent of the Indiana Reformatory at Pendleton.

During these perilous months, there were some officials in the hierarchy of the Indiana Correction Department who "wanted out" before the archaic structure crumbled around their ears. For instance, in June of 1969, Valjean L. Dickinson resigned as head of the women's prison in Indianapolis. The following month, Herschel B. Thomas resigned as superintendent of the reformatory at Pendleton. Said Thomas: "There's no stability in the Department of Correction and no future for any man working there."

As I write this, Russell Lash, appointed to replace George Phend as warden here, has been on the job for only a short time. It is much too early therefore to predict what success he will have. However, one thing is certain, the very fact that he is only twenty-nine years of age and inexperienced in the field of penology will not make things any easier for him. Under the circumstances, it is doubtful that he will be able to steer clear of the quagmire of the "vindictive-punishment syndrome" apparent here and elsewhere in corrections. I hope that he will, but I doubt it. For after all, the "old guard" lieutenants and captains here are already at work on him. I've seen some pretty liberal-minded men fall prey to their "lock 'em up and throw away the key" sickness. But again, I hope that Warden Lash possesses enough wisdom and skill to keep his head above the muck. His only real hope of success lies in the help men like Dean Bolerjack can give him. One thing is certain: Unless legislators like Bolerjack and an aroused public change the system before the system changes him, Warden Lash—like other well-meaning men before him—will become but another "voice in the wilderness" crying for help that rarely, if ever, arrives.

The system of Indiana patronage politics and the lethargy on the part of its citizens combine to make a formidable stumbling block that has stood for years in the way of meaningful progress in corrections. And unless something is done about educating the general public, this will continue to be the case for years to come.

In 1948, Austin MacCormick of the Osborne Association conducted a thorough study of the Indiana Penal System. He found it woefully inadequate. In 1968 a similar study was conducted by the National Council on Crime and Delinquency, successor organization to the Osborne Association. Again existing institutions and practices were found archaic. Yet, despite these findings, little effort has been expended to improve the situation.

Of course, this failure is not confined to Indiana. For with few exceptions, correction systems in this country do not accomplish what they must to protect society: that is, resocialize and prepare the convicted criminal for his return to the free world. And the primary reason for this situation is that the political patronage systems in the fifty states hold fast to archaic practices out of vested interests.

—H.J.G.

18

Notes from a Prison Journal

(I)

On my way to the small paneled visiting room I am eager with anticipation. A gate clangs open. I move inside. Give my name. Take off my shoes. Empty my pockets. Everything out in the open on a small table.

Impersonal hands pat loosely over my body in search of some hidden item. The hands cannot feel my surge of excitement at entering this room. This ritual of degradation is lost upon me now. My thoughts are hidden; he cannot paw through them like my meager possessions laid out before him on his small table (like to kill the sonofabitch!).

Wait over there by the gate. Be with you in a minute. That stupid bastard. Can't he read my impatience to be done with him? Or is it, perhaps, exactly that he can. Careful now. Don't let the bitter anger surge up from inside your trembling. Here he is now. See? Only a few tortures later.

He signals a sharp-eyed brother hawk in blue. A buzzer frazzles, another gate swings slowly open. Another wait until hawkeye is sure I am permitted to enter this small sanctuary which like none other in this barren place will bring me face to face with those apart from prison.

Goddamn this interminably prolonged aggravation. Ah. Another buzzer. Won't be long now. By some unintentional pattern of construction design I am privileged to watch Her unseen as She walks those first dozen steps from Her world into mine. Yes, this is my only secret pleasure with Her now. One that I have guarded jealously. I savor this stolen glimpse each month. She uses these last few steps to compose Her secret self. At times I have been ashamed of this selfish little secret I keep from Her. It gives me a slight advantage to see Her struggle for control. (She cannot see my struggle!) She seems so helpless now. So small. Ah! There She is. Her frown changes when She enters this room. There is the familiar set to her pretty chin which She is so anxious to present as Her proof of strength over these last four years.

She has bravely suffered my imprisonment, defending me with every breath of Her convictions. She clings to the belief that I am something other than what my presence here in prison says I am. Her smile masks the trembling of Her lips. (Why does this goddamn place make her cry every time?) Are those tears so ill-concealed beneath the sparkle of Her green eyes a sign of Her defeat? Or are they the unashamed flaunting of Her certainty as Woman?

Her reprieve, like mine, is this brief hour of our pretense. We walk the few remaining steps separating us. The distance closes. We meet. Touch. Kiss. My senses are drowned in Her sweet nearness and the soft redness of her hair. We murmur the usual greetings, but our touch at greeting is now our meaning. Across this narrow table, my love envelops Her. She knows. We speak small-talk-happy of many things this summer morning. Of all the things we once were.

Only a narrow wooden divider separates our bodies here. Once it was not so. Her eyes hold mine. Say many things. They hold the message I shall carry with me from this small room this day. They speak of the promise which will be my substance for days to come. No eavesdropping bastard can steal that look from my possession. It is mine alone. A look no other shall ever know. Born here in this very room in isolated time. Our hope, Hers and mine. Our talk this morning will soon be stopped by a guard with a clock on the wall at my back. But he cannot take the re-built assurance Her presence here means.

A lifetime flits before our very eyes this day as the morning sun settles warmly across our oak divider. We must hurry now; our time is near. Yes. There is the signal. A few parting words as we walk selfconsciously together-apart to the small railing where we are required to say our good-byes.

A touch again. Another kiss. Firmer this time. All the standard good-byes. And then her hand comes up in the fragile gesture which I have come to know so well. A timid sign born of prison parting these past four years. We turn and begin the walk back to our separate worlds. I stop short of the door, slyly, for I will not be denied that fleeting look of her as she passes by my secret place. Goddamn, she looks so tiny.

(II)

Under the glass top on my desk is a photograph of a smiling, lean-faced boy—proud and young and aware and about to become a teen-ager. His tanned image stares out at me in reminder of the hurt and bewilderment I burdened him with as heritage.

His mother tells me he does well in school, "an honor

student," the letter said. "He likes to write things, and draw, and has a most amazing memory," she adds.

As I read her words, I am moved to wonder if he can remember those times he expressed an interest in "doing the things Dad does." He was only seven then, a sensitive and self-aware seven, bursting at the seams with curiosity about the Nature of things. (Dad, how do trees grow?)

I wonder, too, if he can recall how eagerly I rushed out to buy all the paraphernalia for a small fisherman—miniature rod and reel, dip net, waders, flies—exactly the way I recalled my father had made certain I learned the "man things" every paternal generation is charged with passing along.

Did I completely hide the bitter disappointment I felt when he cried at seeing a fish hooked and dangling from his line as I coaxed him to put it in his creel. How could I know that his interest—and satisfaction—lay in watching a speckled trout flash across a creekbed, not in hooking it on a line? Months later he would carry a woefully cat-mangled sparrow and ask, "Can you make it well, Dad?" and cry himself to sleep when I couldn't. About this time his fishing gear was relegated to a cluttered corner of the garage, never to be used again.

I never got to really know my son, nor he me. Our time together was too short. But our blood bond still remains. In his memory, like mine, are the weals of disappointment at the ties which should have been, but now, tragically, are lost. And we shall both be poorer for the loss. I because he shall become a man without my counsel; he because I cheated him of his rightful kinship.

When I came to prison I walked from his life and, as his mother once wrote, he walked into manhood years ahead of his time. (Don't worry, Mother, now that Dad is gone I will care for you.) Once he was confused, bewildered by the turn of events which deprived him of his father. (Mother, why did the policeman take Dad away?) Now he sees with clarity, although the maturity for understanding the vagaries of man is not yet his.

Sometimes, too, I plumb my thoughts for some long-forgotten sign which I might have missed, a sign which now I might seize upon desperately and twist to interpret as added assurance to his mother's "Don't worry, he will grow up to be a fine man."

But this, also, is denied me. Our man-boy relationship is unable to reach across the time of prison years. What were once very real qualities of my son have, with the passage of the years, faded beyond recall.

So he smiles out at the world from my desk—in prison—and I look at his image, and hope for him, and speculate upon his potential—and pray.

(III)

Reaching backwards over the years, I'm startled by the vividness with which I can recall those things I saw and heard when prison gates shut behind me.

I saw long shuffling lines of convicts moving, heads bowed, to grimy prison workshops. I thought, "Why, they look like zombies, like creatures devoid of all human feelings."

I saw men pass one another on the prison walks and in the workshops with that stare peculiar to the imprisoned, eyes fixed straight ahead, staring, unseeing, lost in thought about other happier times.

I saw the hurt and humiliation on the face of a young man as he stared across a narrow wooden visiting table at his wife and child, inches apart but worlds separated in heartache and misery. And I felt a wave of remorse rise up in my throat for the hurt and disgrace my own imprisonment would bring upon my wife and children.

I saw two men reduced to haggling like beggars over a package of cigarettes, their tempers exploding, fighting like maddened dogs. Weeks later one would stab the other with a sharpened file because, as he told prison guards, "he wanted to teach the fellow a lesson."

I saw these men in a kaleidoscope of emotions—fear, sorrow, anger, and frustration. I would not allow myself to believe that the impersonality of prison could smother me too in anonymity or fill my eyes with that vacant, unseeing stare.

Yet, somehow, I too have changed. Now I see there is no escape from the total inevitability of despair and hopelessness. It is a despair and hopelessness that reaches into the very bowels of prison; no one person, no single thing escapes the permeation. It hangs over everything like a thick, murky fog.

All men surrender to the despair of prison. The capitulation comes sooner in some than in others, and more subtly; sometimes it creeps stealthily and secretly into the nature of a man, as it did to me. But there is that day when you will awake and look unbelievingly about you, and see that you are one of the shuffling, snarling, half-maddened men called convicts.

Here, then, is a look into the dark nature of one man and the forces of circumstance which conspired to bring him to his particular time and place in prison. Once he was possessed of the same drives, feelings, and ambitions as you and I. Now he is an old man, near eighty I would guess, and his frail hands have the palsied tremble that is common to the very old. His blue eyes are watery and vacant, focused on some faraway scene that is real only in a dark recess of his mind. He sits in the sun, and recalls another era. He makes us uncomfortable.

He is a man apart from his fellow men, a stranger to the world outside prison walls. Long ago he was caught up in the dreary monotony of prison life. Now, in his failing years, even prison life has passed him by. And so he sits quietly in the sun of an October afternoon, head cocked slightly awry, a freak happenstance of no concern to anyone.

He came to prison a young man, violent and uncontrolled. He was a victim of his own dark passions as much as he was a part of the era that spawned our Dillingers and our Capones and bathtub gin. When prison swallowed him, he found his own kind in a special hell of guns and walls and authority and regimentation.

He nurtured his hate on the tangible aspects of his own little private hell, savoring each tortured day, remembering, storing back against the day when he would once more become a part of a world changing ever so rapidly toward concepts he had never known.

Now he relates only to prison events: when they (somehow in all his hopes and longings of yesterday, those apart from his inner world became "they") added the extra fifteen feet to the prison wall; when they enforced the lockstep; when they enforced the silent system; when they released Dillinger.

In his clearly divisive world, his judgments and reflections are biting; he speaks out in jumbled castigations against "they"—against authority—standing brokenly, a ludicrous figure of antiquity. He is a wreck of contradictions.

Sometimes men stop to chat or to pass the time of day with the old man. Some come only to scoff and laugh or to whisper to companions about "the old loony." And for a smoke or candy bar, he may be bribed into reminiscing of times past, of an era unknown to them. They stand by uncomfortably, self-consciously, as the old man hunts through the corridors of his mind until he flushes out an appropriate indignity suitable to his state of mind.

He sits on the low stone abutment along the prison sidewalk and flails his arms. If we have come to ridicule, we are taken aback at his trembling fury. We stand in stunned silence, embarrassed, for his babbling is ours, too. His rage is our rage against our presence here.

He has put our dignity on display for all to see, and even as we cringe at his spewings we hear the echo of our frustrations. The old man is our badge of helplessness. We stand naked in his presence: with compassion for him but a degrading hatred for our own lives . . . reduced to this.

His days spent in frustration span more than forty years. His will is cemented.

Perhaps he has made an easy mockery of us after all. For he sits in the sun, and he smiles and recalls another time, and he makes us uncomfortable.

He is the bone marrow of the cancer called prison.

—A.P.

19

Escape

. . . inevitableness of Destiny can only be illustrated in terms of human life by incidents which in fact involve unhappiness. For it is only by them that the futility of escape can be made evident in the drama.

—ALFRED N. WHITEHEAD

Imprisonment is fraught with sights and sounds calculated to frighten the imprisoned. Yet there is a host of nameless fears inherent in the loss of one's freedom about which little is known.

One of them—the fear of death—is something that you will seldom hear inmates discuss. But if my own experience is in any degree universal—and I believe it is—then the fear of dying while imprisoned dogs the step of every man who is confined—especially those beyond thirty years of age.

I'm not now referring to being pushed off one of the upper tiers of a cellhouse or the sudden death that comes with the thrust of a homemade knife in the hand of a psychopath. I'm referring to the fear prisoners have of the death that results from cancer, leukemia, or one of the many nonterminal, yet chronic, illnesses that can eventually take the life of the afflicted—particularly when he is in prison and denied competent medical care.

So, how does a prison inmate who is serving ten, twenty, or thirty years cope with these fears of dying in prison—especially after he begins to say to himself: "Let's see, I'm thirty-six now and I don't appear before the parole board for another seven years and that will make me forty-three . . . and, if I don't make parole then I'll be forty-four when I see the board again. Damn! That's how old Jim was when he died of a heart attack, and I've been having chest pains myself lately. Better go to the hospital—no, I can't do that, look what they did to Charlie. . . . And then, sooner or later, as it did with me in May of 1962, the possibility of escape emerges. I say emerges because most men at least subconsciously entertain the possibility of escape from the very moment of their arrest. All that's required to nurture that thought into an obsession is time. And worry. And yes, the fear of dying in prison. It's a frightening thought, one that can take possession of a man and cause him to commit all manner of irrational acts.

I didn't seriously consider escaping from prison until Christmas of 1961, when I had already served thirty months of a ten- (flat) year sentence. And perhaps I wouldn't have considered it even then had I not myself begun to entertain thoughts of ill health and what a terrible thing it would be to die in prison.

My notion was to find a way to scale the forty-foot walls that surround this century-old prison, but because I had no Jacob's ladder and wanted to make it *sans* bullet-holes, I soon discarded that idea.

It then occurred to me that if I played my cards right and conned Classification Director Harold K. Joyce—who had previously been the witch doctor (Protestant minister) here—I just might gain trusty status and be transferred to work outside the walls.

Because of my past record and long FBI file of so-called violent crimes (mostly armed robberies), it took several months and some real convincing. But on May 1, 1962, I was finally granted trusty status and assigned as the barber for the sixty inmates who worked and lived at the Summit Dairy Farm, located some ten miles from the prison proper. To my surprise and disappointment, however, I learned upon my arrival there that the large brick dormitory had barred windows, locked (solid steel) doors and that in my job as barber, I would be under the eyeball of "the man" most of the time. In addition, the dormitory was surrounded by a ten-foot woven-wire fence, topped with three strands of ugly barbed wire.

Now mind you, I had not only spent thirty-four months inside the walls, I had also spent six months in the Vanderburgh County Jail in Evansville, Indiana, prior to being sent to state prison. As a result, I was out of shape physically. Consequently, I spent the first week on the Summit farm tuning up, so to speak, for my bid for freedom. I did push-ups and walked round and round the fenced-in enclosure.

On May 15, I was ready to make my play. But instead of running for the fence in broad daylight, as others had in the past, I waited for the cover of darkness, which would make pursuit by the guards and dogs more difficult.

Normally the guards change shifts at 11 P.M.. Then, at about a quarter past, the new guard makes his bed check to be sure everyone is present and accounted for.

After this bed check, I slipped out with my clothing on and followed the guard into the kitchen. I gave him just enough time to seat himself and begin reading a girlie book before I eased up behind him and laid my straight razor on his throat.

"Oh, my God!" he said, "Why'd it have to be me!"

After admonishing him to be very, very quiet, I took him to the basement and tied him up. When I saw how he was shaking, I put my razor away and assured him that he had absolutely nothing to fear so long as he cooperated and remained quiet. Which he did.

After I had tied him securely I went upstairs, cut the telephone line, unlocked the heavy steel door with his key, and let myself out. Then, avoiding a roving armed guard, I scaled the fence. In the process, I completely severed one of the veins on the back of my left hand and lost a pound of hide from sundry parts of my anatomy. But at the moment I didn't feel a thing.

"At last I'm free!" I ran like hell until I had crossed a toll road about a half-mile from the dormitory. At that point, I stopped long enough to cover my shoes with lighter fluid, which I thought would throw off the dogs. I also covered my tracks with black pepper from a tobacco sack.

Because it was one of those moonless nights and I was thoroughly unfamiliar with the countryside, I fixed my "compass" on an airplane beacon some distance to the east and kept away from all roads and railways. The going was slow and, because of briers, ditches, and electric cattle fences, painful. Once I even considered turning back and giving myself up, until I imagined the kind of reception I might get.

By sunrise the next morning I had traveled several miles and was much in need of water and rest. A small patch of woods up ahead looked cool and inviting—and it would hide me from the prying eyes of shotgun-packing farmers and low-flying state police planes equipped with high-powered binoculars.

As it turned out, my Shangri-La was without drinking water but, thankfully, the underbrush was full of wild strawberry plants that were heavy with ripe, lush fruit no larger than blackberries. Ummmm! They were delicious!

When I had eaten my fill, I found a likely spot near the base of a large white oak tree, an ideal place to conceal myself should anyone approach and a fine place to bed-down for a while. But when I found myself unable to sleep—I was much too tense—I began searching for a spider's web, which I knew from experience would stop the bleeding of my injured hand.

Sometime during the afternoon I slept, dreaming of what might have been, with phenomenal good fortune, might be: *As a result of having done all the right things, I was an eminently successful author of several best-selling books and was being courted by publishing houses and film companies for my next project. . . . I had just bought a $100,000-home in San Francisco for my wife, daughter and myself—and another smaller but no less pretentious one for my mother . . . yes, and then a private plane—a jet. . . . I was in New York . . . had a bachelor's apartment there . . . I called it my Shangri-La—my place to be alone and write—and play . . .* And, then I awoke with a start.

It was almost dark. It took a few seconds for me to get my bearings. After remaining motionless for several more seconds, hearing only the chirp of a cricket, I lit a cigarette and inhaled deeply. The taste of the smoke reminded me that I hadn't had a drink of water in nearly twenty-four hours. I didn't realize how stiff I had become until I stood and stretched. Every muscle and nerve in my body rebelled against the prospect of another long night of cross-country walking. But there was no other way, so I began to move.

I loosened up and, although I was thirsty, I soon felt fine. So, I lengthened my stride and quickened my step in order to put at least another ten miles between me and the prison farm.

By morning I had come onto the outskirts of a small farm community where I found a water spigot in the freight yards. After about a half-hour there, I hopped aboard a boxcar of an eastbound freight train and felt my spirits rise as the speed of the train increased. Like the man said in the song, "I was movin' on!"

By midafternoon I was in Fort Wayne, Indiana, where I hocked my wristwatch—a solid gold Bulova that I had paid $130.00 for—for five bucks. From there I went to a Salvation Army store and bought a pair of slacks for fifty cents and a sport shirt for a quarter. After wearing those convict clothes, I felt like a fashion plate.

It is almost axiomatic that if an escaped prisoner in this country wants to remain at large, he must go to work, not frequent bars, and stay out of automobiles. Yet who but a hermit wants to live like one?

Within days I had an automatic pistol (yes, I know, an automatic is a pistol) and was up to no good again. Almost as quickly, I was arrested again for robbing a loan company in Rockford, Illinois. As a result, I served five years in the Menard Branch of the Illinois Penitentiary before being returned here under guard. No, there was no red carpet rolled out for me . . . only an old, thin, greasy-looking mattress in solitary confinement and the loss of three years and four months statutory good time.

If this story has a moral, I suppose it is that going over a prison wall or a barbed-wire fence is only the first— and perhaps the smallest—hurdle for an imprisoned man. After that he must free himself of a host of socially imposed mores and inhibitions that keep him on edge and looking over his shoulder. And that, dear reader, is not freedom!

—H.J.G.

Be out.

Not get out, but be out.

That is the essence of the daydream that pacifies most of us who are doing time. We think of how it was when we were free and how it will be when we are out again, but most of us avoid the uncertainty of how and when we are to get out. There are a few who appeal their cases and hope to be released through court order, but the majority count on the mercy (not justice) of the parole board. Other than dying, the only remaining way out is to escape.

Hollywood portrays an escape artist as a cunning organization expert who enlists the aid of dozens of cons from various departments in a complicated maneuver designed to avoid the close scrutiny of the alert guard staff.

It just ain't so.

First of all, there is very little artistry involved in the average escape. A con keeps his nose clean long enough to warrant trusty status, is transferred to an outside assignment, and simply walks away. There are exceptions, even from outside assignments, but the majority of escapes are simply walk-aways. Secondly, if a con involves more than a very few of his close friends in his escape plans, he will be snitched out before he gets out. Thirdly, both "close scrutiny" and an "alert guard staff" are almost nonexistent. The guards inside the walls spend more time watching for a con to steal a sandwich than they do watching for an escape.

The day that three cons climbed atop a building, threw a board against the wall, and climbed over at high noon—right beside the front gate, right under the main guard tower—and scampered right across the warden's front lawn, that day four white caps were busy setting a trap on the back street to catch the dangerous criminal who had been tossing steaks over the back gate of the messhall. And at the same time, the deputy warden of custody was industriously escorting a "federal man," who had come to inspect the prison's security measures, through the cellhouses.

For days after the escape the newspapers were full of reports concerning the alleged demotion of one deputy warden, the transfer of another, plus the suspension of several guards who were negligent. That was three years ago, and all the employees are still here with the exception of one captain who retired about a year after the escape.

The desire to escape from this prison was with me even before I got here. As soon as I learned that I might get a life sentence, my fantasies of escape began. Those fantasies have continued, with varying degrees of intensity, to this day. And I accomplished this feat on one memorable occasion.

During my first few months here, I frantically searched for a hole. In fact, I almost made my own hole in the Admission and Orientation unit where I was held for about three months. Another con and I spent as much time as possible chipping away at a brick wall that, once removed, would allow us to emerge on a level with the top of the wall and directly under a guard tower. We were on the final layer of brick when we were both routinely assigned to jobs in the population and transferred to a regular cellhouse.

As soon as I became involved in the daily routine of prison (playing football, studying, going to the movies, etc.), I begin to rationalize about escaping. I remembered what my court-appointed attorney said when I asked him if a lifer had to do a certain number of years before he could be released. He stated that, considering my youth (twenty-two) and the fact that I hadn't killed anyone (my charge was Inflicting an Injury During the Commission of a Robbery), I should be released in five or six years if I kept my nose clean. When I pressed him about how many years the law required, he replied that there was no certain number of years and went on to tell of someone doing a double life sentence who had recently been released from here in six years.

I bought it. The man was a *bonà fide* attorney-at-law.

Surely he knew the law on how much time a man had to serve on a given charge before he was eligible for parole.

After those first few months, I tried to settle down and keep my nose clean so I could go home in five or six years. The only good that came of my naïveté was about two years of doing time in sweet, blissful ignorance of how long I was actually going to have to vegetate in this cage.

My coat was pulled gradually by a few well-meaning friends and by observing the many "long-timers" in here. I began to notice the numbers on the jackets of different cons and found that there were many men in here with over thirty years served. My prison number is 30650, so when I spotted a con wearing number 4445, I couldn't resist checking his packet. He had been here fifty years without parole. It was about this time too that the prison newspaper published a list of the average time served at ISP for the various life-sentence crimes. The *average* time served for Inflicting an Injury was seventeen years.

Even now, though, as I look back on my court-appointed attorney's statement concerning how much time I would have to serve, I don't feel that he intentionally lied to me. The dumb sonofabitch probably didn't know any better.

I started looking for a hole again. And wondering how I was possibly going to exist for fifteen or twenty years in this place without losing complete touch with reality. I knew it could be done because I saw men in here who had done it, but I didn't like what I saw. Their contact with reality was strictly limited to this prison—to the petty, conniving, ass-kissing, snitching ways of the Indiana State Prison. It made me wonder if it was worthwhile to survive for twenty years. I still wonder.

The "hole" that I eventually decided to try for was one of the many trips being made outside the walls by various groups in the institution. I was already playing part-time in the band and wrestling. Both of those groups were traveling. I think I went that route because it was the easy way and because I really had no other hope of being allowed to travel. It gave me an excuse not to make a ladder or dig a tunnel as I knew I should have been doing. But it was so easy to fall into the simple routine of the prison and forget about freedom while I kept telling myself that I was just waiting on a chance to make a trip with one of the traveling groups. My fantasies of escape included a pistol in each hand, a boss short under my ass, and several thoroughly corrupt young trim at my side. I would terrorize the countryside and never be taken alive. But of course, neither would I die.

It didn't quite work out that way.

One day after I had served about four years, the clerk in the band room added my name to a trip list, and to everyone's amazement, Warden Lane approved me without even calling me up to interview me. I couldn't believe it. I felt betrayed. Surely the warden knew how dangerous I was! Didn't he know I would be like a raving maniac on the loose? Well, too bad for him!

I began to plan my escape. I had only a few hours before I would be walking out that front gate. Another dim thought kept pushing its way to the front of my mind: If the warden had that much faith in me, if he could see that there was some good in me somewhere, surely someone on the parole board would eventually have equally perceptive vision. Surely.

I walked through the front gate at noon and loaded my drum onto the back of a low boy that would carry the prison band through Michigan City as just another unit in a parade of some sort. The joy of that temporary freedom was somewhat negated by my concern about how to turn it into permanent freedom. There was a guard in the cab of the low boy and two on the back with us. The parade route was lined with policemen. And besides that, no one, not a single person, offered me the pistols I would need.

The problem was solved for me at the high school which served as the marshaling area for the parade units. I was looking around for the best place to jump off the truck and just run like hell (fuck some strategy) when the guard tapped me on the shoulder and grunted, "Someone at da back a da truck wants to talk wit ya."

There, jumping up and down, full of joy and disbelief, about to pee on herself, was my mama.

She and my dad had driven up from Indianapolis to visit me and were told at the prison's reception desk that I was "downtown." Unable to understand how her son, who was doing a life sentence and had a detainer on him, could be "downtown," Mother suspected the prison authorities of having me locked away in some dungeon—chained, beaten senseless, and on my deathbed. (Once when she came to visit and I entered the visiting room with a two-month growth of beard, which was for a wrestling show, she was in tears by the time I walked the short distance up the aisle to meet her and said, "Son! What have they done to you?") At the reception desk, she demanded to know where I was "downtown." When she found out, nothing could keep her from coming. Naturally, that ended my escape plans for that day. If I had made the break, the police would have suspected my parents of aiding and abetting and picked them up. Even though I had disappointed them and caused them grief all my life, I couldn't subject them to that in-dignity.

After making that first trip, I began to hope again. I thought that surely after I traveled for a while and didn't escape, the parole board would realize that I could be trusted in society. Surely?

I was on the road for over a year with almost every group that traveled. I wrestled with the wrestling team, played drums with the band, took pictures for the chess team, and did a recorded play-by-play on the baseball and softball games. The most criminal thing on my mind during that period was stealing something to eat at every opportunity and staring at every broad with thoughts of lewd, lascivious conduct. Once, with the unofficial permission of the officer in charge (who shall of course remain nameless), my family picked me up in their car and took me to a Chinese restaurant for dinner. I had no thoughts of escape. I had no thoughts of returning to crime. I just had that foolish, naïve hope, faith even, that I would be released within ten years.

The illusion first began to go sour when I requested a transfer to a trusty assignment outside the walls. My nemesis, the Classification Committee, turned me down on the ground that I had a detainer on me. I had crossed a county line while committing the crime I am incarcerated for and different charges were filed against me in both counties. Even though I was given Life, the other county wouldn't drop their charges—as my court-appointed attorney had assured me they would. I had written and asked them to drop charges. I had written and asked them to try me. No answer either time. I have since learned that, because I am available for trial, they have denied my right to a speedy trial and therefore the detainer can be beat. But I didn't know that then.

I couldn't understand how Warden Lane could trust me to travel all over the state and those committee men couldn't trust me out the front gate. When I asked them about this, one of those brave souls replied that, just because the warden stuck his neck out didn't mean that they were going to.

I tried three times to change their minds. Three times

I asked them to believe in me and allow me to hope for a future. When they denied me the third time, they read a letter to me that said that because of the seriousness of the charge (kidnaping) the detainers would not be dropped. If I was ever paroled, it was to be to "wanting authorities."

That was hard enough to live with, but my rationalization process broke down completely when rumors began spreading that the governor was going to fire Warden Lane, that a new head of the department of correction was to be appointed, and that all traveling was going to stop. It began to be harder and harder to come back from each trip, knowing that each might be my last.

Finally, on December 23, 1965, after serving six and a half years, I simply walked away. No big deal. No complicated planning or strategy. No pistol in either hand, not even a sense of excitement. Just a sad anger, knowing that I was committing another blunder that would haunt me the rest of my life, but knowing too that I had to do it. Along with another inmate, I walked out of the door of the mental hospital where the band was playing. Within an hour we were in another state.

Within eight hours we had dined well (several times) and were comfortably resting in a motel somewhere in Ohio. Free at last! Living!

Within thirty hours we had foolishly argued with a drunken motel owner until it turned into a fight. The car we were driving had been stolen from us (goddamn joy-riding juvenile delinquents), I had been shot, and my partner had been assaulted by some people who no doubt called themselves law-abiding citizens (after he had been hand-cuffed by the police). Within forty-eight hours both of us were back behind bars. If Hollywood were to do the story of our escape it would surely have to be a musical comedy.

But all that was years ago. I'm not so naïve now as I was then. In fact, since I have ten years in now, I was called out by my counselor last week to give him information for my progress report. You see, I'll be appearing before the clemency board within a month of this writing (the department's policy is to allow all lifers to appear in ten years *if* they file papers), but I have no illusions about being released. I did casually ask my counselor if he had any predictions concerning my release. His candor was refreshing.

He counted on his fingers the number of years that these "law and order" Republicans have left to serve in this state's politics, then he added one to allow the Democrats to set me "just to make it look good." That came to a total of four more years. Hell, that's not half bad if it's true. I can make four more years. Surely he should know what he's talking about, a prison counselor. Surely?

—M.M.

20
Parole

We pardon to the degree we love . . .
—DE LA ROCHEFOUCAULD
Reflections

"Parole granted"—the most breathlessly anticipated phrase in the English language for more than 200,000 individuals now serving time in this nation's prisons. "Parole denied"—the most terribly feared phrase ever uttered to any of the same 200,000 individuals.

For those who walk out the door marked PAROLE BOARD with the longed-for phrase ringing in their ears, there is no mistaking the signs, although they assume many forms, from quiet inner glow and stunned puppet-like upturned mouth to loud hoots, clicking of heels, and clapping of hands.

And there is also no mistaking the signs when the echo of the feared-for phrase still reverberates in the ears of the rejected. Shock at first, followed by grief. All go through the shock phase. It lasts longer for some than others. But for all there is the sickening knot in the pit of the stomach, the dazed—I've been sledgehammered—expression, and the numbness from the neck up.

The parole function is little understood by everyone from the no-nothing troglodytes who cry out that parole boards are "releasing hordes of dangerous criminals to prey upon the public," to those most intimately concerned with the process—the prisoners themselves.

One constant confusion in the minds of many is the distinction between probation and parole. To many they are synonymous. Actually they are entirely different processes. Probation is a judicial decision by which a judge places an offender under the supervision of the court but does not send him to prison or jail. The basic element of probation—suspension of sentence—traces back to antiquity. Roman courts used it during the time of Christ, and the practice is recorded in English Common Law records dating as far back as the fourteenth century.

The modern element of the process—supervision of the offender—began in the U.S. with the work of a Boston shoemaker named John Augustus who began bailing out drunks, vagrants, prostitutes, and petty thieves from Boston's municipal court in 1841. He aided them in obtaining jobs, medical care, food, and lodging, and his home often contained upward of two dozen of his "wards." His record of success with the two thousand individuals he kept from going to jail was, I might add, better than that of most official court-associated probation departments of the nation today.

Parole differs from probation in that it is a process of releasing prisoners, under supervision, before the expiration of their maximum prison sentences. This is handled by an appointed board, not by the courts. Although both the probationer and the parolee have been convicted of a crime, and technically speaking are convicts, the probationer is not assigned by society the status-degradation appellation "convict" or "ex-con." This is reserved for those actually sent to jail or prison.

The word "parole" derives from the French and means "word" or "promise." For many centuries it had been used by the military in referring to the practice of releasing prisoners from custody on their word that they would not resume hostilities against their captors. "Parole" was not used in the penal or correctional sense until Samuel G. Howe, a penal reform advocate from Massachusetts, used it in 1845.

Parole is viewed by penologists and criminologists as a technique by which society can be protected and the offender given aid and supervision while re-integrating himself into the community from which he had been previously torn. Full jurisdiction is retained over the offender by the state, which can—at any time and without having to go through any judicial channels—remove the offender from the community and return him to prison.

The parolee is virtually a ward of the state. As such, he has no rights or privileges, which are not granted him by the state. And any rights or privileges so given can be taken back whenever the state deems it necessary.

When released on parole, the offender signs a parole agreement, in effect a contract, under the terms of which he must live while in the community. An estimated 15 to 20 per cent of all parolees are returned to prison for technical violations, that is to say, violations of these agreed-upon rules.

The parole rules govern the individual's place of abode, his employment, his associations and habits, and his movements within the community. Should a man have special problems he will have special rules. If the man is an alcoholic who has a history of getting into trouble because of drinking, he will not be able to drink while on parole. If the man is an addict, he will be instructed that any use of drugs while on parole will mean his return to prison.

It is assumed, and rightly so in many cases, that by returning these men for technical violations, the society is heading off potentially more dangerous forms of behavior. This is one of the major tenets of the whole philosophy of parole. Checked, supervised, and in some cases guided and assisted in readjustment, the offender is far less dangerous to the society should he be unreformed, than he would be if released from prison with no supervision. Thus it is obvious that the society should demand that all offenders be released on parole and under supervision. Unfortunately, this is not the case.

There are many critics of parole board policies in this country—the general public, the police, the courts and the prisoners themselves. The boards pay a lot of attention to the criticisms of the general public and none to those of the prisoners. All parole boards are extremely sensitive to the miasma which fills the air when they make a mistake in judgment. All parole boards possess acutely sensitive antennas for sensing political vibrations that sweep down from the state capital. They are on the one hand very timorous bodies but, on the other, too, often subjected to completely illogical, unjustified, and unfair criticism.

It was Chief Justice Earl Warren who succinctly stated one of the major problems facing parole boards when he said, " . . . unfortunately for parole, it is one of those terminal procedures which must absorb most of the criticism for the failure of the intermediate agencies leading up to it." The family, the schools, the community, the police, the courts, and the prison have not done their job. But they drop the whole problem in the arms of the parole board.

Much of the public's criticism of the parole board stems from those ex-cons who again run afoul of the law. Since newspaper editors are acutely aware of the value of sensationalism in selling papers, they rub their hands with glee when an ex-con commits a crime. The headline too often reads PAROLEE ARRESTED FOR. . . . This is often the case even though the man was not on parole at all but had served his maximum sentence without ever being granted a parole.

What the public never learns is that the great bulk of men on parole make good and are eventually discharged from their sentence. The rate of recidivism is much higher among those men who have never been granted a parole but have been made to serve out their maximum sentences.

I am sure that the people of the state of Michigan would not be too happy to learn that between 1939 and 1959 the Michigan parole board released 164 convicted murderers. But out of that 164, only four had to be returned as parole violators, and only one of them for committing a new crime. That means roughly a 2.5 per cent failure rate. Ninety-seven and a half per cent were successful. Yet if just *one* of those 164 convicted murderers had committed a sensational new crime, I know what the headlines would have read. The parole board would have been savagely attacked by the press and the public for "turning killers loose wholesale."

It's a well-known fact among all prisoners, prison officials, and parole board members that the man serving time for murder is the best parole risk you can get. If they were to release every man serving time for murder in this country, not one out of a thousand would ever commit another murder in his lifetime, not one out of a hundred would ever commit another crime of any kind, and less than 4 per cent would be returned as parole violators. What is it then that keeps so many of these men in prisons for so long a period of time? Potential public reaction. Fear of public reaction is why thousands of men are forced to serve thirty, forty, or fifty years in our prisons. A large percentage of them die there.

But 95 per cent of the men now in our prisons will

eventually be released to the community. The public has two choices here. Either it desires that all men serve their maximum sentences without parole, thus providing no incentives for good conduct, or the public desires that the majority of men be offered parole, with all the incentives that eligibility involves. If the public fights against a liberal parole policy, the prisons will turn out dehumanized men who most certainly will return to crime in a large percentage of cases. They will also be extremely hard to manage while inside our prisons. What have they got to lose? If the public supports a liberal parole policy, releasing men under supervision and guidance instead of turning them loose at random, prisoners and community alike benefit.

Parole involves two distinct stages. The first is *selection* of inmates to be paroled, and the second involves the *supervision* of these men once they are released. In this country selection is the province of a board of parole, a quasijudicial function performed as part of the executive arm of the government. Supervision is a bureaucratic function of that same executive arm.

Selection is based on two factors—eligibility and suitability. Usually a minimum amount of time has to be served by a prisoner, as provided by statute, before he is eligible for parole. The date of eligibility is a factor involved in the sentencing procedure and fixed by the courts. There are exceptions to this general rule in a few states.

Suitability is the tricky problem, the horn of the dilemma for both offender and parole board. How do you judge suitability? What factors should be considered, and how much weight should be given to the different factors considered? This is, without any doubt, the hottest issue debated in every yard and cellhouse of every prison in the country.

The prisoners ask themselves such questions as: What

does the parole board look for in a man when they consider him for parole? How much weight will be given to my past record? Why do they select Jones and reject Smith when they are both in on the same charge and have almost identical past records?

Many experts in the fields of penology and criminology, both highly educated professionals and those who have come up through the ranks, advocate releasing an offender when he is "ready." That is to say, at the precise moment when he seems most likely never again to commit a crime. As the prison yard scuttlebutt has it, the precise moment is a delicate balance between how many pounds of flesh the society will be satisfied with and the point where the man becomes so embittered that he will be extremely dangerous if *ever* released (although he *must* be released when his sentence expires).

There seems to be a large percentage of experts who believe there is a release time of maximum advantage for both offender and society, a time when the man is psychologically and motivationally ready. This "best time" varies with the individual. To keep a man beyond this "best time" is to reduce his chances of success in proportion to the length of additional time served.

Do I believe this? Yes, with additional corollaries. I know that at least 75 per cent of the men in prisons do not have to be there. They are not violence-prone and can be handled in a safer manner, more cheaply, and much much more successfully in the community. I also know that for a lot of men who come to prison, the "best time" to let them go is within a few weeks or months after they arrive (of course this never happens). Because I know what the prison environment does to a man, I take the position that the faster society gets him out of that environment the better, for the man and for the society.

It seems to me that the parole board should be on the

side of leniency for the following reason. If a man is held within the degrading, dehumanizing, all-corrupting atmosphere of our nation's prisons any longer than is absolutely necessary, that man is being greatly damaged and so is the society. For he becomes less and less a human being with every dreary day, week, month, and year he is confined.

It never fails to surprise me when I read about some "mad-dog" killer who is terrorizing a community and hear people expressing shock and bewilderment over his actions when it plainly states in the newspaper that the man had just been released from some prison after serving ten or fifteen years. I would venture to say that if you randomly selected a thousand men off the streets of any community in the country and placed them in the nearest state prison for a period of ten years, the following would be the result:

90 per cent of the married men would be divorced by their wives.

75 per cent of the men would find that even their own close relatives—sisters, brothers, sons, daughters—would stop communicating with them.

40 per cent of the men would become so inured to the prison way of life, so indoctrinated by the criminogenic outlook on life, that they would be future serious lawbreakers upon release.

80 per cent of them would become bitter, cynical, vengeful, petty individuals and remain so for the rest of their lives.

25 per cent would become so mentally and emotionally disabled that they would be unable to function as citizens and breadwinners upon return to the community.

This is just the way it is. And it is only an infinitesimal part of what our prisons do to the people in them. This just cannot be a deep, dark secret, known only to a few, any more than Hitler's crematoria and concentration camps were unknown to the people of Nazi Germany. The people know. They just don't give a damn. Or they want it that way.

So you see, it is not the physical isolation from the community, or the deprivation of creature comforts, or even the cruelty and sadism and indifference *per se* that hurts you half as much as the degradation and perpetual dehumanization. Too many men leave prison as zombies, not human beings. That is why I think that the faster you can get a man out, the better for both the man and the society.

Parole boards should not have the power to keep an offender in prison for a disproportionately long period of time beyond his minimum sentence on the highly speculative and purely intuitional ground that he represents a "poor parole risk." Being a "poor parole risk" means being an individual whom the parole board believes will probably either violate the rules of his parole agreement or eventually commit a new crime. OK, so with the mere passage of time, as that same "poor parole risk" remains in prison, does he become a better parole risk? Or release risk? How ridiculous. Maybe, just maybe, it would be different if prisons helped people, but only a liar or a fool or an ignoramus would say that they do.

Some parole board members go along with the concept of readiness, but they immediately pose a difficult question, one which has not been satisfactorily answered by those who advocate the readiness concept. How do you determine *when* a particular individual is ready?

An examination of parole decisions suggests that selection for parole is made in terms of estimations not so much of an offender's "readiness" or chances for success as of his chances for failure. This shift of emphasis from positive to negative considerations suggests that parole decisions relate too often to considerations unrelated to the offender's "readiness," motivational state, or personal adjustment, and clearly states that the basic objective is to minimize risks of failure instead of increasing the number of offenders able to profit.

The easiest way for a parole board to increase its "batting average" is to give paroles only to those who are sure to make good and reject all doubtful cases. But this means rejecting for parole a large amount of cases where the men would make good.

So the parole decision becomes an estimate of the likelihood that a given man will or will not increase the board's failure rate. As such it is a measure of the individual board member's confidence in his own ability to judge and has very little to do with what the prisoner has been trying to do for himself or the circumstances of his case. This is a long way from selecting for parole because of positive value judgments based on the convict's background, ability, and state of mind, or his welfare in general.

This brings us to some very serious gripes concerning variables used in parole decisions. The first concerns the amount of weight given that variable called "past record." The gripe is based on the fact that about three quarters of the men in any prison have a previous record and the parole board considers this *the* most important variable to be considered in granting a parole. What is so frustrating to men who keep getting rejected for parole because of "past record" is that there is obviously nothing that the individual can do about it. It cannot be changed, it cannot be expunged. It therefore generates a feeling of helplessness and frustration, especially in men who take seriously what they are told about rehabilitation and perfect institutional records. These men cannot understand the rationale behind parole denials based on past records if the major goal of the correctional system is rehabilitation and if they have tried to take advantage of every rehabilitation program offered by the institution. The men know that merely serving another two or five years is not going to alter or expunge the past record and it is not going to further the "rehabilitative" process. Their realization must be that rehabilitation is meaningless, and punishment pure and simple is the goal of the parole board.

The second gripe is closely related to the first. It is that both the offender and the parole board know that to turn down parole on the basis of low probability of success is not the way to reduce over-all recidivism rates. For if a man has a low probability of success, he will eventually have an even lower probability of success if *not* paroled. In fact, he may eventually be released with absolutely no supervision or aid, after spending an additional number of years in an environment which is hardly conducive to a healthy mental state.

Parole boards know this, but they usually answer that their principal duty is the protection of society, not the well-being of the offender. Inmates, and a large percentage of penologists and correctional officials, answer in turn that keeping a man in prison is at best only a short-term protection. Many men are much more dangerous to the society when finally released after long years in prison. In reality, parole boards are doing a greater disservice to society by keeping men in prison too long.

A third gripe among prisoners is that parole boards are too easily influenced by pressures put upon them by any number of sources: letters written to the parole board by police and prosecutors in which possible parole for a man is opposed; newspaper editorials and letters to the editor opposing a certain individual's parole or opposing parole in general for all incarcerated men; pressure from victims. One such victim was the Cook County druggist robbed of $143. At the trial, when asked to point out the robber, the druggist mistakenly pointed to a police officer. In spite of this, another man was subsequently convicted and sentenced to prison. The druggist sent letters to the parole board instructing the parole board to notify him if the man ever came up for parole so that he, the druggist, could make a personal appearance before the board to argue against release.

Pressures also come from the attitude of local politicians and lawmakers, financial problems of the state, the budget for the corrections department, and whether the prison is overcrowded or has plenty of empty cells. None has a bearing upon any concept of justice or fairness. If the man in the executive mansion is a "lawnorder" advocate, the parole board either sniffs at the prevailing political wind and decides discretion is the better part of you know what, or it is told by the governor or one of his aides to tighten up the reins. If the prison warden feels that too much pressure is building up because of overcrowding or because the parole rejection rate is too high, the parole board will often loosen up for a few months in order to let a little steam out of the pressure cooker before it blows. Parole boards and wardens alike fear the investigations that follow prison riots. When prisoners see such pressures determining parole policies they just become a little more cynical, a little more bitter.

The chaotic, erratic nature of sentencing for criminal offenses in this country adds much to the problems of release on parole. It has been criticized continually for decades by judicial congresses, bar associations, and other interested groups, but nothing is ever done about it. The same offense can get you six months in the county jail in one part of the state and twenty years in prison in another part of the state. Is this a major gripe among convicts? You bet it is. Take a look at a typical case.

Wallace B, a thirty-five-year-old three-time loser for burglary out of Detroit walked into the state prison of southern Michigan with a two-to-five-year sentence for his fourth burglary conviction. There he met Larry C, who had just arrived with a ten-to-fifteen-year sentence for burglary. Larry was only nineteen, a first offender who should have received probation. But he made the mistake of burglarizing a gas station in the boondocks of rural Michigan, receiving a minimum sentence five times larger than the professional burglar and a maximum three times as great. Larry committed a felony in a small town, and the eighteenth-century minds of the community crawled out from under their rocks and saw to it that Larry "got what he deserved."

Now, undoubtedly the parole board is not going to release Wallace B at the end of his two-year minimum since he is now a four-time loser. But he can serve his entire sentence and still beat Larry C out by five years. When Larry finally staggers in to see the parole board, after his ten-year minimum is up, he will have been lost forever to his family, his friends, and the society. And Larry is very likely to want to make "someone" pay. Every month or so, for the whole ten years, he is going to run into a guy in the yard who is doing time for burglary and getting out long before Larry. The salt will be rubbed deeply into the wound, and Larry is going to get very bitter. He is probably never even going to try to "go straight."

What is the parole board going to do with the Larrys in our prisons? And they abound. After a year or two they might want to release him, but they cannot. The court has set his minimum term as ten years, and the parole board cannot assume jurisdiction until the minimum term expires.

All this is a major source of bitterness and disillusionment for prisoners because they take seriously the admonitions to strive for the goals held out to them. They soon find out that they have been fooled, tricked. Good conduct or learning a trade will not get them a parole. Most will be rejected for "previous record." And when they do get out, the goals to which they have been enjoined to aspire are largely unavailable. Unions will not let them in, employers will not hire them, they are discriminated against by the community. It would be far better not to promise these men anything at all than to make offers which the society and its representatives in the prison and on the parole board have no intention of keeping.

Another question that needs serious study and a definite answer is whether an offender should have the right of appeal of a parole board decision. Such an appeal might take the form of an open hearing in the court of original jurisdiction, with the offender having the right to employ legal counsel or other specialized assistance to challenge or rebut the findings of the board.

More than sixty years ago, a young man in the British Parliament by the name of Winston Churchill delivered a statement which is as apropos to the topic of parole as it is to our entire penal system. He said:

> The mood and temper of the public with regard to the treatment of crime and criminals is one of the most unfailing tests of the civilization of any country. A calm, dispassionate recognition of the rights of the accused, and even of the convicted criminal against the state—a constant heart-searching by all charged with the duty of punishment—a desire and eagerness to rehabilitate in the world of industry those who have paid their due in the hard coinage of punishment; tireless efforts toward the discovery of curative and regenerative processes; unfailing faith that there is a treasure if you can find it in the heart of every man. These are the symbols which, in the treatment of crime and criminal, mark and measure the stored up strength of a nation and are sign and proof of the living virtue in it.

Out of 8241 offenders sentenced in England during the year, only 2 persons received a sentence of over ten years. That works out to .2 of 1 per cent. I wonder how civilized the English consider their American cousins?

—E.T.

21

The Ex-Con

The descent to hell is easy
    The gates stand open day and night
But to reclimb the slope
    And escape to the upper air
This is labor. . . .

                —VERGIL
              Aeneid, VI

Hi, Joe! What's that? No kidding? You made parole. Congratulations. When are you leaving? Soon as you get a job and place to live, eh? Well, Joe, that may take a little time. You don't have anyone out there to give you a job, do you? I didn't think so. It's awful nice out there in the free world, Joe, but life ain't no bed of roses for the ex-con. What do I mean? Got a while? Sit down, Joe, and I'll explain some of the facts of life to you.

You see, Joe, you're a convicted felon. Know what *that* means? It means you've been tried, convicted, and sentenced for a crime, a felony. What is it? Oh, burglary. OK, and now you've done your time and are going back into the community. That's fine, Joe, but you're a convicted felon.

That means a whole helluva lot of things. Means you've been labeled, stamped "defective," branded for the rest of your life. They've put you into a bin marked "scrap material," and they're never going to let you forget it. You've heard that old saw about paying your debt to society? Well forget it, Joe, because as far as the vast majority of people in the society is concerned you'll never be able to pay that debt.

Now when you get off parole you can write the governor and ask him to restore your civil rights. And he will. That means you can vote. But that's all you get back, Joe. All the rest of the barriers and obstacles are still up to constantly remind you that "Ex-Con" is indelibly stamped after your name.

In most of these United States an ex-con can never hold public office, Joe. And almost all professions are closed to you. Did you ever hear of an ex-con law enforcement officer, judge, university professor, schoolteacher, lawyer, physician, or accountant? How about an ex-con governor, mayor, senator, or representative? Yah, I know about that guy in Massachusetts, but he had been in office for years before they nailed him. Besides, how long was he on the scene afterwards?

Sure, I know you don't plan on running for President, Joe, but just hear me out, will you? Now you'll find that every state and local government has different laws and customs and practices on the subject of ex-cons. Some places an ex-con can't charter a corporation, other places they won't give you a barber's license, and in still others they won't let you run a public business like a restaurant. You see, any time you need a license for anything and you are an ex-con, you're in trouble.

What'd you say, Joe? A tavern? Forget it. You can't get a license to sell liquor or beer in this state or in any other state that *I* know of. Oh, you used to be an automobile salesman, eh? I think you better look for something else, Joe. You know you have to be bonded. And what bonding company is going to take you on, even if your boss will?

You see, Joe, if you figure it out, about 50 per cent of the jobs and occupations in this country are barred to you by law or practice because of your record. Rule out jobs in local, state, or national government, civil service jobs, the armed forces, all jobs involving a security clearance no matter how low. Add to that all public utilities such as light, power, gas, and phone. Then there are the professions and jobs dealing with the public where you're required to be licensed by any government authority. Top it off with any job that involves trust and the handling of money, and for the cherry, any job in which you need to be bonded. There you have it, Joe. A minimum of half the jobs in the country are automatically and forever out of bounds for you.

You might think that blue-collar jobs would be open to you, Joe, but an awful lot of them aren't. For example, hundreds of thousands of blue-collar jobs are in industries handling defense contracts. That means a security clearance. Almost all truck drivers and deliverymen are bonded today, as are many warehouse men. Did you know that the FBI gets over ten million requests for fingerprint checks every year from employers?

Remember Richie? Locked over in 5 Block? He used to be a schoolteacher downstate, District 37. When he left here he tried to get work again as a teacher. No go, Joe. He's working for his brother-in-law as a plumber's helper. He can't get back into the profession because he's an ex-con.

I don't think you knew Smithy. He left before you got here. Smithy really tried to improve himself while he was here. Studied real estate for two years and took correspondence courses from the university. He's selling books door to door now. Encyclopedias or something. You see, he couldn't get a broker's license from the state, and he couldn't work as a salesman because they wouldn't bond him.

OK, OK, so all you want is a job, period. How many letters have you written out of here asking for a job? Twenty-three, eh? How many answers have you received? Four. That's very good, considering. Any of them offer you a job? I didn't think so. Look, Joe, your letter comes into some personnel office. They open it. Right away they see that little black box for your number and that heavy black line at the top that reads STATE PRISON. In the left-hand corner is the censor's stamp, and then the paragraph concerning rules and regulations for correspondence with prisoners. Well, they may read it out of curiosity and pass it around the office for a laugh. But you're not getting any job, Joe. You're labeled, pigeonholed, stigmatized. And if there was some guy in that office who was sympathetic, what the hell can he do? He's only an employee himself and has to hire according to the guidelines set up by management, doesn't he? How many businessmen do you know that will hire a person through the mail, sight unseen, and from prison as well? See the odds you are bucking, Joe?

Now one way a lot of guys get a job from prison is to have a friend or relative go to bat for them. They go to their boss or someone they know and say, look, my son, or my brother-in-law, or my nephew, is getting out of jail. He made a mistake, but he's really a good boy, and a good worker too. How about it? Can you give him a job? That's how a lot of 'em get jobs.

And sometimes they have to go to a friend or employer and say, look, just *say* you'll give the guy a job. Write a letter to the parole board and tell them you'll hire him. Then when he gets out he can get a job of his own. Sure, that works sometimes, Joe, because you can always find *some* kind of work, even if it's washing dishes, once you are out on the bricks. It's the getting *out* that's rough.

What if you don't have anyone out there to intercede for you? Then it's rough, Joe. Not just in this state but in a lot of 'em. Guys have made parole and are still inside six months, a year, or more later because they can't get a job from inside. And I'm talking now about guys that are young and in good health. What does a guy do if he's like fifty or sixty years old? He rots, that's what he does. He slowly goes batty.

You know that 90 per cent of the guys in here have no trade, no real marketable skills. What can they do that millions of other guys already out there and with no record can't do? So maybe you're fifty years old, have no trade, and are an ex-con too. What kind of future do you think you'd have, Joe? A few of 'em are taken out of here by Sally—the Salvation Army—or by a minister who'll let the guy sweep up around the church in exchange for room and board. But so many of them just rot in prison, Joe. You see that old guy sitting by the wall playing checkers. Yah, that's the one. He's sixty-seven years old. Can go out any time he finds a job and a place to stay. Been eligible for release for two years, but he'll die here. That's what I said, Joe, die here. Sad, ain't it?

It's like that all over too, with a few exceptions. A few states will let you go out without a job if you have money in the bank, or if you're going to live with your parents and they say they'll take care of you until you get on your feet. And a few states have established what they call halfway houses where a guy can go after he gets the green light from the parole board. You live under supervision in these halfway houses, put on a suit during the day, and go out job hunting on your own. It's a fine idea, Joe, but it only affects like 1 or 2 per cent of the country's prison population. California, Michigan, Wisconsin, and Minnesota have this type of program, and the Feds too.

Then there's what they call the work-release program. That's designed especially for guys with families, you know, costing the state a lot of aid money. So they let the guy leave the joint to go out to work and come back each night after work. Then he can support his family while he's doing time. I guess it cuts down on a lot of nonsupport cases, huh?

Of course if you don't have a big family, or if you are doing more than a few years' sentence, or have a long record, or are in for a serious crime, well, you don't make the work-release program. I talked with a guy from your home state the other day, and he tells me that they have had a work-release program on the books for about two years now and maybe fifty guys have been eligible for it. In the last two years that state has processed like six thousand or seven thousand cons and only approved fifty for the work-release program. They screen them so good that if you make the work-release program you should never have been put in prison in the first place—you were already an A-number-one probation risk. Well, it's a start, Joe.

You've got a pretty good thing going, Joe. You're young and got some smarts. You even have a high school education, and that puts you in the top 10 per cent of the convict population. You even have some kind of job skill. Most of the guys in here have been ditch diggers, assembly-line workers, farm workers, waiters, dock workers, such like that. That's the old filtering process at work, Joe. The higher the socioeconomic class, the greater the education, the less it's going to be represented in prison. Most upper- and middle-class criminals are white collar. And the vast majority of white collar criminals don't even get into a courtroom. Out of those that do get hauled into court, a large percentage don't get convicted, and out of those that get convicted, a large percentage get put on probation. That leaves the slobs, Joe, like you and me. We're crude enough to use a crowbar or a pistol, or sleight of hand, instead of the more refined book juggling, misrepresentation, and under-the-table payoff for services rendered.

Now if you're out there on the bricks and looking for work, Joe, don't bother applying for any of those jobs I told you about and you'll save yourself a bundle of heartaches. Whenever you apply for any job, my advice is not to mention your record. That's right, lie to 'em. If they have a place on the employment application where it asks you if you've ever been convicted of a crime, put down N-O, no! If you don't, you're screening yourself out of 75 per cent of all jobs, and damned near 100 per cent of the better jobs. You have to look ahead too, Joe. Big Willie, the trustyland barber, has a brother working for one of the big steel companies. A friend got him the job, white collar too. That was seven, eight years ago. He's still on the same job, but guys who have only been with the company two or three years are moving right up the line to higher job classifications and better pay. Why? His boss told him why. He's got a record, and the company knows it because it's on his original employment application. His boss told him he was terribly sorry, that it wasn't his fault, but the higher-ups passed him up because fifteen years ago he served two years in prison. See, Joe, crime don't pay, because they ain't never going to let you up once they got you down. That's just the way it is.

Go ahead and tell 'em if you want to, Joe. You're taking a chance no matter what you do. If you tell 'em, you don't get the job most of the time. If you don't tell 'em, and they find out, they fire you. You know Louie, the cellhouse clerk? He got a job and didn't tell 'em about his record. Louie's parole officer came around checking on him and blowed the job for Louie. How do you like them apples?

And Gabby, the four block runner, went out and got a job that'll knock you out. He was hired as a credit investigator! Yah, handling confidential financial reports all day long. While he was still on parole too. His parole officer was an OK guy and said more power to 'em. Well, it took about two months because the employment application investigation isn't handled by regional offices but is done by the main office in New York. One day his boss calls him in, red-faced and all, and says to him, why didn't you tell us? Louie says, if I'd told you, would you have hired me? His boss says, of course not! Louie was canned.

Of course landing and keeping a job is only a small part of your problems, Joe. For example? For example, you have your parole officer to contend with, for the next couple of years. They're just like any other group of people, Joe. Some of them are nice guys, very sympathetic and willing to help you all they can. The majority of them are just people putting in their eight hours and look upon you as so much merchandise, so many crates of apples. They are the indifferent ones. Then there are the dogs, Joe. The dogs seem to hate the whole world and especially an ex-con. Some are ex-cops, and they think they are still on the force. Others are guys with eighteenth-century minds, troglodytes who creep out from under rocks and are naturally attracted to the job, as iron filings are attracted to magnets. Sure, they're definitely in the minority, but you gotta know they're out there. You might be unlucky enough to get one for your very own.

If you get one of these guys, Joe, he plays God. He can manipulate you like a puppet on a goddamn string. He'll tell you to be in by ten o'clock, he'll say you can't buy a car, or get credit anywhere, or drink a bottle of beer, or get married, or change your job, or leave the country, or be in the company of any disreputable people, or be caught in a bar or a whorehouse, or . . . well, these are the more or less standard rules, Joe, but your parole officer can make up as many rules as he wants. Maybe he's got a hangup on guarding the community against the likes of you. So you meet a girl, and you both want to get married. Your parole officer tells you to bring the girl into the office so he can talk to her. If he can't change the girl's mind, he contacts the girl's parents and warns them about you. If the parents won't block it, your parole officer says, I want you to wait six months, until you are in better financial condition. Sometimes he thinks you'll ruin the girl, and sometimes it's the other way around and he thinks the girl is no good for you. Maybe he thinks the girl's a whore or something.

Maybe he's got a hangup on late hours, and he says to you, be in by ten at night. That's curfew time, Joe. And so he'll call you at ten-thirty or eleven o'clock, and you better be home or he may send you back to prison. Send you back for two, three years for being out late, and you're a grown man. Absurd, Joe, that's what it is. Say you're making out with a girl, Joe, and it's almost score time, and it's like nine-thirty on a Saturday night. What are you going to do? You know damn well what you're going to do. So maybe you get home at midnight. Midnight, Joe, on a Saturday night. And the next morning your parole officer's got a warrant out for your arrest for parole violation. Bang. Back you come in chains.

Or maybe he's a bug on drinking and says to you, no drinking, period. So he comes by your place one night, and you're sitting there in front of the TV set, feeling no pain. Not bothering a soul, but with a half-empty bottle on the table. He walks in, and bang!

I'm not trying to scare you, Joe. I'm trying to tell you what can happen, because it has happened. Look at Timmy over there by the fence. Been back for almost a year now for having a few beers in a tavern. OK, OK, so he was warned twice by his parole officer. But does the punishment fit the so-called crime. A year in jail for having a couple of beers in a tavern?

Well, chances are you won't get that kind of parole officer, Joe, but you should know what some of 'em are like. Takes all kinds to make this world, kid.

What else? Plenty else, Joe. Say you leave here and go to the bigtown. Small towns are murder. You get into the city and get a place in a neighborhood where nobody knows you. But the cops know you, Joe. When you leave here the cops in the town you go to are sent a bulletin on you, and a fresh picture and set of prints. Also your address. The cops at headquarters send the information out to the local precinct, the one that covers your neighborhood. So the cops know you, Joe, and they keep a pretty good eye on you. That's their job. You've been sent down here for burglary. What happens when the grocery store down the block is broken into by neighborhood punks? You guessed it. They pick you up for questioning. You didn't do it, and maybe you convince them. After seventy-two hours they let you go. But now you've lost your job because you have not reported to work for three days and weren't able to make a phone call. What do the cops care. And your parole officer asks you what the hell are you doing getting picked up? Can't you keep out of trouble? OK, you get another job, maybe, and a few months later another place is broken into in the area, and it looks like your MO. Bang, they bust you. They smack you around a little to loosen you up, and tell you if you cop out they'll drop charges and just send you back as a parole violator. You scream, you holler. Your parole officer starts to think, where there's smoke, there's fire, and meanwhile you lost another job. The cops and the prosecutor see you as an easy conviction and you can clear up their books. If you get out of it, or if they happen to catch the guys that did it, you go out and try to get another job, if you can. It's a merry-go-round, Joe.

The cops. Well listen, Joe, police harassment is a very serious problem in some areas, and in other areas it's practically nonexistent. It all depends, like getting the right or wrong parole officer. You have to avoid areas where you will be harassed.

Then there are your friends and relatives to contend with. It's not just strangers who will discriminate against you. No indeed. Some of your so-called best friends will put you down like right now. Even relatives. Why, my own sister hasn't spoken to me in years. You see, Joe, most people have to have somebody to put down, somebody to feel superior to, and you're a natural. Society has singled you out as the schmoo that they all can legitimately kick around. You're an official whipping boy for all the "decent" and "upright" folks.

Guys you went to school with, worked with, were in the service with—many of them won't know you when you get out. Be careful about speaking to them first, or you'll be embarrassed more times than you can count. They'll cut you dead. No use telling 'em, hey, I'm the same old Joe you once knew. I just made a mistake, but I paid my debt. Forget it. You are not going to be able to wipe out the stigma. You will never pay off that "debt."

You'll find things have changed a lot, Joe. Lots of the people you knew have moved away, or gotten married, gone into the service, what have you. Out of those that are still around, some will snub you, and a lot of the others will feel uneasy in your presence, especially in public. Yah, it's a shame, Joe, but that's the way it is.

So you may be pretty lonely for a time after you get out, until you get in with a new set of friends. And of course you can always find companionship if you want it, in the person of an ex-con or a gangster. There are hundreds of ex-cons and thieves running around out there. But, Joe, it's better to be a loner until you can establish new friendships, than to start hanging around with a bunch of ex-cons and thieves. Sure, some of the ex's are going straight and wouldn't commit a jaywalking offense in your company. But there are always some that are not trying to straighten up. And they are always looking for rap buddies to share the danger, and later the time, when the old judge gets around to passing it out.

It's too easy for a couple of ex-cons to sit around feeling sorry for themselves and getting madder at the world with each passing day. Then, one day when your defenses are way down, maybe you're out of work and broke, and have lots of debts to pay, and—well, that's when you might take the first step, that first little job, and then you're on the old merry-go-round. One thing about the merry-go-round, Joe. Once you get on it, you can't get off. The "easy" money coming in, and going out, fast. It's as hard to get off that merry-go-round as it is for an alcoholic to stop after that first drink, or an addict after that first fix. You just can't take that first little step or you're lost. Choose your companions wisely, Joe. Look at me. I'm a living example of what I just told you. Started messing around with an ex-con after I'd been out for six months, and six months later, back I came.

Is that all? Hell no, that ain't all. But I guess that's all the major problems, except one. And that one is your biggest problem, Joe. What's that? It's *you,* Joe. Yah, your biggest problem will be you. I'm talking about the way you're thinking and acting when you go out of here. I'm talking about negative attitudes, thoughts about striking back at the society, chips on your shoulder. And I'm talking about the effect this rotten joint has had on your mind.

You know and I know that a prison never did anyone any good. Those that have come through here and never come back, they did it in spite of the system, not because of it. No one knows what the rate of return is in this country, because all the agencies that are supposed to tabulate such things keep such sloppy records that even the experts are confused. There's a reason for it too. The reason is that the correctional system is protecting itself from the wrath of the public. If accurate statistics were kept, and made public, something would be done. Maybe not much, but something. We'll take a generally agreed-upon figure of 60 per cent nationwide, and in some areas it's pushing 75 per cent. That's a terrifically high failure rate for the nation's "rehabilitation" institutions. The nation's prisons aren't doing any kind of a job. They're a big bust. Any other institution, public or private, that had as great a record of continuous failure, decade after decade, hell, it wouldn't have lasted out one year. Too many people just don't give a damn.

What I'm getting at, Joe, is that one reason it fails is because prison only influences a man negatively. The longer a man stays in prison, the smaller his chances of staying out and adjusting to life in the free world. They put you through a status degradation ceremony, stripping you— deliberately and with relish in some cases—of all self-esteem, self-respect, human sensibility, and sense of responsibility. This is designed to punish you, humble you, humiliate you, and shame you. And it destroys a little part of you, Joe. I've seen guys in here that have been literally destroyed, broken, turned into a mass of jelly, into vegetables. The society would be more just if they went ahead and killed them. And they regiment you, Joe. Every minute of every hour of every day of every week of every month, year after year. And when they get through they boot you out the gate to live in the free world. Sure, a lot of guys fail to make it. It ain't surprising.

You see, Joe, when any living organism is immobilized, its vitality is impaired. Even if this immobilization is thought necessary for the future welfare of the organism, like a cast on a broken leg. But the society denies any responsibility for the impairment of the organism that results from imprisonment. It is this destruction of the personality, of the functionalism of the organism, that prevents a lot of guys from making it on the streets.

Yah, Joe, I know. As one wise old prison warden put it, you can't train men for freedom in conditions of captivity. What the guy going out of here needs is self-respect, self-discipline, and confidence. But the system denies this to him. That's why these places fail, Joe, and will always fail in the most miserable manner. Prison automatically precludes what you need for the street.

Well, Joe, there goes the yard whistle, time to line up and march back into the cellhouse. I'm hungry too. They ring the dinner bell in twenty-two minutes. Better button your shirt, Joe, or some screw will write you a bad-conduct report. I didn't mean to depress you, Joe. I just thought you ought to know that the world outside is ready and waiting with less than open arms.

—E.T.

22
Last Day

When I lie down, I say,
    When shall I arise, and the night be gone?
And I am full of tossings to and fro
    Unto the dawning of the day.

                     —JOB 7:4

Midnight. The NBC time-tone made my earphones ring, and I pulled them from my head. I am not interested in the news. I go home today.

I've been waiting thirteen hundred and forty-three days for this moment, this going home, and it's so sensuously delicious I don't even *want* to sleep. I want to savor the next few hours. I've sweated out the weeks and months and years, the degradation and the scorn, the barbarity— and in *just* a few more hours it will be all over. All over. I hope to God it'll be all over. I hate this cancerous blot on the midwestern prairie. It's ten after twelve. I go home today.

In the yard this afternoon I exercised as much as I could in the hope that I would sleep this night. But it didn't work. I rolled over on my side. My eyes flicked about the familiar darkened corners of my cell and slid quickly over the shadows etched in the half-light. I counted the bars for the jillionth time and listened to the noise of captive men. Coughs and groans, the rumbling of the plumbing, and the creaking of the bedsprings. Night was the worst time of all in prison. You stopped all the memory-numbing activity that every man engages in to prevent thinking. Night was the time for reflection and dreaming and regretting, the time for sorrow.

I got up and fumbled for a cigarette. The flash of the match momentarily blinded me, and I moved the flame around in the general vicinity of the cigarette until I got a hit.

Sitting on the little wooden stool by my bed, I could feel my left leg trembling slightly. I smiled. Shortitus, they call it. Short-timer's nerves. The sociologist calls it the short-timer's syndrome. Most guys get it when they are approaching their release. Nervousness, flightiness, preoccupation. Some get positively giddy. A few get irritable and cranky. But most are just so damned overwhelmed with a cross-grained mixture of joy and fear that they merely seem more alive, less like the rest of the automatons and zombies walking around behind the wall, the ones who aren't going anywhere.

It had started, my shortitus, about three months before, when the screw brought around my pre-parole papers with the evening mail. Two mimeographed sheets stapled together. They wanted to know what I had done to "prepare" for release and where I had a job and where I was going to live.

If your problem was alcohol, you were supposed to have gone to Alcoholics Anonymous and have a good attendance record. If your problem was narcotics, you should have gone to Narcotics Anonymous meetings and done the same. If your "Main Maladjustment" was lack of education

—that covers about 90 per cent of the men—you should have gone to school or taken correspondence courses in the cell. If you possessed no marketable job skill, you were supposed to have gone to the vocational school and learned something. If your hangup was anything else, like sex, or status seeking, or a Johnnie Dillinger complex, or what have you, well, you were just screwed, baby. About half the inmate population was screwed.

And of course you couldn't get paroled unless you had a job waiting for you and a place to stay, both of which had been approved and checked out by the Corrections Department. Well, I got shortitus that night they brought the pre-parole papers around, and I'd had them ever since. I shuddered through the next sixty days until the parole board met, going over in my mind every night all the things they could hold against me, and trying to judge my chances. I studied the actions of previous parole boards, comparing my own case against that of men who were released and men who were turned down, trying to detect clues to the board's decision-making process, trying to figure out what kind of chance I had.

How in hell can you be objective in trying to figure out your own chances with the parole board? No one who walks into that conference room knows for certain what they will get. If they had ten convictions, thirty arrests, and fouled up six paroles, they still walk into that room with hope in their breasts. Oh, they laugh and say, "They'll turn me down, I know." But you knew, and they knew, that they were hoping—against impossible odds, perhaps—for some kind of miracle. Why not? Once in a while a miracle happens.

It's a great morbid game. The guy next door to me got a three-year flop last month. Narcotics case. He's a user, not a seller, but they know he'll start sticking a needle in his arm again when he gets out, so they won't let him go.

Oh, he tells them never again, but they've heard that story so many times their ears are cauliflowered.

It's one o'clock. I don't have to look at my watch. The screw just walked by again. The stool is getting hard, so I get back in bed, lie on my back, and stare at the ceiling.

The parole board meets the first of every month, but they don't tell you anything at that time. They just listen to you and nod their heads and say that's all. About three weeks later the papers come back from the state capital: Parole Granted or Parole Denied. If you've made it, they send a pass for you and you half-run, half-skip up to the administration building to sign some papers and find out when you can leave. If you don't make it, you don't get a pass. You'll never know why, mind you, but you'll know what. Your denial slip will arrive at your cell with the evening mail.

Everyone knows when the papers and denials come back. The grapevine is faster than the speed of light. Four hundred pairs of eyes watch the screw deliver the mail that night, and when the lights go out at nine o'clock there'll be tears in some of those eyes. The tears don't come until the lights go out and the men are lying on their backs, staring at the blackness of the ceiling, and that blackness descends and seeps through every pore of your body and fills your soul with misery. You won't be able to hold your wife in your arms or romp with the kids—how they've grown since you've been away—and then, well, then the eyes grow moist in some of the strongest of men.

But for those who have made it, it's a night of happiness. Not the pure joy of walking out that gate on the last day, but a happiness. Some make up lists of things to do: get Social Security card, get birth certificate, write home, write employer; tell the wife or sister or mother to get the old clothes out of the basement or the attic or the closet and air the naphthalene-laden fabric, soak the shirt collars in bleach to remove the yellow of age, check the shoes for cracks in the dried leather and for run-down heels. That's what some do if they have anyone to go out to, or any clothes to wear. For others, there are no lists, not even any plans. They will have twenty-five dollars in their pockets—compliments of the state—and a prison-made suit and shoes, and a room at the YMCA or the Salvation Army.

The night I got the green light, I made no list. Instead I thought about how things must have changed out there in four years. And I wondered how I could make it for two weeks until I got my first paycheck with the fifty dollars I'd have (twenty-five from the state and twenty-five saved from my five dollar monthly wage).

I rolled over on my stomach and stared through the bars at the screw's tower in the middle of the cellhouse. He was coming down to make his two-o'clock rounds. I guess I dozed off then because the first thing I knew a key was slammed into the lock of the next cell and I was wide awake. It was five o'clock and the kitchen worker next door was being let out for work. My mouth tasted like blah—I'd smoked too many cigarettes during the night, and tailor-mades at that. Street cigarettes would be a real luxury after four years of that sawdust they call state tobacco. To the convict *cognoscenti,* smoking free-world cigarettes is synonymous with distinction. I'd been saving that pack for my last night and now had just four left to make it to the front gate.

At six o'clock the breakfast bell clanged, and there was the din of three hundred doors banging open as we filed out to the messhall. I just had a cup of coffee and gave my breakfast roll to the guy next to me. He knew this was MY DAY and asked me to phone his wife when I got to Chicago. I said I would and kept repeating the phone number all the way back to the cell. They searched you going out, so I had to memorize a dozen phone numbers and addresses during my last few weeks.

They let me take a shower before I put on the dress-out clothes and didn't even time me. I figured I was up on them because I'd already had my weekly three-minute shower a few days before.

The white shirt was stiff with newness. I had a hard time with the buttons, and had to think before I attempted a half-windsor in the tie.

The pants were pressed and even had a zipper. I hadn't had a pair of pants with a zipper or crease for years. The shoes smelled of new leather and dye and were stiff. I used a piece of cardboard as a shoehorn to get into them. As I laced them, I wondered how long they would last. Rumor was that the first time the shoes got wet they would sort of collapse and you would have black dye all over your socks and feet. Later I found out it wasn't just a rumor.

Decked out in my prison-made underwear, shirt, suit, and shoes, I picked up my prison-made topcoat, which strongly resembled an old army blanket in shape and texture, and stood in front of the huge mirror in the dress-out section of the clothing room admiring myself. Why, I didn't *look* like a con at all. I looked like a free person. It was a shapeless, ill-fitting suit I guess even Khrushchev himself wouldn't have been caught dead in. But to me at that moment, after years of denim, it was Brooks Brothers and I pictured myself . . .

A screw jolted me out of my reverie with the order to line up. The four of us walked behind the screw up to the administrative building at the other end of the prison, acknowledging with a wink or a nod the grins and waves of the denim-clad men we passed. Each man hopes to make the safari we were on, and each man gets a vicarious satisfaction from viewing the almost daily trek of the fortunate ones about to step through the gates into the sunshine. Sometimes you get to thinking you'll just never get out. It's a good if slightly melancholy feeling, to see living proof that they do let some guys go.

They took many pictures and six sets of prints, then placed us on a bench in front of gate number 2, to await the opening of the business office so we could get our money and papers.

Across the hall from me was the door to the parole board room. Was it just a month ago that I had been on this same bench waiting to see the Great Powers behind that door?

It had been a hot, sticky day in late August. Our shirts were wet with perspiration and sticking to our bodies like gummy wallpaper. I looked again at the No Smoking sign. I'd be fine if I just had a cigarette. I had thought about that cigarette with one part of my mind while I listened and watched with the rest.

He's calling me now. That's *my* name. I stood quickly, with a jerk, and swallowed, trying to get some saliva in my mouth. He waved me forward. I stood in front of the door and tapped on the glass. A heavy voice rumbled out at me. I turned the knob and walked in. It was a pleasant, almost relaxed sort of office, considering it was a part of the prison, albeit a part I had never seen before. There was a rug on the floor—wonderful, as extraordinary in a prison as a Communist in a cathedral—and the luxurious feeling seemed to penetrate my boots and slowly seep up through my body. But the room still had the atmosphere best described as jailhouse impersonal.

He was about fifty, short, muscular, big shoulders— ex-football player flashed through my mind—with a face pitted with scars, and a shock of pure white hair cropped short. A female stenographer sat next to him, fingers poised above her machine.

"Sit down," he told me in a voice like a lawnmower chopping weeds. He asked the standard questions in a monotone, slowly, flipping the pages in the folder in front of him. Name, age, offense, sentence, institutional progress, last place of employment—all information he had in the folder, but it was part of the ritual.

Then he asked me why I did it. I told him I didn't really know. He smiled and said I was a strange case. I agreed. He said it was an irrational act. I agreed. He asked me what led up to it, and I told him. All the time I talked I watched his face and knew he knew I was rationalizing. I really didn't know. When I stopped talking he leaned back in his chair, clasped his hands behind his neck, and stared at the stenographer, who was getting my last sentences down on her machine. When she stopped and looked up, he reached across the desk and closed my file.

"That's all," he said.

"You know," he said, as I opened the door, "you can't be a highwayman all your life. There's no future in playing with pistols."

I didn't say anything. I nodded and stepped into the corridor and closed the door very softly behind me.

Waiting across the road from the prison for the bus to Chicago, I loosened my tie and tugged at the shirt collar until the top button suddenly popped out and fell in the dirt. Another man was going to Chicago too. Tom Corning was a short, heavy-set Negro, about fifty, with rheumy, bloodshot eyes, half-concealed by a perpetual squint.

I had known Tom for the last two years, ever since he had been transferred up from the Menard Branch Prison downstate. He had fallen in 1936 for armed robbery and received a sentence of one year to life. Seven years later he had been paroled into the U.S. Army in the middle of the war. But he went AWOL, and they brought him back as a parole violator for another five years. His second parole lasted nine months before they caught him running a whorehouse.

Well, this was Tom's fifth parole on a sentence that began way back in '36 with a twenty-dollar stickup, and I don't think the old man was capable of making it now. Too many decades in prison had ruined him for the free world. Who was going to hire him? Who could make contact with him? Who was going to tell him when to get up, go to bed, launder his clothes, set his alarm clock? He had adjusted beautifully to the artificial environment of the prison. Over-regimented and brainwashed by the prison system, he couldn't handle responsibility. They'd broken Tom. He talked out of the side of his mouth, with his lips hardly moving, and glanced nervously over his shoulder every few minutes. I wanted to tell him that he wasn't inside any-more, but I knew it would do no good. The defenses he had erected for so many years were built in now, and like Pav-lov's dog, he wouldn't get hungry until he heard that bell.

The bus came bouncing down the road at last, and we climbed aboard. As it pulled away I walked quickly toward the back and sat down next to a window. Tom sat beside me. We didn't say much, just looked and listened. There were about a dozen people on the bus, mostly women and children. I listened to their chatter for several moments, drinking it in great gulps. I had to fight back a rising flood of emotion. Years without hearing the sound of laughing children, of never hearing the sound of women's voices. The kids' voices had a merry, tinkling sound that made me smile. I looked at Tom, and he was smiling too. "It's music, man," he said. Crazy wonderful music.

I nodded and closed my eyes. You don't realize, I thought. You don't realize how much of life you are missing—the simple things are so goddamn beautiful—until you've been deprived of them for a long, long time and then suddenly exposed. Here I was, almost speechless with emotion because I was hearing the sound of laughing children for the first time in four years.

The bus stopped. Two women and three kids got off. It was quieter now—a few murmuring feminine voices and the *tickety-tick* of the gravel under the fenders of the bus. A mixture of strange smells filled my nostrils. Old, worn leather, gasoline, exhaust fumes, and . . . and perfume and powder. How sensitive one becomes to strange—yet long-ago familiar—sounds and smells. I inhaled deeply the heady mixture and settled back contentedly in the seat.

The old bus moved with what seemed like incredible speed down the highway. "Seems like we're moving pretty fast," I said to Tom, and he nodded, lost in his own thoughts. The sun caromed off the windows of the bus, and off the land, giving the whole landscape a freshly laundered look, bouncing and sparkling a myriad of tiny points off the highway, the shiny passing cars, and the neat, brightly painted houses set back on wide lawns from the highway. I thought of the pointillism of Seurat and the paintings of the Impressionists. Why didn't the sunlight look this way yesterday. Or the day before?

All your senses become numb and flattened and unresponsive in prison. They'd better. Otherwise you'd soon be shipped off to the psychiatric section or booby hatch, a blithering idiot. Who wants his sense of smell to remain normal when all around you is the stench of prison. Who would ask that his hearing remain acute in order to hear the constant voices echoing through the concrete bins and bouncing off the cellhouse walls. Or the clanging cell doors, the groaning of the master brake lock. Or the rattle of the brass keys, the shuffling of hobnailed shoes on concrete, the moans and groans, the curses and screams that penetrate the night as half a dozen men experience nightmares, or the occasional hysterical laughter, or the . . . . As for the sights that pass in front of your retina, better left unsaid.

Now the bus plunged down a ramp and onto an expressway gouged out of the terrain. I watched the cars flash by and attempted to identify them. The new models all looked so much alike, and so strange. I gave up. The expressway took us right down to the loop, and by the time the bus roared up the exit ramp we were surrounded by tall buildings, reaching up toward the sky like clusters of missiles on their pads.

Now we were in the heart of the city. A thousand sights slammed into my vision. Cars, taxicabs, buses, trucks, elevated trains, subway entrances, store fronts filled with everything on earth. Men in shirtsleeves, men in sport clothes, men in suits, men in topcoats, hurrying, scurrying, ducking, dodging, a vast blur of people in motion. And the women . . . ah, the women, bless them all. They were streaming by in a vast panorama: short ones, tall ones, fat, skinny, young, old, well dressed and shabby, some in skirts, some in slacks, pretty ones and not so pretty ones, but all so beautiful.

I felt a rising surge of near panic as we rode through the bustling streets. The pace was making me nervous. I worried now about having to leave the safety of the bus and join that frantically animated throng. Everything was so delightful and so confusing.

But it was the end of the line. The bus driver watched us through his mirror as we rose and then descended the steps to the street. Suddenly I felt very self-conscious. Of course he knew. He'd picked us up right in front of the prison. And then there was the clothing. I momentarily felt as if I had a neon sign on my breast, flashing on and off, announcing to one and all: Ex-Con! I looked around at the clothes people on the street were wearing, trying to determine if what I wore was so obviously prison-made. No, I concluded, I'll pass—I think.

Tom tugged on my sleeve, and I followed him down the street. He knew where the parole office was: he ought to, by this time. The pedestrians scared me almost as much as the traffic. They seemed to flow along the street in a controlled hysteria, determined, set upon goal and destination, and when one of them approached, I didn't know whether to jump to one side, freeze, or keep right on walking toward the inevitable collision. You didn't have all this confusion in prison. There everyone walked in neat, orderly lines in a sort of half-shuffle. The noise of the traffic, the horns, the whistles, the music coming from somewhere, coupled with the clatter of high heels and the chatter of voices welled up, a cacophonous crescendo. Hey! I'm free! Goddamn, I'm free!

The parole office was in the State of Illinois Building on LaSalle. I swear the elevator operator snickered as we got off on our floor. Why not, he'd probably taken hundreds of parolees up to this floor, and if the average person couldn't spot a prison suit, he could.

A receptionist took our release papers and told us to wait on a bench. Twenty minutes later she directed us to a conference room down the hall.

There were two of them in the conference room. One had an unlit cigar in his mouth and wore a baggy tweed suit. Middle-aged, pulpy around the middle, a rumpled look. The other wore a black suit of a silken sheen. He was extraordinarily thin, a taut face with no flesh on the bone. He looked like an undertaker as he sat doodling on a legal-sized yellow pad, very much within himself. We hadn't arrived in the room yet as far as he was concerned. I didn't like him.

The one with the cigar finally lit it and glanced up soberly. "Sit down, boys," he said, nodding to a row of chairs in front of the conference table. We sat down. No one said anything, and the undertaker eyed us with a slightly speculative stare as the silence built toward the beginning of tension.

The one with the cigar told us he was the district supervisor and that as long as we kept our noses clean and stayed out of jail we'd have no trouble. He said our parole officer would call on us in the next few days to get acquainted. Then he rose and nodded toward the undertaker. As soon as the district supervisor left the room, the undertaker jumped to his feet and ran it down to us. I mean, he told it like it was: what we could do and could not do, and what would happen if we didn't go along with the program. I imagine he had given this pat speech countless times and should have been pretty bored with the whole thing. But he seemed to relish the role of Inquisitor General, and I left the office a little shook. Tom told me not to worry, that it was SOP to scare hell out of new parolees, but it didn't do much to calm my fears. We parted downstairs with a handshake and a doughty smile.

I went sightseeing. It was great. Better by far than a movie. I walked into Marshall Field and just sauntered up and down the aisles. The sights were magnificent, but the smells really knocked me out. New leather and tobacco, food and cologne, wax and oil and polish, perfume and powder, everything. After half an hour on the main floor I got on the escalator and rode and rode and rode. Well, about like the twelfth floor I got off and walked around some more. By the time I'd worked my way down to the main floor again, I'd killed all of three hours.

I never saw so many well-dressed people, especially the women. I don't think I ever did. Maybe I had. After all, it had been only four years. I walked over to Michigan Boulevard and stared in all the windows, block after block. It didn't matter what was in the window, it all fascinated me. Jewelry, furs, clothes, food, antiques, rugs, paintings, sport goods, travel displays, it was all great. It must have taken me an hour to go four blocks. And all the time I was so very conscious of the women, of the powder and the cologne, the perfume and the scented hair spray.

It was rush hour now, and the streets were jammed with quadrillions of people pouring out of buildings and

heading home. Long snakelike queues formed at every corner, waiting for buses. The subway entrances seemed to
swallow them up like a whale swallowing minnows. I got
out of their way.

The restaurant wasn't fancy, but it had real silver,
flowers on the table, a rug on the floor and tablecloths—
beautiful, soft, white tablecloths. I ordered a sirloin steak
with onions and mushrooms. It was going to put a real dent
in my fifty bucks, but I'd waited too long for this moment
—I didn't care. I'd eat bologna sandwiches for the next two
weeks.

It was chow time now back at the joint, and they
would be silently filing into the big top, that barnlike dining
room, by the thousands, to eat out of tin dog-plates on bare
wooden benches with huge tablespoons. The rattling of
nineteen hundred plates and spoons, the banging of tubs
and vats and pitchers, the hands raised to call the waterboy
to fill the tin cups with tepid liquid, the screws pacing up
and down the aisles, the riot guns jutting out from the
barred windows of the gun turret over their heads—all aids
to digestion. And they ate their beans, sopping up the juice
with coarse chunks of bread, and maybe a scoop of Jello
for dessert.

I looked up from my salad at the wood-paneled walls
of the restaurant and smiled. No, there were no gun turrets
in sight, no pump gun pointed at my belly, not a screw in
sight. I suppose I had a silly grin on my face. Why not? I'd
survived the hellhole of the Midwest reasonably sane and
healthy. I was free.

About the Authors

H. JACK GRISWOLD grew up near Fairfield, Illinois—home of the notorious Shelton Gang—where his father was a bootlegger and thief, and he himself began stealing milk and fuel coal at age ten. "It wasn't right or wrong but a matter of necessity and a question of doing it without being caught." He *was* caught though—several times—and as a result has spent more than fifteen years of his life behind bars—five in Washington State Prison, five in Illinois prisons, and five so far of his present confinement in the Indiana State Prison. From those first thefts he graduated to stealing cars and armed robbery, but he is quick to point out he has also worked on construction jobs on the Aleutian Islands and Alaska's mainland. While serving time he has earned a high school diploma, fifty college hours, and is presently a selling free-lance writer. "I've traded my gun for a typewriter."

MIKE MISENHEIMER was born in North Carolina and attended "about a dozen schools" in North and South Carolina, California, and Louisiana before joining the Paratroopers at seventeen and obtaining his high school diploma through GED tests. At nineteen he jumped from the 82nd Airborne Division to the North Carolina pen with a two-to-three-year sentence for Common Law Robbery. He is now serving a life sentence for Inflicting an Injury During the Commission of a Robbery. After six years in Indiana State he escaped, staying out just long enough to "eat three good meals" before being caught and returned. Mr. Misenheimer reports no illusions about his future.

ART POWERS was born in Seymour, Indiana, in 1927. His convictions range from first-degree larceny at age twenty-one to his present ten-to-twenty-year burglary term at Indiana State. Powers lied his way into the Navy during World War II and served aboard two Navy destroyers before being honorably discharged after thirty-one months. A high school dropout, he has since completed prison correspondence courses from Indiana State University, earning his high school diploma, and twelve semester hours of college credits. During this time he has had modest success free-lancing articles for Sunday supplements about prison and prisoners, but he says, "It's rather difficult to see anything past this ten-to-twenty-year sentence."

EDWARD TROMANHAUSER was born in 1932 in Minneapolis, Minnesota. After elementary school in Minneapolis and high school in Detroit, he spent a year and a half at Wayne State University, then graduated from Chicago City Junior College and Northern Illinois University, where he majored in history, with some additional graduate studies at the University of Illinois. He has worked as a car salesman, auto assembly-line worker, railroad gandy dancer, draftsman, radio-TV repairman, and schoolteacher, writing free-lance sporadically since 1959. Tromanhauser's criminal career began with armed assault, quickly followed by robbery convictions and sentences in Illinois and presently in Indiana. He recently completed a 160-page programmed study guide for the Chicago City College and is now completing a laboratory workbook in psychology.

FUNDERBURG LIBRARY

MANCHESTER COLLEGE

365.9772
Ey31g